DISCARD

Reading
the Korean
Cultural Landscape

Reading the Korean Cultural Landscape

Je - Hun Ryu

www.hollym.com

HOLLYM
Elizabeth, NJ · Seoul

Note:
The McCune-Reischauer system of romanization has been applied in this book.

Copyright©2000
by Je-Hun Ryu

All rights reserved.
No part of this book may be reproduced in any form without the written permission of the author and the publisher.

First published in 2000
by Hollym International Corp.
18 Donald Place, Elizabeth, New Jersey 07208, USA
Phone (908)353-1655 Fax (908)353-0255
http://www.hollym.com

Published simultaneously in Korea
by Hollym Corporation; Publishers
13-13 Kwanchol-dong, Chongno-gu, Seoul 110-111, Korea
Phone (02)735-7551~4 Fax (02)730-5149, 8192
http://www.hollym.co.kr

ISBN: 0-56591-156-3 (hardcover)
ISBN: 0-56591-159-8 (softcover)
Library of Congress Catalog Card Number: 00-106349

Printed in Korea

To my late mentor,
Dr. Paul Ward English (1936 - 2000),
who taught me how to think and
write about geography.

Preface

This book is indeed a sort of product from my academic life in the past 24 years. Before I entered the master's program at Seoul National University in 1976, I did not really know of the existence of a subfield in geography named cultural geography. I was a little surprised when Dr. Chan Lee, who is retired now, but at that time was active in educating graduate students, suggested the graduate study in cultural geography to me. Until that time I had never thought that geographers could study culture, and upon his proposal changed my original plan to major in cultural geography. Dr. Chan Lee is now 77 years old, but still has influence on my research program by giving me the advice either directly or indirectly. I still remember that I was reading the book, titled *Readings in Cultural Geography* (1962) edited by Wagner and Mikesell, in his office while working for him as an assistant from 1976 to 1978. This classical book in cultural geography provided me with the basis upon which I could write this book in later years.

By the time that I was about to finish my master's degree, I was wondering which university in the USA to go for my doctoral program studies. I was working as an assistant for Dr. Joseph E. Spencer, an emeritus professor at UCLA, who was visiting Seoul

National University in the fall semester 1979. During this time, Dr. Spencer kindly told me about his experience in studying Chinese cultural geography, and the information about graduate program on cultural geography in the USA. My dialogue with him helped me choose the University of Texas at Austin where I would study cultural geography in the doctoral program.

After all, in 1981, I decided to have Dr. Paul Ward English as my advisor for my doctoral program at the University of Texas at Austin. The theme of cultural ecology was in vogue among cultural geographers at that time, and the geography department at Austin was not the exception. My doctoral dissertation, "Institutionalization and Cultural Adaptation on the Honam Plain of South Korea, 1789-1982 (1987)," was also not free from the influence of cultural ecology. My mentor, Dr. English, taught me how to be scientific and analytic in my research, and how to be innovative and creative in my thinking. The courage, confidence and love that he gave to me became the mental cornerstone upon which my professional career would build after coming back to Korea in 1987. Dr. Terry G. Jordan influenced me in a different way, but as great as anybody. His textbook, *Human Mosaic: A Thematic Introduction to Cultural Geography* (1986), much loved worldwide by geographers, has been used as the primary reference in the composition of my book. His words, "You had better study folklore at first when you return to Korea," has served as a guide for my research in Korean cultural geography since 1987.

However, as my experience in research and field work on Korean cultural geography accumulated day by day, I gradually became skeptical about the utility of theories and concepts that I had learned in the USA. I came to realize that the Korean cultural landscape is too complicated in its social context to be explained only in terms of cultural diffusion or cultural ecology. It is at this time that the so-called new cultural geography, rapidly developing in the UK, attract my attention. Peter Jackson's book, *Maps of Meaning: An Introduction to Cultural Geography* (1989), made me rethink the whole structure of cultural geography that I had cherished in my mind. It occurred to me that the new cultural geography might have the theories and concepts to explain the aspects of the Korean cultural landscape which the Berkeley-style cultural geography might not. With the Korean examples in my mind, I thought that neither the American nor the British side could win in the debate about traditional and new cultural geographies. In my opinion, an integrated cultural geography wherein traditional and new theories and concepts are combined, is necessary for the study of the Korean cultural landscape.

Korea has a long history of over 5,000 years, and her cultural phenomena has been complicated in many ways. It is, therefore, difficult to explore the Korean culture in terms of its origin and spread or human adaptation to environment. Even in the pre-modern era, social structure was very sophisticated, and cultural politics were extensively elaborated. The ruling class utilized ideology and knowledge as political means to excercise their own power and dominate the subordinate class in the society. A distribution pattern of a cultural element becomes overlapped with another, and its boundary is hard to draw clearly whether in a line or zone. Such a cultural region, often difficult to trace its origin, varies from small to large in size depending upon its continuity and density of distribution. To the westerners, Korean traditional culture may be seen as self-contradictory because it consists of post-modern as well as pre-modern elements.

What I look forward to seeing in the future is geographical discussion on the Korean culture that would spread wide among Korean people in general as well as Korean geographers specifically. Koreans themselves have regarded their own land as too small to contain national culture with much regional variation.

Koreans have focused on the unity of national culture with little consideration over the diversity. They tend to suppose that Koreans as a single nation have lived on the Korean Peninsula for quite a long time, using the same language and script. This view may be proved to be true only if Korean culture is seen as composed of a dominant culture or an elite culture. However, if it is seen from both sides, the dominant and the dominated, it will certainly demonstrate regional diversity. Regionalism recurrent in the national elections and mutual distrust between both North and South Korea may be due to such a regional differentiation of Korean culture. I propose that these national problems will be solved if Koreans come to understand the regional diversity of Korean culture, that is the Korean cultural geography. If such a geographical discussion on the Korean culture is diffused in and out of the country, Korean national development will be achieved much more easily and rapidly than ever expected.

Nonetheless, this book is nothing but a beginning: an introductory discussion about Korean cultural geography. Since it does not mention anything from North Korea at all, I must admit that this book is a half-completion of the introduction to Korean cultural geography. I believe that such an incomplete discussion will provide the grounds upon which further studies can be carried on by other scholars. With further studies in the future being accumulated, I hope that national consciousness will be formed in a greater width and depth about Korea as a nation with more cultural diversity as compared with her small land size. The 21st century is the age of culture, and thus cultural competition will be ever tense among countries. The internal or regional diversity in a national culture is the necessity for a nation to develop its own cultural capability. If Koreans comprehend their own national culture as a mixture of many regional cultures, they will be more prepared to adapt themselves to the process of globalization.

Acknowledgement

English is not my native language. When I returned to Korea in 1987 from my doctoral study in the USA, I felt more or less relieved because I would not have to write a book in English ever again. It was not only a burden, but also a headache for me as a foreigner to translate cultural ideas from Korean into English. Moreover, when I had to translate my doctoral dissertation from English into Korean and publish it as a small book from 1992 to 1993, I confirmed to myself that it was like torture to swing back and forth between two different languages.

It is the 29th International Geographical Congress to be held at Seoul in August 2000 that made me change such an idea and write a book in English. In June 1999, I decided to use Korean materials that I had accumulated to write a book in English on the cultural geography of Korea. I remember that I telephoned to Ms. Julie Han, the editor at Hollym Corporation; Publishers to ask the possibility of publishing a book in English on Korean cultural geography. Ms. Han encouraged me so much by replying that to write such a book would be a good idea and introduced me to the president, Mr. Ki-man Ham. President Ham kindly showed me in advance several important directions to which I would have to pay attention in writing a book in English as a

Korean. The most important of them was to find a native English speaker who would correct my English writing.

What I felt the most difficult was the placement of articles and preposition in the middle of sentences, which do not follow any consistent grammar rule. It was not an easy task to meet with an American with the qualification to improve my English writing. Even if I might find such a qualified person, the next problem would be his or her time and commitment to my work. While I had a hard time to locate such a person, Ms. Fran Eitel, the visiting English professor at Korea National University of Education, caught my eye one day. To my surprise, she consented without hesitance to my request for correcting my English writing during the winter vacation. She devoted her time and energy wholeheartedly to the correction of my first draft, four to five times, from December 1999 to February 2000. Even after then, she did a superb job in proofreading upon my request as if she were an author of my book. Her thorough and friendly way of commenting on my draft did make a wonderful contribution to the improvement of my writing. As I look back upon the moment that I met with her, it was really an unexpected fortune for me to have her correct my English writing.

Around January 2000, I was almost exhausted due to endlessly sitting up in front of the computer. I began to feel numb around my neck and fatigue in my legs, and felt like falling down all of a sudden. It was at this time that Mr. Sŏn-Jŏng Kwon, my doctoral student, came to be engaged in correcting the first draft that Ms. Eitel made comments on. Ms. Sŭng-Ja Pak, my master's student and Mr. Chong-hwan Chŏn, my doctoral student, also painstakingly drew the many maps to be displayed in my book. Mr. Chin-Sŏng Ch'oe, my doctoral student, did an excellent job in romanizing Korean terms into English and typing the bibliography in English and Korean. Without their loyalty and sincere assistance, I might have become sick of writing a book in English and could not have finished my writing.

Many materials and sources in this book were drawn from the master's theses that I had supervised at Korea National University of Education from 1987 to 1999. Upon the basis of these theses, I was able to develop a geographical perspective on the Korean culture and the idea of regional diversity in Korean culture. I would like to appreciate those graduates' commitment to field work and mapping while they wrote their own master's theses under my supervision. As most of them were attending graduate school as school teachers, they had to divide their time carefully to do research in cultural geography. I want to thank them for their hard work by listing their names: Ju-sŏp Kim, Kil-nam Kim, Su-dong Kim, Pŏm-ki Kwon, Ch'i-gyu Nam, Chae-ch'ŏl Park, Mun-gyu Park, In-jŏng Song, and Yŏng-sik Yang.

In February 2000, when I was close to the end of the first draft, some sad news was unexpectedly delivered to me. The news said that my former doctoral advisor, Dr. Paul Ward English, had become fatally ill because of lung and liver cancer. It was really sad news to me as I had always felt that I owed him many mental debts in my academic career. Such a feeling was also strengthened while I was writing the first draft. The sad news happened to come at a time when I was again appreciating his grace and love that he gave to me while I was his doctoral student. I was in such a hurry to fly to the USA and see him in the hospital in early March. There I presented to him the first draft as a special gift. He was so delighted to receive it, and said, "Thank you for being my student, Je-Hun." He said to me that he would like to survive until my book was published and write a book review on it. Despite his hope, he died on March 30 2000. Therefore, I want to dedicate this book to him upon my promise to him at that time. Once again, I would like to appreciate his spiritual legacy in me, and pray for his safe journey to eternity.

My lovely wife, Soon-Jong Kim, wholeheartedly took care of my health and consistently inspired me all along during the entire period of writing this book. The reassuring words that she told me with a warm heart whenever I was lingering on writing recreated my mind and body. Without her support and encouragement, my mind and body might have gone bankrupt completely. She has stayed around me all the time in 20 years of our marriage, while sharing loneliness with me and compensating for my weakness as a scholar. I would like to dedicate my highest compliments to her endless contribution and sacrifice in our lives. In the end, my two sons, Il-hwan and Sŭng-hwan, deserve my due thanks. They have constructed firmly for me a family surrounding within which I have been able to enjoy the ordinary pleasures from my daily life. Their youth and enthusiasm have always turned the home into a wonderful world where I have been able to refresh myself.

CONTENTS

Preface ———————————————————— 6
Acknowledgement ———————————————— 10
Contents ———————————————————— 14
Figure list ——————————————————— 16
Photo list ———————————————————— 18
1. Introduction —————————————————— 21
2. Religious Landscapes ———————————— 43
    1) Catholic Churches around Ansŏng Town · 46
    2) *Sŏwon* (Private Confucian Academies) around Andong City · 56
    3) Protestant Churches around the Yŏngdŭngp'o District in Seoul · 66
    4) T'ongdo Temple at Yŏngch'wi Mountain · 75
    5) Songkwang Temple at Chogye Mountain · 82

3. Folk Landscapes ——————————————— 91
    1) Shamanistic Halls in Kyeryong Mountain · 95
    2) *Ponhyangdang* (Main Spirit Halls) on Cheju Island · 104
    3) *Sŏndol* (Standing Stones) around Okch'ŏn Town · 112
    4) *Tolt'ap* (Pebble-Piles) around Kŭmsan Town · 123
    5) *Tangje* (Village Rituals) on the Islands in the Tadohae (Southwestern Sea) · 130

4. Linguistic Landscapes ——————————— 137
    1) Isoglosses on the East Coast · 142
    2) Isoglosses on the West Coast · 148
    3) Linguistic Islands on the Southwest Coast · 154
    4) Place Names in Kyŏnggi Bay · 160
    5) Place Names on Chiri Mountain · 165

5. Rural Landscapes ——————————————— 175
   1) *Yangban* Lineage Villages around Andong City · 180
   2) *Chŏngja*s (Pavilions) in the Upper Reaches of the Namhan River · 187
   3) Folk Housing on the West Bank of the Nakdong River · 195
   4) Irrigation Networks on the Honam Plain · 203
   5) Village Forests on the Southern Coast · 214

6. Urban Landscapes ——————————————— 223
   1) The Royal Landscape in Seoul during the Chosŏn Period · 228
   2) The Colonial Landscape in Seoul under Japanese Occupation · 237
   3) The Royal Landscape in Chŏnju City during the Chosŏn Period · 246
   4) The Colonial Landscape in Chŏnju City under Japanese Occupation · 254
   5) The Royal Landscape in Kyŏngju City during the Chosŏn Period · 261

7. Conclusion ——————————————————— 273

Bibliography ———————————————————— 295
   Bibliography 1 · 296
   Bibliography 2 · 302

Appendices ————————————————————— 311
   Glossary · 312
   Place Name Index · 330
   Topic Index · 334
   Photo Credit · 340

Figure List

Figure 1. Locations of cultural landscapes in Korea · 25
Figure 2. Locations of religious landscapes in Korea · 47
Figure 3. The growth of Catholic parishes around Ansŏng Town · 54
Figure 4. The increase of Catholic churches around Ansŏng Town · 55
Figure 5. The diffusion process of *sŏwon* (private Confucian acaemy) around Andong City · 61
Figure 6. The regional structure of the Andong Culture Area · 62
Figure 7. Protestant churches in the Yŏngdŭngp'o District before 1945 · 72
Figure 8. Protestant churches in the Yŏngdŭngp'o District in the 1990s · 73
Figure 9. Locations of folk landscapes in Korea · 94
Figure 10. The spatial distribution of Shamanistic halls on Kyeryong Mountain before 1975 · 102
Figure 11. The spatial distribution of Shamanistic halls on Kyeryong Mountain after 1975 · 103
Figure 12. Individual territories of *ponhyangdang* (main spirit halls) on eastern Cheju Island · 110
Figure 13. The spatial distribution of *sŏndol* (standing stones) around Okch'ŏn Town before and after the 16th Century · 117
Figure 14. The spatial distribution of *tolt'ap*s (pebble-piles) around

Kŭmsan Town (in the upper valley of the Kŭm River) · 124
Figure 15. The spatial division of islands in the Southwestern Sea called Tadohae · 131
Figure 16. Locations of linguistic landscapes in Korea · 141
Figure 17. Isoglosses based on vocabulary · 143
Figure 18. The linguistic boundary between northern and southern dialects in Korea · 149
Figure 19. Isoglosses based on grammar · 151
Figure 20. Dialectic boundaries on the Southwest Coast · 157
Figure 21. The coastal lines around Kyŏnggi Bay · 161
Figure 22. Locations of rural landscapes in Korea · 179
Figure 23. The site and layout of Hahoe Village · 183
Figure 24. The spatial spread of *chŏngja* (pavilion) in the upper reaches of the Namhan River before and after the 18th century · 188
Figure 25. Floor plans of "—" and "ㄱ"shaped houses · 198
Figure 26. Floor plans of a *kyŏpjip* (double- room house) · 199
Figure 27. Drainage Systems on the Honam Plain · 204
Figure 28. Irrigation networks on the Honam Plain before 1920 · 208
Figure 29. Irrigation networks on the Honam Plain in the 1980s · 211
Figure 30. The village forest called Ŏburim on the south coast · 226
Figure 31. Locations of urban landscapes in Korea · 227
Figure 32. The site and layout of Seoul in the Chosŏn Period · 229
Figure 33. An old pictorial map of Seoul in the late Chosŏn Period · 234
Figure 34. Another old pictorial map of Seoul in the late Chosŏn Period · 235
Figure 35. The layout of Chŏnju City in the late Chosŏn Period · 248
Figure 36. An old pictorial map of Chŏnju City in the late Chosŏn Period · 252
Figure 37. The layout of Chŏnju City under Japanese occupation · 258
Figure 38. The layout of Kyŏngju City in the late Chosŏn Period · 264
Figure 39. An old pictorial map of Kyŏngju City in the late Chosŏn Period · 269

Photo List

Photo 1. A Memorial Catholic Church at Paet'i Pass · 49
Photo 2. Graveyards for the martyred at Paet'i Pass · 50
Photo 3. Kup'o-dong Main Catholic Church in Ansŏng Town · 52
Photo 4. The side wall of Kup'o-dong Main church · 52
Photo 5. Sosu Academy (*sŏwon*) beside a stream · 59
Photo 6. Tosan Academy (*sŏwon*) on the slope of a valley · 60
Photo 7. Yŏŭido Sunbokŭm (Full Gospel) Church in the Yŏngdŭngp'o District · 67
Photo 8. Yangp'yŏng Presbyterian Church in the Yŏngdŭngp'o District · 69
Photo 9. Kŭmganggye-dan, or the Diamond Ordination Platform in T'ongdo Temple · 77
Photo 10. Kuryong (Nine Dragon) Pond in T'ongdo Temple · 79
Photo 11. The spatial arrangement of buildings in Songkwang Temple before and after the Korean War · 87
Photo 12. A series of peaks on Kyeryong Mountain · 98
Photo 13. The forest surrounding a *ponhyangdang* (main spirit hall) on Cheju Island · 108
Photo 14. A main crater called Paekrokdam on the summit of Halla Mountain during the winter time · 109

Photo 15. A *ponhyangdang*, or main spirit hall around Kujwa Town on Cheju Island · 111

Photo 16. A road icon, or a totem pole, called *changsŭng*, at a village entrance · 114

Photo 17. A *sŏndol* (standing stone) as a mountain deity around Okch'ŏn Town · 115

Photo 18. A dolmen, called *koindol* in Korean, located in the upper reaches of Kŭm River · 116

Photo 19. A male *sŏndol* (standing stone) around Okch'ŏn Town · 118

Photo 20. A more typical shape of a male *sŏndol* around Okch'ŏn Town · 119

Photo 21. A female *sŏndol* (standing stone) around Okch'ŏn Town · 120

Photo 22. A *tolt'ap*, or pebble-pile, around Kŭmsan Town · 125

Photo 23. A *sŏnangdang* with a small pile of pebbles on the trail passing over Mungyŏng Town · 126

Photo 24. The peak called Nogodan on Chiri Mountain · 171

Photo 25. The shrine for the female deity called Mago or Sŏndosŏngmo on Chiri Mountain · 172

Photo 26. A front view of Hwaŏm Temple with the Main Worshipping Hall, pagoda, lantern and stairway · 172

Photo 27. An aerial view on Hahoe Village and its surroundings · 184

Photo 28. Yangjindang, the clan-head house in Hahoe Village · 185

Photo 29. Ch'unghyodang, the clan-head house in Hahoe Village · 185

Photo 30. A pavilion situated on a cliff · 189

Photo 31. A pavilion situated in the village · 190

Photo 32. A *yangban* house with a *maru* (veranda) installed into a guest room called *sarangch'ae* · 196

Photo 33. A folk house in the shape of "—" with a *maru* around Mungyŏng City · 201

Photo 34. The extensive paddy-rice fields on the Honam Plain · 205

Photo 35. An old irrigation canal called Tokjuhang-suro on the Honam

Plain · 206

Photo 36. A traditional reservoir called Nŭngje on the Honam Plain · 212

Photo 37. Kyerim, or the Chicken Forest, in Kyŏngju City · 214

Photo 38. The village forest called Ŏburim on the south coast · 221

Photo 39. Kŭnjŏngjŏn, or the Throne Hall, located inside Kyŏngbokgung, or the Main Palace · 236

Photo 40. An overview of Seoul from Nam Mountain under the Japanese occupation · 238-239

Photo 41. The building for Chosŏn-ch'ongdokbu, or the Japanese Government-General in Korea · 240

Photo 42. Kwanghwamun, or the Gate of Radiant Transformation, before its relocation in the early Japanese rule · 242

Photo 43. A Shinto shrine called Chosen Jingu on Nam Mountain · 245

Photo 44. The south gate called P'ungnammun in Chŏnju City · 249

Photo 45. Japanese-style shops remaining on the street in Chŏnju City · 256

Photo 46. The old city walls remaining in the center of Kyŏngju City · 263

Photo 47. The Stone Chamber from the United Shilla Kingdom in Kyŏngju City · 266

Photo 48. Taenŭngwon, or Tumulus Park in Kyŏngju City · 268

Photo 49. Ponghwangdae, or the Chinese Phoenix Height in Kyŏngju City · 270

1. INTRODUCTION

1. Introduction

Cultural geography explains culture from a geographical perspective, focusing on the location and spatial variation of cultures. It has been one of the fastest expanding, and the most interesting sub-disciplines in geography over the last fifteen years. The "cultural turn" in contemporary geography has demanded new ideas of culture, making cultural geography more exciting than ever. A new group of cultural geographers has emerged to challenge the old group of cultural geographers, calling itself "new" cultural geography.

Definitions of "culture" are, by nature, diverse and complex, and these two schools are fiercely conflicting over the concept of culture. Defining the word culture is a complex and difficult task which has produced a variety of definitions. New cultural geography has proposed the concept of a "plurality of cultures," taking up ideas of Marx and humanism. It criticizes traditional cultural geography for sticking with the old concept of culture. Against this criticism, however, adherents of the traditional school argue that the new school is casting aside virtually all of the traditions that have long distinguished American cultural geography. In their view, the new school intentionally misrepresented the traditional one, with an attempt to construct a foundation for a British cultural geography.

In concepts other than culture, these two schools also reflect some friction between American and British geographies. The new school, with its close affiliation with British cultural geography, is contrasted with the traditional school, with its historical legacy in American cultural geography or so-called Berkeley school. The former criticizes the latter that the rural and historic bias of the work did not take urban life and experience into consideration. In the study of cultural landscape, too, the new and traditional schools are assuming very different theoretical standpoints: the former follows the thinking from cultural materialism or symbolism; the latter draws the ideas from cultural diffusionism or evolutionism.

After all, in this book, an experimental effort will be made to test which of these two schools would be better suited to the study of cultural landscapes in Korea. To test the cultural theory in the real world is the contribution of geography, looking at cultures (plural) as locatable, specific phenomena. Moreover, Korea, abundant in cultural landscapes with different origins, will provide a good laboratory where the validity of cultural theories can be tested. With her long history over thousands of years, Korea has a variety of cultural landscapes as the outcome of cultural diffusion and adaptation to physical environment, social and political processes, and power relations. Some of the cultural landscapes, especially regionalized or localized, await geographical study, sensitive to the spatial variation of cultures.

Cultural landscapes in Korea can be classified into religious, folk, linguistic, rural and urban landscapes, occupying their own territories, with specific meanings in space and time (**Figure 1**). In reality, however, these landscapes have not been formed individually, but in relation to one another. In the process of formation, for instance, folk landscape in the countryside has to do with the rural landscape. Some of them, though their distribution patterns are regionalized or localized, may be found universally all over Korea. Therefore, to explain the real histories and meanings of cultural landscapes in Korea requires an invention of cultural theory, or an integration of cultural theories.

In this book, another effort will be made to examine whether traditional and new cultural geographies can be brought together in the real world. Cultural landscapes in Korea are so complex in their forming processes that they cannot be studied only from the standpoint of traditional cultural geography. Both traditional and new cultural geographies have their own merits to be exploited in the study of cultural landscapes in Korea.

Cultural landscapes to be dealt with are those that have been regionalized or localized mainly in the countryside, and the initial theories to be consulted are those on cultural diffusion and adaptation to physical environment in traditional cultural geography. When these theories are not complete in exploring the forming processes of cultural landscapes, theories from new cultural geography focusing on social forces may be applied to their study. In Korea, there are many traditional cultural landscapes, fully embedded with meanings and symbolism, transcending the scope and capability of traditional cultural geography

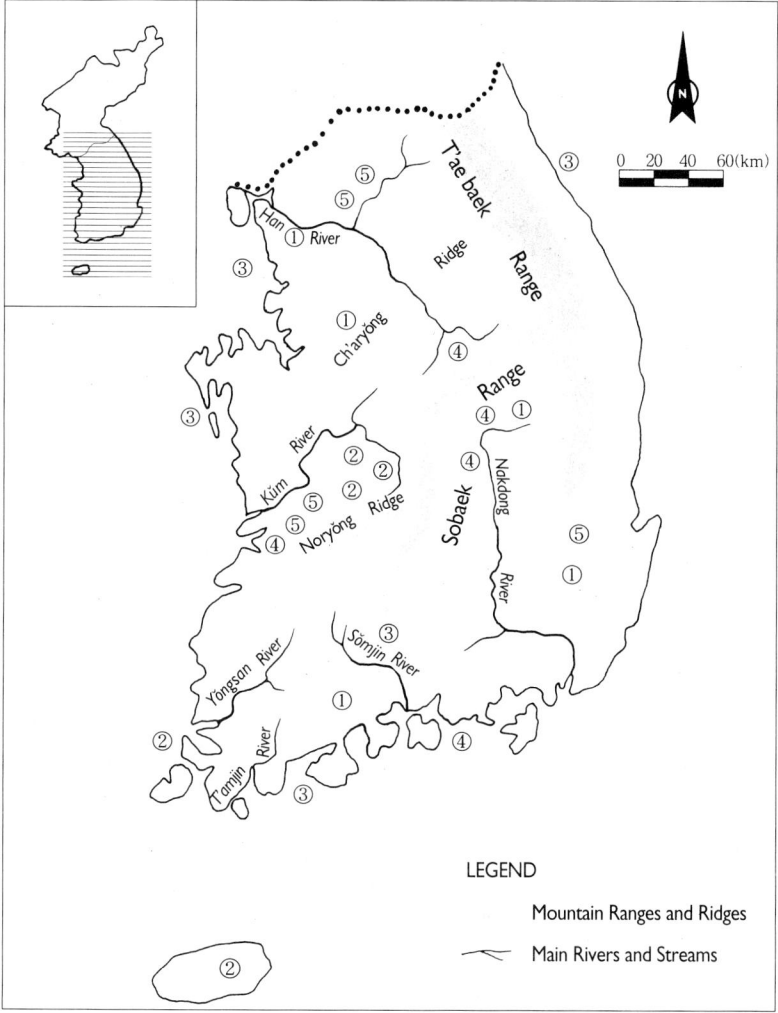

Figure 1. Locations of cultural landscapes in Korea:
　　① Religious landscapes
　　② Folk landscapes
　　③ Linguistic landscapes
　　④ Rural landscapes
　　⑤ Urban landscapes

1) "TRADITIONAL" CULTURAL GEOGRAPHY

In the simplest term, culture is defined by traditional cultural geographers as a total way of life held in common by a group of people. Learned similarities in speech, behavior, ideology, livelihood, technology, value system, and society bind people together in a culture. Because cultures are formed by groups of people, the cultural geographer is necessarily concerned with humans in aggregate. According to Jordan (1986 : 4), cultural geography is the study of spatial variations among culture groups and the spatial functioning of society. Geographers are trained to observe spatial patterns of all kinds, both human and environmental. Therefore, they are particularly well qualified to describe and interpret spatial variations of culture.

Geographers, as experts at spatial questioning, can make contributions to the study of Korean culture which historians or anthropologists cannot. However, there have been few geographical studies on Korean culture in comparison to historical or anthropological studies. Under these circumstances, this book may be the first step in the study of Korean culture utilizing theories from both traditional and new cultural geographies.

The scarcity of geographical studies on Korean culture may be due to either the lack of theoretical knowledge in cultural geography or the shortage of geographical knowledge itself. At first glance, Korea, small in size and homogeneous in language and ethnicity, does not seem to have any significant areal differences within the country. However, a closer examination on cultural landscapes from the geographical viewpoint would reveal the regionalized or localized cultures with quite an old tradition. This book, therefore, will try to open new visions onto two kinds of horizons: theoretical knowledge in cultural geography and geographical knowledge in Korean culture.

The ideal form of geographical description is the map. Anything that has unequal distribution may be expressed by the map as a pattern of units in spatial occurrence. According to Sauer (1941 : 6), the spacing of phenomena expresses the general geographical problem of distribution, which leads to questions about the meaning of presence or absence, massing or thinning of anything. Because many limits of distribution coincide or come close together, a cultural boundary may appear as a "bundle of lines" on the map. A simple objective procedure for localizing cultural boundaries is to superimpose as many maps as possible of different traits, and establish boundaries where "bundles" cluster. Within these "bundles" of lines, taken as cultural boundaries, it would be possible to find "culture areas."

In general, such a mapping method of cultural boundaries is frequently used in drawing linguistic or dialectic boundaries. In Korea, a mountainous country with a long coastal line, dialectic differences are significantly large enough to be used in dividing cultural boundaries. The linguistic boundaries clearly appear as a "bundle of lines" on the map, especially between northern and southern dialect areas. The zone where the bundle of lines crisscrosses does not simply show a transitional or mixed character but a distinctive personality. In this book, how these "hybrid dialects" have been developed on the west and east coasts will be discussed.

The investigation of the past and present distribution of cultural traits constitutes the basis for recognition and delimitation of culture areas. According to Wagner and Mikesell (1962 : 5), a culture area, herein, may be defined as territories inhabited at any given period by human communities characterized by particular cultures. The culture area, in geographic terms, may constitute a "region," forming a definable unit in space. Wagner and Mikesell (1962:9-10) also suggest that the typical association of geographical features within a region may be described as a "landscape."

The cultural landscape, then, connotes the geographical content of a determined area, and serves as criteria for regional classification. It is the artificial landscape that cultural groups create in inhabiting the earth. Cultures have shaped their own landscapes out of the raw materials provided by the earth. Every inhabited area has a cultural landscape, and each uniquely reflects the culture that created it. Jordan (1986:25) argues that landscape mirrors culture, and the cultural geographer can learn much about a group of people by carefully observing the landscape. Indeed, so important is this visual record of cultures that some cultural geographers regard landscape study as the core of geographical concern.

In Korea, above all, religious landscapes serve as criteria by which cultural regions can be recognized and delimited. The architectures of Buddhist temples, private Confucian academies, and Catholic or Protestant churches provide material elements whose distribution patterns can be measured in terms of density. The investigation of past and present distribution of these landscapes may lead to the discovery of cultural regions dominated by Zen Buddhism, Neo-Confucianism, Catholicism and Protestantism, with different histories of origin and diffusion. It is assumed that physical environment has influenced the distribution of these religious landscapes and thus development of these cultural regions.

The identification, description, and interpretation of landscapes has long been a major geographical enterprise. There is substantial agreement that landscape study is one of the important themes of geographical research, most notably in the subfield of cultural geography. Based on this agreement, old and new approaches on landscape study will be introduced in this book. It is suggested that the landscape approach will offer a foundation for future geographical study on Korean culture. The identification and description of landscapes will be able to present which landscapes should be interpreted in more detail. In the end, the interpretation of cultural landscapes in Korea will contribute to the understanding of Korean culture.

However, methodological objections were raised against the definition of geography as landscape science, and they were centered on two issues: the vagueness of the term and certain philosophical difficulties. According to Mikesell (1968), landscape had been employed by geographers to refer to the impression conveyed by an area, to the objects producing that impression, and to the area itself. In other words, the dual meaning of "scenery" and "area" was carried over from the popular use of the term "landscape." Traditional cultural geographers have focused on the concept of area, whereas new cultural geographers have paid attention to the meaning of scenery.

Mikesell (1968) proposes that the cultural landscapes studied most often by geographers are those which have to do with the occupation and utilization of land. Such landscapes include the form and arrangement of settlement (houses and other buildings); field patterns, roads, paths, and other communication lines; crops and the "wild" or "tame" vegetation associated with settlements; irrigation works; and surface modifications. In Korea, rural landscape, in particular, reflects the way that land has been occupied and utilized. *Yangban* lineage villages, irrigation networks, folk housing and village forests in Korea contain local histories of occupying and utilizing the land. In this book, special attention will be given to the relationship between these cultural landscapes and the physical environment.

The evolution of a landscape is a gradual and cumulative process -- it has its own local history. The stages in that local history have meaning for the present landscape as well as that of the past. Moreover, the present landscape may reflect local history of migration or diffusion. It is, in fact, logically impossible to prove that a given landscape has been invented or introduced in a place without external influence. In Korea, foreign religions, such as Buddhism, Neo-Confucianism and Christianity, were introduced into one locality, and from there diffused into other locations. Without knowledge of the diffusion process, therefore, it is almost impossible to understand religious landscapes in Korea.

In reality, both by internal evolution and by diffusion, a culture grows and spreads. A culture often spreads when those who share it move about, and come to prevail over those of other cultures in new territories. The simplest demonstration of the spread of culture is the proof of movements by people who possess it. Migration, however, is often naive assumption rather than a demonstrated fact that can mislead research. Individual cultural landscapes can become widely distributed through contact of peoples, without any population movements taking place. In Korea, where folk cultures could spread without as well as with migration, it is difficult to relate the origin and diffusion of a certain folk landscape directly to migration.

According to Wagner and Mikesell (1962:12-15), the problems of diffusion versus independent invention can be investigated by geographical methods: the plotting of single and joint distributions and densities of given landscapes; the delimitation and comparison of regions by various criteria; the mapping of the spatial arrangement and organization of related landscape elements; the charting of movements; the identification of physical and biotic zonation. Cultural geography, then, seeks to discover four kinds of facts: the origin in time and place of given landscapes; the routes, times, and manner of their dissemination; the distribution of former culture areas; and the character of former cultural landscapes.

But, in reality, it is not always possible to unveil these facts without obtaining written records or oral tradition on migration in the field work. In Korea, it is difficult to chart the routes of movements and the manner of dissemination in folk and linguistic landscapes, because they have very few written records and oral traditions, testifying to their own histories: origin and diffusion. Without knowing precisely the routes, times, and manner of their dissemination, it is difficult to explore the former character of folk and linguistic landscapes as well as the distribution of former folk or linguistic regions.

The cultural landscape is a concrete product of the complicated interplay between a human community and its natural conditions. It is a heritage of many years of cultural evolution or many generations of human adaptation to the physical environment: the overall pattern of mountains, hills and rivers; the climate; and the ocean coasts. In Korea, folk and rural landscapes have developed in close association with physical environment. A particular folk region tends to correspond with a natural region: river basin or climatic zone.

The deities worshipped in village rituals are often made of local materials that are available in the vicinity. Irrigation networks, large in scale, have evolved in the process of introducing technology that enabled people to overcome natural conditions. Folk housing of mixed type emerged as an outcome of cultural exchange and adaptation to climatic conditions. For this reason, this book will make an inquiry into the characteristics of physical environment within which these cultural landscapes have been developed.

2) "New" Cultural Geography

Historians usually refer to culture as the artistic and intellectual product of an elite. However, in "new" cultural geography, culture is not the safe preserve of an elite who dominate a country's major institutions and lead its national culture. Jackson (1989:2), suggests that it is a domain in which social relations of dominance and subordination are negotiated and resisted. In other words, new cultural geographers look at cultures of socially marginal groups as well as the dominant, national culture of the elite.

After all, they define culture as the way that social relations of a group are structured and shaped. This definition of culture may be helpful to explain cultural landscapes in Korea as a whole. The transformation of Buddhism or Shamanism in the Chosŏn Period cannot be examined without knowing the social relations of its believers with those in Neo-Confucianism.

I. Introduction

Understanding the regionalization or localization of a folk landscape also requires the knowledge of social relations of dominance and subordination. Shamanism, in particular, has served as a domain within which socially marginal groups, including women, resisted the elite culture.

New cultural geographers also criticized that "traditional" cultural geographers played down the wider social context in which cultures are constituted and expressed. In their view, cultures involve relations of power, reflected in patterns of dominance and subordination. According to Jackson (1989:3), the concepts of ideology and hegemony are therefore central to their landscape study, focusing on the processes through which dominant meanings are imposed, negotiated, and registered. Ideology, in particular, serves a crucial role in the reproduction of society, disguising the inevitability of class conflict and representing the interests of the ruling class as the interests of the whole society.

As stated by Williams (1977:55-71), ideology may refer to any system of beliefs that has characteristics of a particular class or group. An ideology operates favorably for a dominant social group by systematically promoting certain meanings in preference to them. In this sense, an ideology can be defined as the way in which ideas come to represent certain interests or conceal them in a more or less consistent way. In Korea, Buddhism under the Koryŏ Dynasty and Neo-Confucianism under the Chosŏn Dynasty, indeed, served as ideologies that represented the interests of the ruling class. The dominant, military elite group in the Koryŏ Period systematically supported Zen Buddhism, while the *yangban* group in the Chosŏn Period publicly favored Neo-Confucianism.

To explore the connection between ideology and power requires a knowledge of the concept of hegemony. In common usage, hegemony refers to a situation of uncontested political supremacy. In Gramsci's work, however, it refers to the power of a dominant class to persuade subordinate classes to accept its moral, political, and cultural values as the natural order. In this sense, the hegemony refers to the power of persuasion as opposed to the power of coercion through the use of physical force. Gramsci (1971; 1973) argues that from the standpoint of a ruling class in a capitalist society, the excercise of hegemony is a much more efficient strategy than coercive control.

Then, in Korea, even prior to the development of capitalism, social relations in the countryside were already complicated with the excercise of hegemony as a political strategy. The ruling class, called *yangban*, in the Chosŏn Period adopted Neo-Confucianism as an ideology to persuade the subordinate class, called *sangmin*, to accept their values. The meaning of rural landscape such as pavilion, for instance, cannot be interpreted fully without considering Neo-Confucianism as an ideology which had once dominated social relations at that time. It is assumed that when Neo-Confucianism as an ideology grew in social power, the territory that pavilions occupied might have expanded.

Nonetheless, however powerful the elite became, their dominance would always be challenged by those in subordinate positions. The dominant values of any social elite might be aspired to by the middle class, but they were likely to be rejected by those lower down the social hierarchy as unobtainable. In Korea, believers in folk beliefs including Shamanism, mostly in remote locations, were capable of rejecting the dominant mores of the ruling class. In the isolated mountains and islands, cultural landscapes in association with Neo-Confucianism are relatively few today.

Jackson (1989:54) suggests that subordinated groups can use cultural or symbolic strategies to resist subordination from the ruling class. The rituals, with various styles of dress and patterns of verbal and non-verbal behavior, may imply an attitude of resistance to those in power. Style is a secret language, and can be a form of cultural insubordination that expresses an attitude of defiance and disrespect to those in authority.

In Korea, rituals in folk beliefs, including Shamanism, show areal differentiation in terms of performance style. How much a particular ritual was assimilated into Neo-Confucianism or Buddhism seems to be in relation with geographical location and social position that its performers had once occupied in the past. Village rituals, indeed, vary so much in style from village to village that one cannot recognize a typical form among them. The regionalization or localization of village rituals, then, should be explained in terms of capability of resisting cultural subordination power.

New cultural geographers believe that cultural geography must go beyond the mapping of languages towards the study of language itself as a medium through which intersubjective meaning is communicated. According to them, it will need to explore the way that language reflects and reinforces social boundaries, constituted in space and time. A linguistic community is formed around shared meanings which reinforce a group's identity and mark it off from neighboring communities.

In Korea, place names have been linguistic media through which communication takes place within linguistic communities, characterized by the possession of shared belief systems, myths, and ideologies, as well as a common language. Place names demonstrate an areal differentiation in assimilating into the Chinese style, depending upon the geographical locations and social positions that their users occupied. In this book, place names will be examined from this viewpoint to assess their values in the formation of group identity.

There is a growing recognition that there are many ways of seeing and reading the landscape. For new cultural geographers, one of the interests is the investigation of multiple discourses about place and identity, uncovering previously ignored senses of place and visions of landscape. Indeed, landscape is object and subject both personally and socially. If traditional studies of landscape stressed the outsider's view and concentrated on the morphology of external forms, recent studies seek to reverse this by discovering the identity and experience of the insider.

A landscape has such symbolic dimensions -- the symbolic and cultural meaning coined in landscape by those who have produced and sustained them, and who have come into contact with them. Cosgrove (1984:15) insists that landscape represents a historically specific way of experiencing the world, which is meaningful to certain social groups. The ways in which symbolic representation of landscapes reflect power relations, including relations of class and colonial domination, are also becoming the focus of examination. In Korea, even prior to the development of capitalism, urban landscapes, particularly in administrative centers, were embedded with symbolic representation of power relations.

Moreover, Cosgrove (1984:15) claims that landscape is an

ideological concept. It represents a way in which certain classes of people have signified themselves and their world through their imagined relationship with nature. The rulers of the Chosŏn Dynasty imposed ideas from Neo-Confucianism and Feng-shui on the city planning to signify their own social role with respect to external nature. These ideas were often directly projected on the composition of street and gate names as well as the spatial arrangement of avenues and public buildings. The Japanese colonialists, then, tried to erase these urban landscapes and establish those of their own ideal versions. In this book, therefore, how important Neo-Confucianism and Feng-shui were in the formation of urban landscapes and how the Japanese colonialists ignored their significance will be questioned in more details.

Recently, the emphasis of the landscape studies has shifted towards problematizing the ways in which landscapes have been represented in written texts, art, maps or topographical surveys. According to Cosgrove and Daniels (1988:1), a landscape is a cultural image, a pictorial way of representing, structuring or symbolizing surroundings. The landscape geographers have turned to work in developing ways of reading the landscape as though it were text. It has been argued that cultural geography may treat landscape as a text embodying a range of discourses that affect how people act.

Reading the iconography of landscape, through art and architecture, cartography and design, represents one of the most prominent new directions in cultural geography. In Korea, the pictorial maps drawn in the Chosŏn Period may serve as fine texts through which one can read the inner world of meaning and experiences about urban landscape. A careful reading of an old map would enable the reader to interpret "the way of seeing" the world, the iconography of urban landscape, at that time.

Cosgrove and Daniels (1988:2) recognize that iconographic study seeks to probe meaning in a work of art in its historical context, and in particular, to analyze the ideas implicated in its imagery. It may consciously seek to conceptualize pictures as encoded texts to be deciphered. In geography, it might attempt to read the symbolism of the urban landscape, and the values of the people who shaped it.

The iconography in geography, then, is to study how the landscape represents and embodies patterns of power relations, and this is in turn represented in art, pictures and descriptions. On old maps of walled-cities in Korea, cultural landscapes, such as man-made mounds and forests, were often depicted in exaggeration, which represent the ideal visions of Feng-shui. These maps, thus, provide the clues to decipher the iconography of urban landscape shared by the city dwellers.

3) An "Integrated" Cultural Geography

In traditional society, in which the friction of distance is a significant social barrier, religion, superstition and social beliefs are part of the "social glue" that holds a people together. Here, diffusionist thinking may be proven more useful in the study of cultural landscapes. In Korea, many folk, linguistic and rural landscapes can be classified into this type, whose regionalization or localization has to do with cultural diffusion. However, this traditional approach may not be suited perfectly to the study of religious and urban landscapes in Korea, complicated in the history of power relations.

Regardless of any recent advances, traditional cultural geography is deservedly criticized for relying on a poorly developed concept of culture. Even the scholars from Berkeley School admit that Sauer, the founder of the traditional school, devoted little effort to the question of culture, with the fear that defining culture rigorously would lead to mindless reductionism (Price & Lewis, 1998:11). Accordingly, he loosely employed the term "culture" only to describe and distinguish the range of human diversity. For traditional cultural geographers, it was a heuristic tool, not an explanatory concept.

Admittedly, until recently there have been few from the traditional school who were concerned with the "inner workings" of culture. In their analyses, they clearly neglected the wider social, economic and political structures of society, and the ways in which cultural practices reflect, reinforce or challenge accepted cultural norms and standards. Certainly, there is an explanatory limit of Sauer's diffusionist thinking.

In geographical usage, landscape is an imprecise and ambiguous concept whose meaning has defied many attempts to define it with specificity. As a term widely employed in painting and imaginative literature as well as environmental design and planning, landscape carries multiple layers of meaning. Landscape, for all its vagueness, retains currency in geographical writing. Genetic morphology found favor in historical, cultural and physical geography, all of which have employed the landscape concept extensively. Under the morphological method, however, landscape becomes a static, deterministic object of scientific enquiry. Formal morphology as an account of landscape, to a certain extent, ignores such symbolic dimensions -- the symbolic and cultural meaning embedded in these forms.

Now there is a need to further integrate the investigation of social processes with the study of landscape, by incorporating social theory and political concerns into the older approach. In order to improve an explanatory ability, cultural geographers should be mindful of complex social and cultural processes. Traditional cultural geography will profit from a greater sensitivity to social theory, while retaining its own merits in research methods. It is advised to grapple with some of the sophisticated social-theoretical constructs now being offered by the new school.

New cultural geography has attempted to place cultural geography within recent developments in critical social theory, adopting a theoretical definition of culture. This new school is to view culture as the medium or idiom through which meanings are expressed. Based upon the premise of a plurality of cultures, culture is the domain in which these meanings are contested. Starting from this point, new cultural geography has tended to focus on subordinate groups, without losing attention to the relations between dominant and subordinate groups.

In this context, an "integrated" cultural geography should not ignore dominant cultures whose agenda remains to be investigated. Because cultures contain a multiplicity of meanings, it is always possible to arbitrate among them by means of the interests they represent. According to Jackson (1989:185) dominant cultures are not identical with subordinate ones, neither is popular culture the equivalent of elite culture: they vary in terms of the scale of cultural power. An integrated cultural geography would be just as interested in seeing how dominant values are institutionalized through the operation of hegemonic forces at the national level as it would be in tracing the detailed contours of particular subcultures at the local level.

There must be a common ground between traditional and new cultural geographies that can be developed. The best of cultural geography has always been, and will always be, oriented to empirical issues, but concern for empirical inquiry by no means entails an empiricist epistemology. It would be possible to conduct a genuinely empirical, but theoretically sensitive research in the study of cultural landscapes. Korea, abundant in traditional cultural landscapes, may serve as a laboratory within which this experiment can be carried out. To fulfill this duty in this book, religious, folk, linguistic, rural and urban landscapes in Korea will be carefully examined one by one, from an integrated viewpoint on cultural geography.

2. Religious Landscapes

2. Religious Landscapes

Korea has many distinctive religious characteristics, and the harmony in pluralism is one of them. In Korea, Confucianism has pervaded all layers of ordinary life, and the degree of pervasion is even greater than in China and Japan. Korean Buddhism is famous for its syncreticism that holds a synthetic view on the Buddhist doctrines. Korean Christianity, in particular Protestantism, is also noted for its fundamentalism which is even more active than in American Christianity. These three religions which were brought into Korea from the outside are now coexisting in harmony.

If Confucianism is not viewed as a religion, the total religious population in Korea amounts to 51.1%, and Buddhism, Protestantism and Catholicism occupy almost all of it. Confucianism has affected Koreans in the realm of social behavior such as ancestor worship rather than in the practice of praying. Many Koreans would prefer to see Confucianism as a social ideology to share with their fellow Koreans than as a religion to depend on for their own eternal lives. The number of believers in Confucianism amounts to 91% of the total population, but most do not identify themselves as Confucianists in terms of religion.

Moreover, Confucianism and Buddhism are less organized than Christianity, and the boundary between them cannot be clearly drawn. Some Koreans are both Confucianists and Buddhists or both Confucianists and Christians or both Buddhists and Shamanists. Within only a century, Protestantism and Catholicism have grown rapidly enough to challenge the hegemony of Confucianism and Buddhism. The number of Christians is now slightly less than that of Buddhists, but in terms of membership with active participation in a congregation the number is considerably higher.

In general, Koreans have been resilient in accepting foreign religions with ease, and adapting their lives to their doctrines smoothly. They have been adept at reconciling indigenous religions with foreign religions, and allowing various religions to intermingle with one another. Koreans have demonstrated an open-mindedness to foreign religions, and even to interpretations of doctrines within a religion. Today Buddhism, Confucianism, Christianity, and other religions are growing together influencing one another. These religions sometimes conflict with each other, but in general coexist in harmony. This religious plurality is very peculiar to Korea in world history, and even the overlapping of various styles of faith within a religion has been permitted in Korea.

Such a remarkable motive for harmony, rather than conflict against religious pluralism, may not have been from religious interests per se, but secular ones. These secular interests may have been concerned with social and political relationships in association with hegemony, ideology and power. Some Koreans may have used religious doctrines as ideology to seize hegemony in social and political power. A foreign religion itself, once it was adopted by an elite group, may have been used as an ideology separating the dominant from the dominated. As a result, one can read the secular history of ideology or power in the various religious landscapes in Korea.

The evolution of religious landscape, moreover, is a gradual and cumulative process which has a history. The religious landscape is a tangible expression of the changing nature of the religion itself. Some sects disappeared, while others changed subtlely, and so their impact on the religious landscape is complex. The imprint of religious ideas on the landscape takes various forms and intensities, but it is most strongly felt at religious centers. The site characteristics, orientation, and types of structures and their spatial arrangement are the major components of the religious landscape in Korea (**Figure 2**).

1) CATHOLIC CHURCHES AROUND Ansŏng TOWN

Catholicism was introduced into Korea in the late 18th century, but was confronted with suppression from the government. The Chosŏn Dynasty armed with Confucian principles severely persecuted Catholics. As Catholicism regards God as the only absolute being, it was inevitably opposed to Confucian ethics. In particular, Catholicism prohibited the Confucian ancestor ritual, the practical expression of loyalty to the king and filial duty to parents. The persecution was very intense from 1801 to 1869. The official persecution began in 1801 when hundreds of Korean Catholics were executed, and afterwards the level of execution was even stepped up in 1839, 1846, 1866, and 1869. During this period, about 10,000 believers and 10 priests were mar-

2. Religious Landscapes

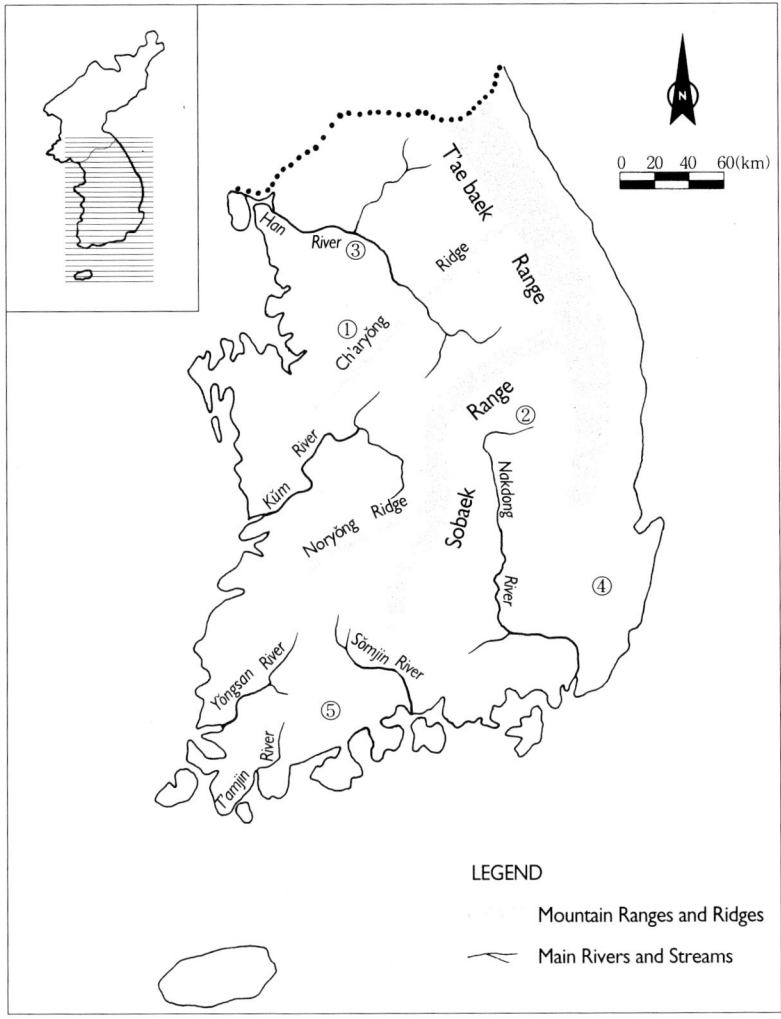

Figure 2. Locations of religious landscapes in Korea:
① Catholic churches around Ansŏng Town
② Sŏwon (Private Confucian Academies) around Andong City
③ Protestant churches around the Yŏngdŭngp'o District in Seoul
④ T'ongdo Temple at Yongch'wi Mountain
⑤ Songkwang Temple at Chogye Mountain

tyred. After Japan forced the Chosŏn Dynasty to open its doors in 1876, the persecution was substantially weakened and finally ceased in 1898.

During these decades of persecution in the 19th century, Korean Catholics hid themselves in remote mountain valleys where they established Catholic villages (Koo & Nahm, 1977:182). Herein, they grew tobacco or made the earthenware pots in which Korean housewives stored food. Their contacts with non-Catholic Koreans were made through infrequent trips to rural market towns to sell their goods. In this context, Ansŏng Town and its vicinity was one of the places with the geographical conditions ideal for Catholics to locate their own villages. To the eastern side of Ansŏng Town run mountain ridges, while to the western side the plains are spread out along the streams. Catholics were secluded in these mountain areas, except for commuting to the market in Ansŏng Town. Among the villages where earthenware pots were made, only one remains today near Ansŏng Town. In this village named Chŏm-mal, one can see how Catholics lived in the 19th century (Kim, 1996:51-52).

During the Chosŏn Dynasty, Ansŏng Town was well known as one of the biggest commercial centers in Korea with a periodic market. It was situated in a favorable place where the main transportation routes of land and water interconnected. With Ansŏng Town as a center, the water routes ran from west to east in contrast to the land route from north to south. Catholics in the mountain valleys were able to visit market places in Ansŏng Town and sell what they made and purchase what they needed. What they really wanted in the market places was possibly, however, information about the government.

2. Religious Landscapes

From the high Ch'ilhyŏn Mountain (516m), the mountain ridge branches out into three directions: northwest, east and southwest. When Catholics escaped from persecution in Seoul into remote mountains, they fled along the Kwangju Ridge running from north to south. Some of Catholics moving southwards settled down around Paet'i Pass where they could easily hide themselves and escape in time of emergency. Catholics thought that once the official ban on Catholicism was lifted they could return to Seoul from this mountain pass, not far from Seoul. A Catholic church was established temporarily in Paet'i Pass to serve as headquarters for Catholics taking refuge in the mountain valleys nearby. Today a newly constructed Catholic church stands, including the graveyards of those who were captured and martyred while retreating into the mountain valleys

Photo 1. A Memorial Catholic Church at Paet'i Pass: The church was built on the spot where a legendary priest named Yang-ŏp Choi, supervised in secret the missionary activities around there. Today, a Mass is performed every year to commemorate his sacrifice and feat in spreading Catholicism during hard times.

Photo 2. Graveyards for the martyred at Paet'i Pass: Once the government knew about the hiding place of Catholics, it raided them. At that time, many of them, even women or children, were captured or killed, and the killed were buried there by their surviving fellow Catholics.

(**Photo 1, 2**). This place is one of the most famous destinations for Catholic pilgrimage in Korea. Once a year this Catholic church holds a memorial service for Catholics who were martyred around Paet'i Pass.

Moreover, the mountain ranges in the east of Ansŏng Town attracted Catholics who lived on or along the western coast and wanted to escape from persecution. Large and small ports were developed in the bay areas on the western coast in connection with China as well as Seoul. Some of French priests from China traveled across the Yellow Sea and landed in these ports. These ports were the places in Korea where Catholicism was introduced from China. Tae-gŏn Kim, ordained as the first Korean priest and martyred in 1846, was a native of this western coast, and many other martyrs in the 19th century came from here.

Herein, the main Catholic churches built in the late 19th century can be seen even today. Among these the most famous are the Wangrim Main Church, the Kuhapdŏk Main Church and the Kongse-ri Main Church. These churches are worth visiting because of their peculiar building materials and architectural styles. It is believed that they accurately reflect the ways that Catholic churches were built during the 19th century in China. It is even said that red bricks were imported from China to build the Kongse-ri Main Church in 1895. As more Catholics from the western coast sought their own refuge in the mountain valleys, the number of Catholics decreased on the western coast.

In spite of the persecution, Catholicism in Korea continued to grow and in 1831 the Chosŏn Diocese was established. Foreign missionaries from Paris were sent to support Catholic churches in Korea. For the first time, in 1898, Catholics and Protestants alike were allowed to move and preach throughout Korea. In 1900, the Korean Catholic community was over 40,000 in number under the guidance of conservative priests from France, concentrated in the countryside.

The Chosŏn Diocese decided to establish a main Catholic church in Ansŏng Town, and in 1901 dispatched a French priest named Gombert there. He built the Kup'o-dong Main Church in 1901, and it is well known to the public for its building materials and architectural styles. What made this building so peculiar was the combination of two different building methods: Korean and Western. The entrance, including a tower, was built in western style, while the main hall was in Korean style (**Photo 3, 4**). Besides this building, there are more cathedrals that were built in the early 20th century around Ansŏng Town. These

Photo 3. Kup'o-dong Main Catholic Church in Ansŏng Town: Since it was built in 1910, the church has retained a mixed style of architecture, half Korean and half western.

Photo 4. The side wall of Kup'o-dong Main church: The roofs, windows and poles are all combined to have a mixed outlook.

buildings are also worth visiting and seeing because of their uniqueness in architectural style (**Figure 3, 4**).

After Priest Gombart came to Ansŏng Town, Catholic churches increased in number rapidly, along with Catholics, in the plain areas along Ansŏng Stream. Priest Gombart persuaded the Chosŏn Diocese to purchase the swampy lands along the stream, and reclaim them into agricultural lands (Kim, 1996 : 46-51). A large part of these swampy lands were exposed to salinization from sea water during the full tide, and were vulnerable to floods from river water during the rainy season. Most of these lands were left without cultivation, and their price was very cheap. Priest Gombart thought that he could purchase these lands with little money and reclaim them into agricultural lands for Catholics to cultivate. The reclamation of swampy lands certainly secured means of livelihood for many Catholics and contributed to the increase of Catholics. In these lands, Catholics established villages for their own with Catholic churches within, and cultivated wet-rice and other crops.

It was also Priest Gombart that introduced into these lands the planting of grapes from France. He decided to grow grape vines by himself to supply wine for Mass, or Catholic rituals, in his church. On his way back to Korea from France in 1901 he brought with him 32 German species to experiment with planting grape vines in Ansŏng Town (Kim, 1996 : 56-57). It is said that at first he planted grape vines in the foothills at the rear of his church. Among these species, one named Muskat or Black Hamburg adapted well to local soils and climate and still survives today. Since then the planting of grape vines has been widely spread, and now many horticultural gardens for grapes can be seen around Ansŏng Town. The major belt devoted to

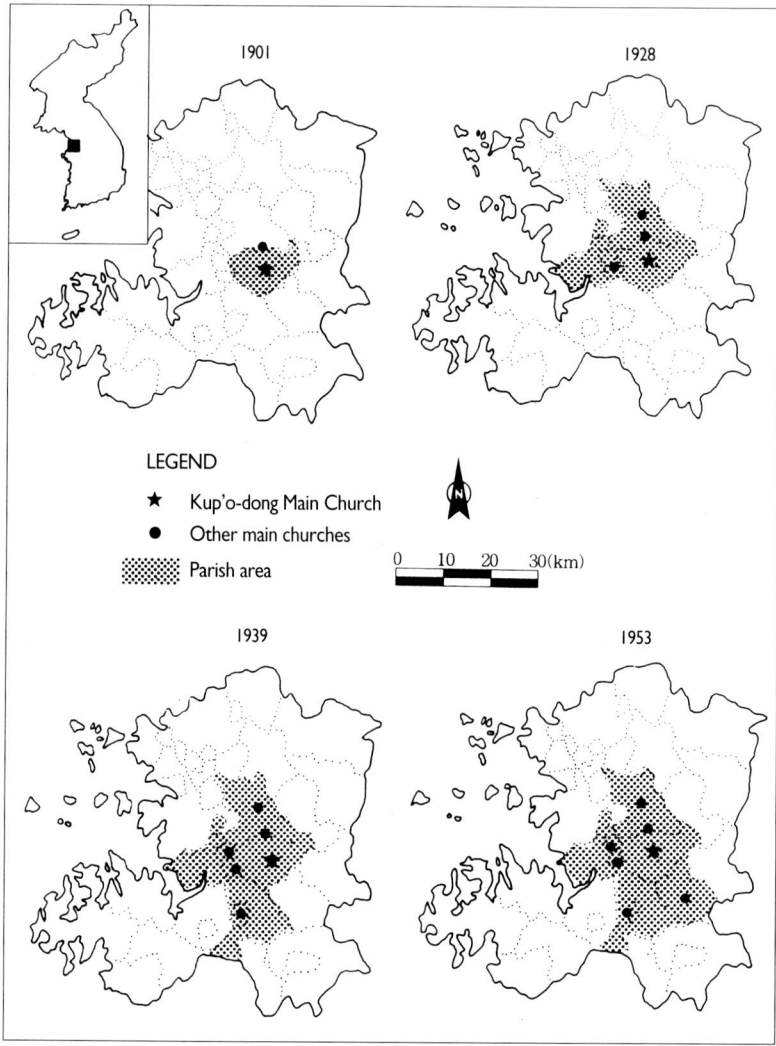

Figure 3. The growth of Catholic parishes around Ansŏng Town: The area of parishes grew rapidly between 1901 and 1939 with its center in Ansŏng Town. (Source: Ju-sŏp Kim, 1996, "The Growth of Catholicism around Ansŏng Town," Unpublished Master's Thesis, Department of Geography, Korea National University of Education, p. 43.)

2. Religious Landscapes

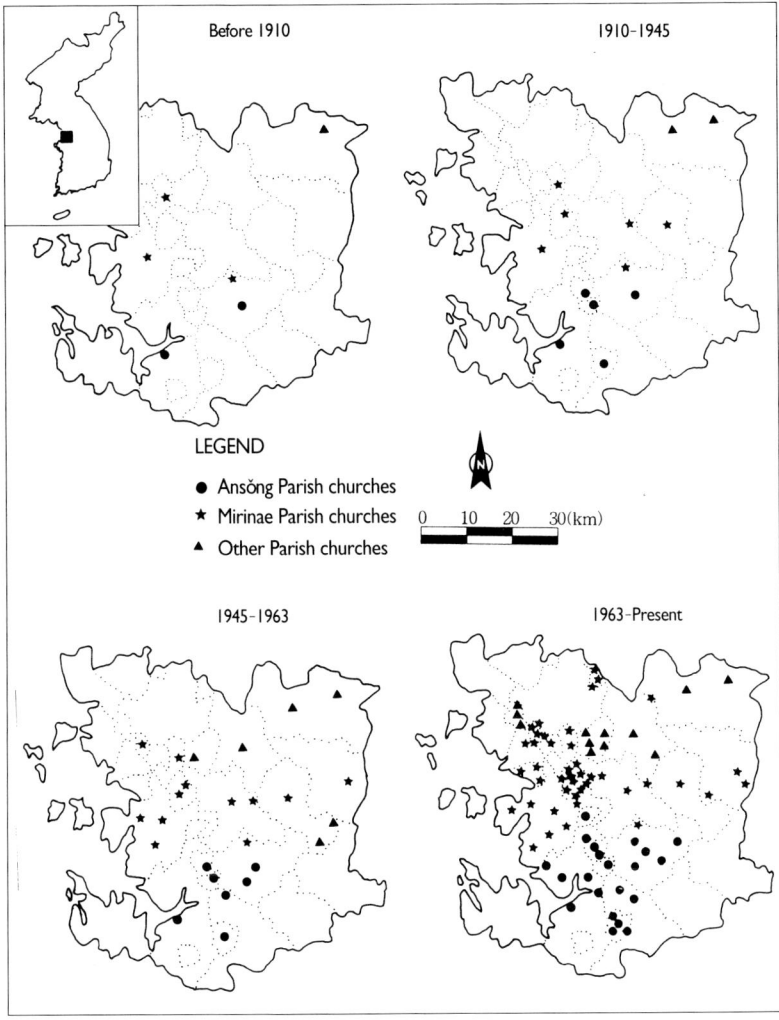

Figure 4. The increase of Catholic churches around Ansŏng Town: In Kyŏnggi Province, there are three headquarters that have supervised the growth of Catholic churches, and two of them are within the boundary of Ansŏng County. (Source: Ju-sŏp Kim, 1996, "The Growth of Catholicism around Ansŏng Town," Unpublished Master's Thesis, Department of Geography, Korea National University of Education, p. 17.)

growing grape vines for marketing has been formed in the mountain valleys to the east of Ansŏng Town. Interestingly enough, most farmers growing grape vines around here today are not Catholics.

2) SŎWON (PRIVATE CONFUCIAN ACADEMIES) AROUND ANDONG CITY

Although Confucianism has had more impact on Korean life than any other religion or philosophy, its influence is pervasive and even hidden when compared with Buddhism, Christianity or Shamanism. Buddhist temples abound in Korea and are ornate and beautiful. Christian churches are found almost everywhere in the countryside as well as in cities. Yet few visitors to Korea can see Confucian shrines or temples in cities or even in the countryside. In general, Confucian architecture is fairly simple, and its iconography is not as rich as that of the Buddhists. Large percentages of Koreans claim to be Buddhist or Christian or followers of Shamanism, but everyone in Korea, to one degree or another, is Confucian. Even those who believe in other religions perform Confucian rituals on a regular basis and adhere to other Confucian values in their everyday life.

Confucianism was first introduced into Korea in the 4th century (the Three Kingdoms Period), but began to make a fundamental impact on people's life when a "new" Confucianism was adopted during the Koryŏ Period. This Neo-Confucianism was finally proclaimed as the official ideology for the dynasty by the Yi household in 1392. Since then Neo-Confucianism has been valued as the perfect ideology in educating the common people

2. Religious Landscapes

as well as running the government. Neo-Confucianism, starting as political ideology, gradually became a religion that ordinary people should practice even in daily lives. After the Chosŏn Dynasty (1392-1910) decided to implement Confucian principles, the impact was felt throughout the society as a whole. In the late Chosŏn Period, Korea became the most Confucian society when compared with China and Japan.

There is no doubt that the most important ceremony in Confucianism was for Confucius himself, and famous Confucian sages. National Confucian ceremonies were held at the Sŏnggyunkwan, or National Confucian Academy, in Seoul. Here, the spiritual tablet of Confucius is enshrined together with those for the four disciples of Confucius, sixteen Chinese and eighteen Korean sages. This ceremony, at national level, was given a special name, the Sŏkjŏn Ritual, which was the most elaborate of all the Confucian ceremonies in Korea. At the county, lineage, and family level, Confucian ceremonies were also performed, and the most frequent were those at family level. The county level ceremonies were held at either the *hyanggyo* (the local Confucian schools) or at the *sŏwon* (private Confucian academies). Both the *hyanggyo* and the *sŏwon* served the dual function of an educational and a ritual center.

At the *hyanggyo* as a public institute, the honored were Confucius himself and eighteen Korean sages admitted into the national Confucian shrine at the Sŏnggyunkwan, while at the *sŏwon* as a private institute, the enshrined were one or several Korean sages or prominent scholars with a certain relation to the county. At that time, the relation did not necessarily mean that the Korean sage or prominent scholar was from the county. Sometimes his disciples from the county were also enshrined along with the Korean sage or prominent scholar.

When not working for the government, Neo-Confucian scholars liked to retire to the mountains and forests in the provinces where they were respected by their fellow clan members and academic followers. While staying there, they could form strong social and political groups on the basis of common ancestral and academic ties. The *sŏwon* in Korea, originally modeled after the private Confucian academy of Song China, began as a local center for Confucian education, and gradually developed into a local base for social and political power. This phenomenon, peculiar to Korea, emerged as a trend in the early 16th century, and afterwards became widespread all over the country. The local *yangban*, retirees or descendants of scholar-officials, used the *sŏwon* as a means for them to enlarge or maintain social and political power. The royal court in the Chosŏn Dynasty with strong emphasis on Confucian learning sometimes provided financial support for the *sŏwon* where a national hero or sage was enshrined. Increasing steadily from the early 16th century, its number reached more than 650 by the middle of the 19th century. It is not surprising, therefore, that among these, 264 were well-off, endowed with land and slaves by the royal court (Joe,1997 : 284-285).

It is known that in the upper reaches of the Nakdong River including Andong City, the distribution density of the *sŏwon* was the highest in Korea. Even the first *sŏwon*, named Sosu Academy (originally named Paekundong Academy), was established in a location not far from contemporary Andong City in 1542. This Sosu Academy is now relatively well-preserved in the original location, a foothill with a stream encircling around it (**Photo 5**). It is said that this place was originally

2. Religious Landscapes

Photo 5. Sosu Academy (sŏwon) beside a stream: Built on the former site of a Buddhist temple, the academy did not have the typical spatial arrangement of buildings that can usually be found in other sŏwons.

occupied by a Buddhist temple, named Suksusa, in the Koryŏ Period. In the Chosŏn Period, the upper reaches of the Nakdong River served as a Confucian seed-bed where the *sŏwon* proliferated after the first introduction. The number of the *sŏwon* grew substantially, with the heaviest concentration in Andong City, between the late 17th and the early 19th centuries. During this period, Andong City emerged as a core of the so-called Confucian culture area (**Figure 5, 6**).

Two reasons can be found why Andong City and its surrounding area contained more *sŏwon* than any other area: a sage named T'oegye or Hwang Yi and natural conditions. After Hwang Yi died in 1570, his disciples established the Tosan Academy in 1574 at the location where Hwang Yi had lived and

Photo 6. Tosan Academy (sŏwon) on the slope of a valley: Building were located on the spot from which one could look down upon the stream.

taught Neo-Confucianism (**Photo 6**). Today, this private Confucian academy is also well-preserved with a fine museum containing Hwang Yi's personal belongings. Its physical location and spatial arrangement seem to conform better to the general principle in the construction of the *sŏwon* than Sosu Academy. After 1574, his disciples and their disciples as well, kept on establishing the *sŏwon* at new locations where they could secure land. Under the name of a great scholar, Hwang Yi, they found a legitimate cause to ask for public approval from the royal court on the opening of the *sŏwon*.

Hwang Yi is even today respected as one of the two most prominent scholars on Neo-Confucianism, and is regarded as the founder of a Korean Confucian school named Yŏngnam-hakp'a or T'oegye-hakp'a. To spread Hwang Yi's

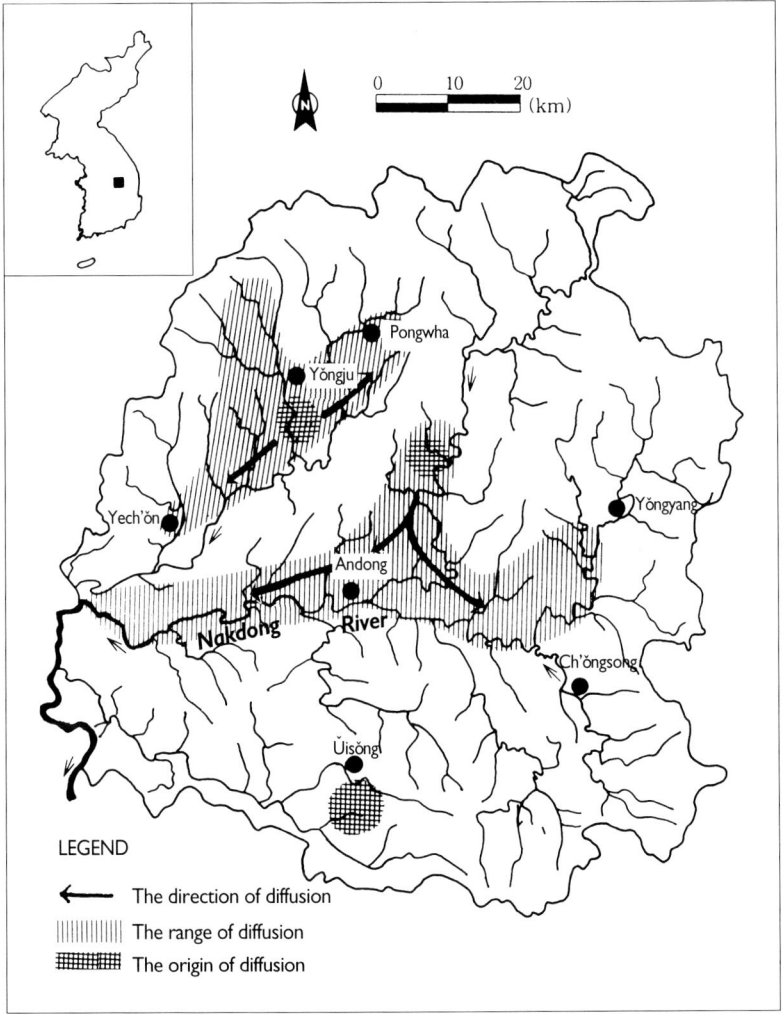

Figure 5. The diffusion process of *sŏwon* (private Confucian acaemy) around Andong City: In the initial stage of diffusion, there existed two centers from which *sŏwons* branched out, and each spatial unit of diffusion approximated each spatial unit of a stream valley. (Source: Pŏm-ki Kwon, 1996, "The Formation of *Sŏwon* Cultural Region around Andong City," Unpublished Master's Thesis, Department of Geography, Korea National University of Education, p. 53.)

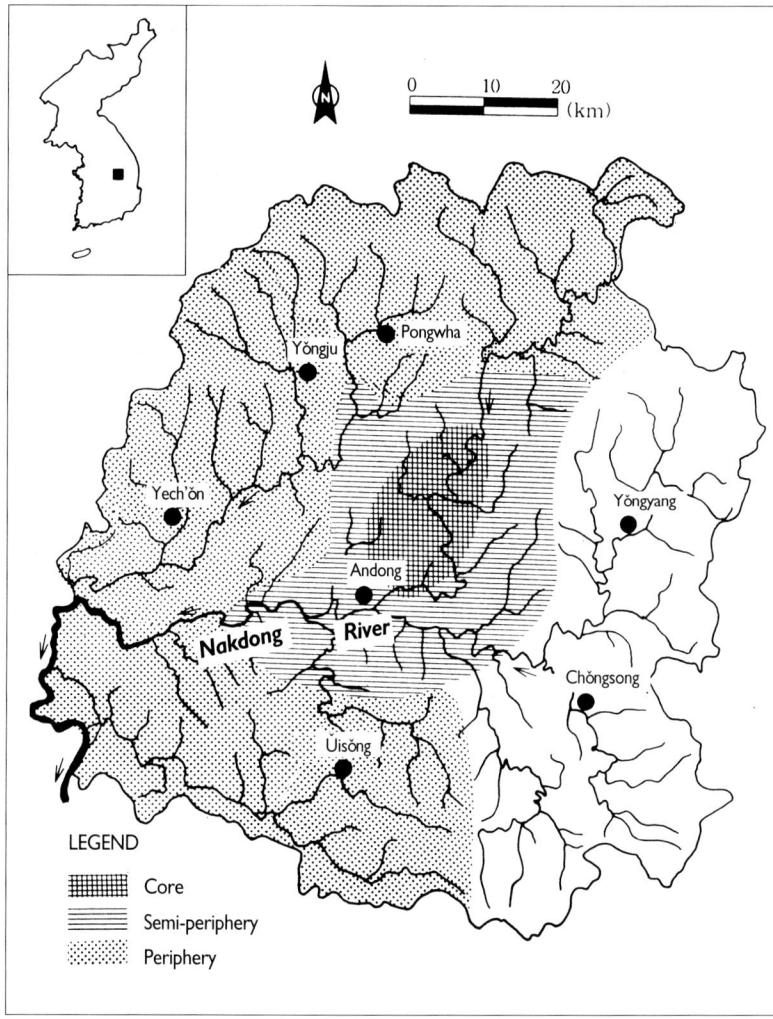

Figure 6. The regional structure of the Andong Culture Area: In the final stage of diffusion, Andong City and its vicinity emerged as the core of the Sŏwon Culture Region. The diffusion, however, was not so much successful to the east of Andong City. (Source: Pŏm-ki Kwon, 1996, "The formation of Sŏwon Cultural Region around Andong City," Unpublished Master's Thesis, Department of Geography, Korea National University of Education, p. 57.)

teachings was good for the people as well as the royal court because it contributed to the construction of society based on Neo-Confucianism, the political ideology adopted by the Chosŏn Dynasty. However, in reality, their hidden motivation in establishing the *sŏwon* was to strengthen relationship by birth and teacher-disciple relations enabling them to excercise extralegal powers in their respective local area (Kwon, 1996:25;31).

In the upper reaches of the Nakdong River are many valleys opening southwards with streams flowing in a curve. According to Zhu Xi, the Chinese founder of Neo-Confucianism, such a site was endowed with a physical environment ideal for studying with self-reflection. In the 12th and 13th centuries, Zhu Xi and other philosophers in Song China worked on the reinterpretation, and later their philosophy came to be known as Neo-Confucianism. They were concerned with broader questions than those answered in the Confucian classics. According to their view on the metaphysics of this world, the roots of all life rest in *li* and *chi* (pronounced *yi* and *ki* in Korean). *Li* is understood as "mental principle" or "reason," and *ki* is often regarded as "material force" (Koo & Nahm, 1997:141-142). Each creation has its own appearance because of its *li*, and each comes into being through *chi*. If one were to understand Neo-Confucianism, one ought to study the way that *li* and *chi* work together in the universe.

Confucius said that those with wisdom or knowledge enjoy streams while those with virtue or tolerance like mountains. Zhu Xi elaborated on this Confucian idea about nature, suggesting that a curving valley through which a meandering stream flows downwards should be ideal for studying the metaphysics of this world. He said that the mind of a person who knows thoroughly all the principles of the universe can be compared to a clean stream flowing gently, but without stopping. He insisted that Confucian scholars must not be isolated so much from the human world as Buddhist monks. Confucian scholars should not stay too far distant from the human world, while at the same time trying not to meddle in human affairs. Unlike Buddhist or Taoist monks, they avoided too remote mountains with turbulent streams as their place for practicing self-discipline. To practice their own discipline, Buddhist or Taoist monks liked to find deep mountain valleys with mystical rocks and water pools or falls.

Moreover, Zhu Xi himself once described the place, ideal for the study of Neo-Confucianism, as slopes or foothills of gently-sloped mountains or hills through which streams are gently zigzagging nine times. He gave a generic name to this valley with a stream curving nine times as *kugok*, or nine-curves, with a specific name in front of it. He also offered to each curve a specific name, usually symbolic in its meaning. In the upper reaches of the Nakdong River, the places with such topographic conditions can be found more easily, and Hwang Yi and his disciples located these places to practice their own self-discipline. Chukkye Nine-Curves and Sŏnyudong Nine-Curves were stream valleys which Hwang Yi found similar to Zhu Xi's description, and Panbyŏn Nine-Curves and Wagye Nine-Curves were what his disciples located as copies of Hwang Yi's Chukkye Nine-Curves. In case that Hwang Yi's disciples and their disciples could not find nine-curved stream valleys, they at least located their *sŏwon* beside streams, following Zhu Xi's ideas. Pyŏngsan Academy, a private Confucian academy which Sŏng-ryong Ryu, one of the best of Hwang Yi's disciples, built in

2. Religious Landscapes

1613, was located at a depositional or defensive hilly slope inside a meandering stream, and faced picturesque cliffs with an image of a folding screen.

The basic principles in the spatial construction of a *sŏwon* were similar to those in Sŏnggyunkwan or *hyanggyo*. It consisted of a lecture hall, two dormitories (in the east and west), a library, and a shrine hall. In the shrine hall, spiritual tablets for one or more prominent Confucian sages or scholars were preserved. When it was large in size, a *nugak*, or a multistoried pavilion, as an entrance was built in the front. If small in size, only a shrine hall stands without a lecture hall, dormitories and libraries. The *sŏwon* with only a shrine hall and sometimes with a lecture hall, began to appear from the late 18th century when the *sŏwon* lost its original function as an educational institute. From the late 18th century, the *sŏwon* became more important as a monument demonstrating social prestige and maintaining the social power of a family or lineage group. This type of the *sŏwon* was a private Confucian academy owned by a lineage group, sometimes nothing but a religious temple containing only the portraits or spiritual tablets of ancestors as distinguished scholars. To these sacred ancestors, seasonal rituals were dedicated in common by their descendants to solemnize their authority. In terms of building style as well as religious elements, the *sŏwon* was even shabbier than a Buddhist temple. The number of these academies tends to increase in the locations distant from the Sosu Academy and the Tosan Academy where Hwang Yi's school's influence decreased (Kwon, 1996:49-50). These are also frequently found in the midst of villages or foothills without a stream flowing through.

3) PROTESTANT CHURCHES AROUND THE YŎNGDŬNGP'O DISTRICT IN SEOUL

The first Protestant missionaries did not arrive in Korea until 1884, a hundred years after the first conversions to Catholicism. There were more Catholics than Protestants in Korea until the early 20th century, but from the early 20th century Protestants began to outnumber Catholics (Koo & Nahm,1997:183-184). After the Korean government publicly recognized religious freedom in 1898, Protestant converts continued to be much more visible in public than Catholics, reinforcing the idea of Protestants as representing Christianity. As a result, in the early 20th century Koreans thought that Catholicism and Protestantism were two separate religions, rather than merely two different versions of Christianity. Even today when Koreans talk of Christians, they usually mean Protestants.

After the Rev. H. G. Underwood, from the United States, established the first Presbyterian church in Korea, named Saemunan Church in 1887, the number of churches continued to grow more rapidly than any other religion. Immediately, Methodists and other denominations of American Protestantism followed Presbyterians to come to Korea. Today, about twelve million Koreans call themselves Christians, and this is a remarkable phenomenon in a nation which had only half a million Christians in 1940. Christianity, in particular Protestantism, achieved its status as one of the three major religions in Korea in slightly over one hundred years. If someone visits Seoul for the first time as a foreigner, he or she may be astonished by the Christian cross soaring in the sky over thousands of Protestant churches. The large number of Christians in Korea, over 20% of

Photo 7. Yŏŭido Sunbokŭm (Full Gospel) Church in the Yŏngdŭngp'o District: Situated in the midst of buildings and apartments, the church boasts of the largest membership in the world. Its members come from distant areas, as well as near to the church, in Seoul.

the population, heavily concentrated in large cities, is surprising as compared with China and Japan.

In the Yŏngdŭngp'o District, with its center in the Yŏngdŭngp'o Railroad Station, are also seen plenty of Protestant churches, either old or new. Here the urban landscape is dominated by factories and stores, gray in color, and dotted with churches, red in color. The red-colored brick buildings and crosses of churches can be easily recognized in the middle of the gray-colored cement buildings of factories and stores. This area, as a subsidiary urban center in Seoul, is one of the earliest where Protestants missionaries began to erect churches in Seoul. In 1903, Rev. Underwood erected a Presbyterian church, named

Yŏngdŭngp'o Changro Church, near the Yŏngdŭngp'o Railroad Station (Park, 1999:59). Moreover, the Yŏngdŭngp'o District hosts the largest church in Korea, named Yŏŭido Sunbokŭm Church. This Full Gospel Church which Rev. Paul Yong-gi Cho established in 1973 has had an explosive growth and records the largest congregation in the world with over 70,000 members (**Photo 7**).

It seems that Protestantism has grown hand in hand with urban population in Korea. From the beginning, Protestant missionaries focused on large cities such as Seoul where urbanization was in rapid progress. They always paid much attention to centers of transportation networks, residential areas and manufacturing zones with high population density as potential locations for churches. Protestant churches were more advanced than Catholic churches or Buddhist temples in occupying wherever these geographical conditions came to meet. In the Yŏngdŭngp'o District, Protestant churches also started their missionary activities much earlier, and grew in numbers more rapidly than Catholic churches. The first Protestant church was established in 1903, while the first Catholic church was in 1936. Buddhist temples are the most modest in occupying locations, and the first Buddhist temple was established as late as 1978. In 1995, the religious population occupied 52% of the total population in the Yŏngdŭngp'o District, out of which Protestants were the majority, 47.8%, in contrast to Buddhists with 34.7%, and Catholics with 15.7% (Park, 1999:10). Considering that many Buddhists may be classified into the category of Shamanism mixed with Buddhism, pure Buddhists in reality can be much less in percentage than 34.7%.

Presbyterian churches were the most advanced in seizing

2. Religious Landscapes

Photo 8. Yangp'yŏng Presbyterian Church in the Yŏngdŭngp'o District: Built with red-bricks, the church appears somewhat different from the ordinary churches built in modern times. It continued to thrive by catering to people's basic needs changing along with industrialization and urbanization.

their strategic locations and extending their spaces all over the Yŏngdŭngp'o District. With financial support from the Yŏngdŭngp'o Church, the first Presbyterian church established in 1903, the Yangp'yŏng Presbyterian Church was erected in 1907, and the Torim Presbyterian Church in 1926. In Yangp'yŏng Church, one hundred-year-old tree still stands, which Rev. Underwood planted in 1902 (**Photo 8**). Before the liberation from Japanese colonialism, Yŏngdŭngp'o Church, the first Methodist church established in 1936, was the only non-Presbyterian church in the district. Particularly in the 1970s and 1980s, Presbyterian churches grew explosively in number along with the urban population. Today, Presbyterian churches maintain the prime position, and Methodist churches come next in terms of church membership. Churches from other denominations such as the Holiness churches, Baptist churches, Salvation Army, and Anglican churches were first erected after the liberation in 1945, and hardly compete with Presbyterian or even Methodist churches.

Until the late Chosŏn Period, only a small part of land in the Yŏngdŭngp'o District was hills without danger from flood, and the rest was lowland vulnerable to flood (Park, 1999:17-20). Anyang Stream, a branch stream flowing into the Han River, and the Han River itself, extensively developed flood plains with swamps, natural levees and back marshes. The areas in Yangp'yŏng-dong and Torim-dong, adjacent to Anyang Stream, were exposed to flood, being deserted without settlement and cultivation. It is said that a harvest was possible there only once in four years due to the devastation of fields by flood. A perennial cultivation was only possible around Shingil-dong with hills, 30-40m above sea level, which was safe from flood. In other small and isolated hills on the flood plains near the Han River, such as Tangsan-dong, a few people were engaged in fishing, boating and commerce.

2. Religious Landscapes

In 1899, the Kyŏngin Railroad was constructed between Chemulp'o in Inch'ŏn City and Noryangjin in Seoul. In 1900, it was extended to Seoul Main Station over a steel-made bridge crossing the Han River. From this time, the Yŏngdŭngp'o Railroad Station which had gained its importance as a transportation center connecting the southern to the northern part of the Han River. Yŏngdŏngp'o-dong around Yŏngdŭngp'o Railroad Station, once sparsely populated, began to grow as a boom town bustling with goods and people. Rev. Underwood, who came to Seoul in 1885 from the United States, kept an eye on this situation and decided to erect the Yŏngdŭngp'o Presbyterian Church in 1903. This church continued to attract Koreans who migrated into Yŏngdŭngp'o-dong to work as laborers in Japanese factories. From the 1910s to 1930s, the Japanese built large factories in reclaimed lands such as Yŏngdŭngp'o-dong. As manufacturing and residential areas expanded into other reclaimed lands such as Yangp'yŏng-dong and Torim-dong, new Presbyterian churches were established: Yangp'yŏng Presbyterian Church (1907) and Torim Presbyterian Church (1926) (**Figure 7**).

From 1929 to 1937 Japanese colonialists built dikes along Anyang Stream to protect lowlands from floods. These dikes provided a physical ground for rapid urbanization coming after liberation from Japanese colonialism in 1945. Until the 1960s, urbanization went on with the influx of many migrants from overseas, North Korea, and even rural areas. During the Korean War the Yŏngdŭngp'o District became a spot for refugees due to its location on the crossroad in Korea and in the vicinity of downtown Seoul. For instance, Yŏngŭn Church in Yangp'yŏng-dong was established in 1960 to satisfy the religious needs of refugees from North Korea. However, from the 1970s, urbaniza-

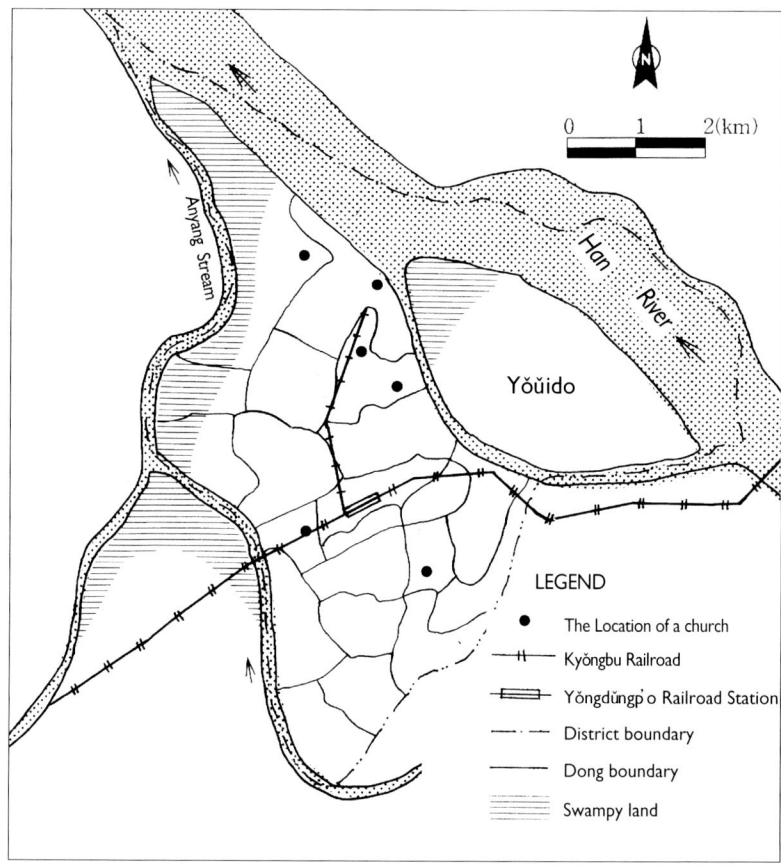

Figure 7. Protestant churches in the Yŏngdŭngp'o District before 1945: Under Japanese occupation, Protestant churches were mostly erected at the manufacturing and commercial areas with high accessibility to a railroad. (Source: Mun-kyu Park, 1999, "The Humanization of Religious Spaces in the Yongdŭnp'o District," Unpublished Master's Thesis, Department of Geography, Korea National University of Education, p. 60.)

tion was accompanied by industrialization as many factories favored their locations within the district. Large companies such as Haet'ae, Lotte, Miwon, and Paekyang located their own factories in Yangp'yŏng-dong, Munrae-dong, Torim-dong and Shindorim-dong. The number of Presbyterian churches also

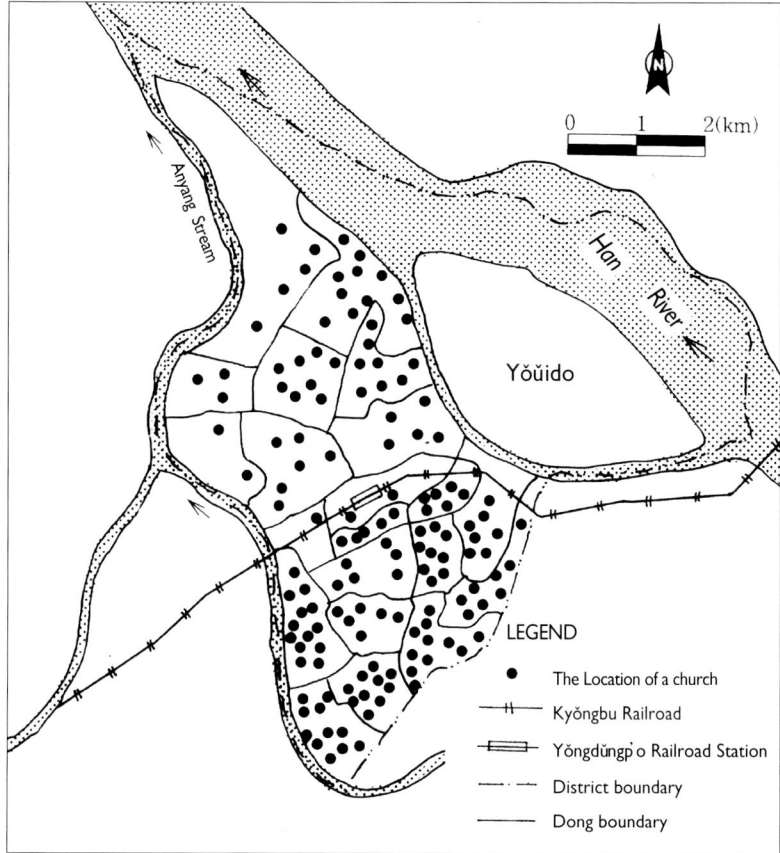

Figure 8. Protestant churches in the Yŏngdŭngp'o District in the 1990s: After the liberation from Japanese colonialism, Protestant churches spread out into every direction and became the most dominant religion in the Yŏngdŭngp'o District. (Source: Mun-kyu Park, 1999, "The Humanization of Religious Spaces in the Yongdŭnp'o District," Unpublished Master's Thesis, Department of Geography, Korea National University of Education, p. 70.)

increased with urban population growing in these manufacturing and residential areas (**Figure 8**).

Presbyterians have been strategic experts at not only securing favorable locations, but also applying missionary tactics. Under Japanese colonialism Presbyterian churches appealed to nationalism, and in the 1950s and 60s they paid attention to the sense of homeland in the Korean mind (Park, 1999:96-109). It is said that under Japanese colonialism Torim Presbyterian Church protested against the colonial law and allowed members to read the Bible and pray in Korean. By contrast, migrants in the 1950s and 60s found themselves placed in an impersonal environment without family or friends. As the rapid urbanization with industrialization went on with the influx of rural migrants, no places like home-villages could be easily recreated in the ever-changing man-made environment. Churches could provide a place for "feeling oneself at home" for those who moved into the city from the countryside. To some of the immigrants, in particular refugees from North Korea during the Korean War, churches could be seen as oasis-like places in the middle of a desert-like city.

In the 1970s and 80s, churches assumed a leadership role in the battles for laborer's rights and democratization (Park, 1999:64-65). Ministers in Yangp'yŏng Presbyterian Church and Torim Presbyterian Church were particularly outspoken against injustice, corruption and exploitation of workers under the dictatorial regime of President Park, named the Yushin. At that time, these churches were even considered to be a mecca for a nationwide labor movement in Korea. These churches indeed fought for the laborers to obtain the legal right for one free day a week and eight-hour labor a day. During this period, factory workers converting into Protestantism, including the Presbyterian Church, increased remarkably. Even today, Protestants are more heavily concentrated in Yangp'yŏng-dong and Torim-dong than in other areas, representing a Protestant core in Korea.

4) T'ongdo Temple at Yŏngch'wi Mountain

The hundreds of church steeples that pierce the sky over Seoul easily mislead foreign travelers into an impression that Korea is a Christian country. This false impression is all the more probable at night when church steeples, lit in red, seem to cover the sky. Even a sightseeing tour would be unlikely to alter this first misinformation, since the largest building in many villages is, more often than not, a Christian church, not a Buddhist temple. Yet, surprisingly enough, there are more Koreans who call themselves Buddhists than Christians all over the country, even though there are more Christians than Buddhists in Seoul.

Moreover, Buddhism in Korea has been a part of ordinary life much longer than Christianity, and has become an integral part of Korean civilization. The history of Buddhism in Korea began as early as the Three Kingdoms Period: Koguryŏ (372), Paekje (384), and Shilla (572). During this period, Buddhism was seen as one or more ideological tools in strengthening the royal authority, and was not treated as a religion for the masses (Koo & Nahm, 1999:159). From that time on, Buddhism gradually penetrated from the royal family and the higher level of aristocracy into the lower levels of aristocracy and the common people.

The ruling class found the ideas of Buddha as a sovereign ruler on Buddha's land useful for justification and rationalization of divine kingship. Kingship was identified with Buddhahood, and building an ideal nation was considered to be the same as realizing Buddha's land on this earth. This tradition of state-sponsorship in Korean Buddhism, nationalistic in character, continued for about 1,000 years from the Three Kingdoms

Period through the Unified Shilla Period until the Koryŏ Period. The relationship between Buddhism and the state was closer than ever during the Koryŏ Period. Until the Koryŏ Period, in fact, Buddhism had occupied the core of Korean life in close association with political and social power.

Over the five centuries of the Chosŏn Period (1392-1910), however, Buddhism no longer received much of the official patronage that it had earlier enjoyed. Temples lost most of their tax-free land and monks were no longer invited as royal advisors to the court. Both temples and monks in clerical robes were officially prohibited from Seoul, the capital city. Buddhist beliefs and practices, along with Shamanism, were despised as an outcome of superstition and ignorance by the new Neo-Confucian ruling elite. During this period, Buddhism, without linkage to political and social power, managed to survive with popular support from the common people including women. It was also during this time that Buddhism was partly incorporated into folk beliefs which prevailed among the mass of people.

T'ongdo Temple is one of the three main temples which represent Buddhist tradition in Korea: T'ongdo Temple, Haein Temple and Songkwang Temple. It is said that Buddhism consists of the three main elements (Buddha, Buddhist Script and monk), and these three main temples represent each of these elements in Korea: T'ongdo Temple, Buddha; Haein Temple, Buddhist Script; and Songkwang Temple, monk. Among them T'ongdo Temple is the oldest in tradition with its origin in the Three Kingdoms Period, and has survived many difficult times from the Chosŏn Period up to today. If someone visits T'ongdo Temple anytime of the year, he or she can see a thriving temple that is filled with many buildings and prayers inside.

2. Religious Landscapes

Photo 9. Kŭmganggye-dan, or the Diamond Ordination Platform in T'ongdo Temple: Originally built in the Shilla Period, but rebuilt right after being destroyed by the Hideyoshi Invasions, the platform has fences with a gate, Confucian in architectural style.

The founder of T'ongdo Temple was Chajang who received much royal support in the Shilla Period. He came back from Tang China in 643 upon Queen Sŏndŏk's request, and served as her major advisor. The queen named him Taeguktʻong meaning the highest rank in priesthood. He was also called Chajang Yulsa, or the Teacher of Discipline, adopting the ideas of early Indian Buddhist orders and instituting the Shilla Kyeyul Sect. He brought with him the relics of Sakyamuni from China and restored them at the Kŭmganggye-dan, or the Diamond Ordination Platform in T'ongdo Temple (**Photo 9**). He, then, made it mandatory that all clergymen receive their ordination in front of this sacred platform. This platform has provided a material basis upon which T'ongdo Temple has distinguished itself from other ordinary temples in Korea.

Chajang decided to locate the temple beside a stream flowing at the foothills of a mountain, resembling a mountain in India where in a cave Buddha used to practice his own discipline (Ch'oe, 1994:69). The name of the mountain was also changed to Yŏngch'wi Mountain, a Chinese translation of the holy mountain in India, named Kisagul Mountain. Even today, the cave remains on the mountain where Chajang is said to have practiced his own discipline. Moreover, he might have highly valued the merit of its location, not too distant from Kyŏngju City, the capital of the Shilla Kingdom.

Another physical element mystifying T'ongdo Temple as a sacred place was a pond with a folk tale. The folk tale says that in the Kuryong Pond, literally meaning the Nine Dragon Pond, beside the Kŭmganggye-dan, lived nine dragons, which were defeated by Chajang. It is said that only one out of nine dragons was allowed to stay in the pond, while the others had to run away. When Chajang dispelled the nine dragons in the large pond and reclaimed it into land for construction of T'ongdo Temple, one dragon wholeheartedly begged Chajang to be allowed to stay there and guard the temple. Chajang left only a small portion of pond without reclamation, and let this one dragon remain there. This small pond is now in an oval shape with a bridge over it (**Photo 10**).

In Memorabilia of the Three Kingdoms, called *Samguk Yusa*, written by a Buddhist monk named Il Yŏn in the late 13th century, a story appears about what Chajang heard while praying in China. According to this story, a Buddhist monk, a reincarnation of Bodhisattvas Munsu, gave Chajang a piece of robe, one hundred pieces of *chinshinsari* (a part of a brain and the finger

2. Religious Landscapes

Photo 10. Kuryong (Nine Dragon) Pond in T'ongdo Temple: The pond is located in the rear of the Main Worshipping Hall, or in front of Sanryŏnggak (Mountain Spirit Hall) and Samshjngak (Tree Saint Hall).

bones of Sakyamuni), sutras (an ancient revered text which Buddhists treat as scripture) and a *yŏmju* (a Buddhist rosary of 108 beads). The monk, then, told him to go back to the Shilla Kingdom and find a pond where evil dragons lived. These dragons blew rainy wind, ejecting a poison to annoy people and devastate crops. Then the monk said that if Chajang reclaimed the pond and built the Kŭmganggye-dan storing the relics of Buddha over it, these dragons would turn into good ones protecting people there from the natural hazards of water, fire and wind. This story, of course, symbolic in expression, attaches a special meaning of place to T'ongdo Temple where a part of Sakyamuni's body and belongings reside.

As T'ongdo Temple managed to grow even through the Chosŏn Period, many other worshipping halls were built in dedication to other kinds of Buddha or Bodhisattvas other than Sakyamuni. The Main Worshipping Hall in front of the Kŭmganggye-dan, was originally built in the Shilla Period, and since then has been reconstructed many times up to this day (Yi et. al., 1991 : 38-40). Inside the Main Worshipping Hall no kinds of Buddha are arranged including Sakyamuni, because it faces the Kŭmganggye-dan with Sakyamuni's body and belongings. Other worshipping halls are those with Buddha or Bodhisattvas: Vairocana, or the primordial Buddha and Lord of the Cosmos; Amitabha, or the Buddha as Lord of Paradise, the Clean Land in the West; Bhechadjaguru, or the Buddha as Master of Medicine; Maitreya, or the bodhisattvas who promised a better world in the future; and Ksitigarbha, or the bodhisattvas rescuing the dead from falling into hell. These halls are also said to have been originally constructed in the Shilla or Koryŏ Period. Only the hall with Avalokitsvara, or the bodhisattvas of unlimited compassion in this world, was first built in the Chosŏn Period.

By the time Buddhism reached China around five centuries after Sakyamuni Buddha's death, the various images of Buddha were carried on with bodhisattvas, analogous to saints in the Christian tradition. It is believed that many buddhas had appeared in the past before Sakyamuni Buddha, and would also appear after Sakyamuni Buddha. Bodhisattvas are beings who have attained the state of liberation from sufferings, but, out of compassion for the suffered, have postponed their own emancipation in order to assist those who wait to be emancipated. In Korea, the pious devotion to Avalokitsvara and Maitreya were the most popular among the common people during the Chosŏn Period.

Other important halls first built in the Chosŏn Period were those associated with Confucianism and Shamanism, very popular at that time. In 1727, an ancestral hall called Kaesanjodang, Confucian in architectural style, was built in commemoration of the founder, Chajang (Yi et. al., 1991 : 52- 53). The main gate, in particular, with three separate doors resembles those which were popular among the *yangban* class believers in Neo-Confucianism. Inside the hall a colorful portrayal of Chajang is hung on the wall in much the same way with anyone in the *yangban* class believing in Neo-Confucianism. Ancestral hall of Confucian style, named *yŏngdang*, a symbol of ancestor worship, began to be widespread all over Korea in the late Chosŏn Dynasty. In the time of Neo-Confucianism as a dominant political ideology and social power, Buddhism could not but adopt Confucian symbols, contradictory in morality, into the Buddhist landscape in order to appeal to the public.

Another effort to survive hardships in the time of Neo-Confucianism with hegemony in power can be read in the buildings of Shamanistic or Taoistic halls such as Sanryŏnggak or the Mountain Spirit Hall, and Samsŏnggak or the Three Saints Hall. The Sanryŏnggak was first built in 1761, and the Three Saints Hall in 1870 (Yi et. al., 1991 : 45- 46). In the Sanryŏnggak, a portrait of a *sanshin*, or mountain spirit, with a tiger beneath him is hung on the wall. On the walls of the Samsŏnggak, a portrait of three eminent monks, Chigong, Naong and Muhak, are hung in the center, while *ch'ilsŏngshin*, or the Big Dipper deity, is to the right and *doksŏng*, or the lonely saint, is to the left. The situation of these two halls in front of the Kuryong Pond as well as behind the Main Worshipping Hall, suggests a hidden intention to allure the common people to the temple. This spot, indeed, adjoining the Kŭmganggye-dan, occupies the core of T'ongdo Temple, the most sacred space. In the time of Buddhism with hegemony in power, such as the Shilla and Koryŏ Periods, the inclusion of Shamanistic or Taoistic halls into a temple was absolutely unthinkable. According to Buddhist doctrine, in fact, the idea of situating them in the most sacred space in T'ongdo Temple was totally unacceptable.

5) SONGKWANG TEMPLE AT CHOGYE *MOUNTAIN*

Korean Buddhism is less sectarian than Buddhism in Japan or traditional China. Korean Buddhists often point with pride to their unique ecumenical spirit of syncretism, with its origin in the legacy of two outstanding monks: Wonhyo (617-686) of the Shilla Dynasty and Chinul (1158-1210) of the Koryŏ Dynasty.

Wonhyo, who never visited China to study Buddhism, insisted that different teachings of various doctrines were all essentially nothing more than different manifestations of the same, underlying "the only one mind" in Buddha. He wandered through villages, encouraging illiterate peasants to adopt Chŏngt'ojong (the Pure Land Sect) of reciting the name of the Amitabha Buddha (the Lord of Paradise in the West).

Based on Wonhyo's tradition, Chinul reconciled two contradictory approaches to religious practice, and founded Chogyejong, or the Chogye Order, the largest Buddhist denomination then and now in Korea (Joe, 1997:212-213). Even under the suppression of Buddhism in the Chosŏn Period, the Chogye Order could maintain its prime position and prosperity due to the support from the royal court. Eminent monks such as Muhak (1327-1405) and Kobong (1305-1428), as royal advisors, actively participated in the opening of the Chosŏn Dynasty in search of political protection from kings and their families.

By the time of Chinul, in the 12th century, Sŏnjong, or the Meditation Sect, introduced in the 7th century from China, became popular enough to challenge the prevailing approaches, using knowledge to enlightenment. This new sect, better known in the West by its Japanese name of Zen, argued that an overemphasis on the written words of sutras made it more difficult to transcend the sutras into the wordless state of enlightenment, which Buddha himself once suggested. Meditative Buddhism incited that monastics should devote less time to studying doctrines and more time to meditation, eradicating their desires by stilling their mind.

Sŏnjong entered the United Shilla Kingdom around the middle of the 7th century, but its influence remained dormant until the 9th century when it emerged as a main sectarian movement. From the middle of the 9th to the early 10th century, nine centers of Sŏnjong Buddhism came into being all over the country. With support from local elites, these centers located their temples invariably in scenic mountain valleys, advocating their own brands of Sŏnjong which were imported from China. With the challenge from Sŏnjong, all the traditional sects with emphasis on the scriptural authority were grouped under the name of Kyojong, or the Teaching Sect, which gradually lost its vitality as well as popularity. Sŏnjong, on the other hand, became the main current of Buddhism in the Koryŏ Period.

Upon royal request, Chinul led the way to bring these two contrasting approaches together. He believed that the lengthy and intensive study of sutras was essential for effective practice in meditation. While holding the two orders of Hwaŏmjong, or the Flower Garland Sect, and Sŏnjong as pillars, he constructed the Chogye Order, within which learning doctrines and meditation were in reciprocity. Since then, Chinul's integrated approach, within which two different approaches to enlightenment were combined, has become the dominant model for monastic life in Korea. The Chogye Order has also been the largest denomination of Buddhism in Korea up to this day.

In his movement, Chinul was strongly supported by the Ch'oe family, which seized political power with military strength (Joe, 1997:213). Kyojong, such as Ch'ŏnt'aejong and Hwaŏmjong, had been patronized by the royal family and the aristocratic class before the Ch'oe family dominated the royal court. The Ch'oe family, then, might have wanted to replace Kyojong with Sŏnjong for their own political ideology. Moreover, iconoclastic Zen tenets, without emphasis on letters of doctrines, might have been palatable to the military-minded men supporting the Ch'oe family with less or no taste in Kyojong's metaphysics.

The Chogye Order borrows its name from the mountain where Chinul established his first community of practitioners, called Susŏnsa. The royal court organized this community in the present location of Songkwang Temple, where Chinul was invited to stay as a master monk (Ch'oe, 1994 : 14). However, it is said that the mountain giving its name to the Chogye Order was not Chogye, but Songkwang in the first place. The name "Chogye" was borrowed from the holy Chogye Mountain in China where the southern tradition of meditation originated. The royal court, with an intention to make it a sacred place, imposed a foreign name, Chogye, upon an indigenous name, Songkwang. In the early Chosŏn Period, the name of the temple, Susŏnsa, was finally altered to Songkwang Temple, borrowing from the previous name of the mountain, Songkwang Mountain.

The Ch'oe family might have viewed that their rival's political background was Kyŏngju City, the capital of the Shilla Kingdom, in southeastern Korea. It is quite probable that they wanted to secure their political background in southwestern Korea to challenge his rival's background in southeastern Korea. By then, moreover, four of nine Sŏnjong temples (Porim Temple, T'aean Temple, Ssangbong Temple, and Shilsang Temple) had already firmly taken root in southwestern Korea. They might have thought that Songkwang Mountain was in a favorable position where Sŏnjong and Kyojong could be integrated under the banner of the Chogye Order without being influenced from Kyojong in southeastern Korea with its center in Kyŏngju City.

It is said that Chinul built Songkwang Temple, once called Susŏnsa in the Koryŏ Period, reflecting the ideology and world views of Hwaŏmjong and Sŏnjong. Chinul placed emphasis on sudden enlightenment into Buddha's mind, the source of all forms of life and inherent in all human beings. According to him, enlightenment is nothing but transcending into the realm of Ultimate Emptiness, which Hwaŏmjong calls the Void or the Law-Realm. In all its inclusive syncretism, Hwaŏmjong taught that all phenomenal existences partake of the Law-Realm, the ultimate reality, in which even the moment of thinking is rooted.

The buildings in the temple were arranged in concentric circles or squares around the center of the Main Worshipping Hall.

This concentric pattern of spatial arrangement conforms to Pŏbgyedo, or Diagram of Law-Realm, in which Ŭisang (625-702), the founder of Hwaŏmjong, had once visualized the ideas of Hwaŏmkyŏng, or Sutra on Flower Garland, in a diagram. It is said that this diagram was borrowed from the symbol of 卍, meaning the Law-Realm in Buddhism. Even today, the temple's ground, within which buildings were located, seems to resemble a circle or square in shape (Kim, 1997: 59-60). When taking a march as a means of practicing monastic life, monks should walk along the lines of 卍 within this entire ground rectangular in shape. They walk from Ch'imkyeru (the Entrance to the Main Worshipping Hall), through the rear and front of the Main Worshipping Hall, Sŭngbojŏn (Monk Treasure Hall) and Chijangjŏn (Ksitigarbha Hall) to the Kuksajŏn (National Monk-Masters Hall). On the way they turn around once on the ground in front of the Main Worshipping Hall, while stepping on the lines of 卍 which were drawn on the ground.

Prior to the Korean War (1950-1953) Songkwang Temple, the headquarters of the Chogye Order, remained as a large temple jammed with 60 buildings, small and large (Ch'oe, 1994:20). In 1951, 20 buildings including the Main Worshipping Hall were burned down by communist guerrillas who found a refugee in this temple. As most of the ruined buildings were concentrated around the Main Worshipping Hall, it became very hard to relate the spatial design of Songkwang Temple with the Pŏbgyedo (**Photo 11**).

Until today a series of efforts have been made to reconstruct the ruined buildings, but only with limited success. A large part of the space around the Main Worshipping Hall is still unoccu-

2. Religious Landscapes

Photo 11. The spatial arrangement of buildings in Songkwang Temple before and after the Korean War: Before 1950, the temple maintained its own spatial design, reminiscent of Pŏbgyedo, or the Diagram of Law-Realm, though many years had passed since the foundation of Songkwang Temple; the upper level is before 1950, and the lower level is after 1950.

pied by buildings. Before the destruction by communist guerrillas, this part of the temple was most densely occupied by many buildings. Herein, buildings are now sparsely distributed around an empty ground in front of the Main Worshipping Hall, extremely large in size. This awkward appearance of spatial arrangement evokes strange feelings that many visitors to Korean temples have never experienced.

The other thing peculiar to Songkwang Temple is that there are none of the stone pagodas or lanterns inside the temple, and Susŏnsa (Meditation Practice Hall) and Sŏlppŏbjŏn (Law Lecture Hall) are situated in the highest spot behind the Main Worshipping Hall. These two halls, designed for monks who practice monastic life through meditation and sutras, attach special meaning to Songkwang Temple which claims itself to be the principal temple for monks. Even higher than these halls are located pudo (stupas) of 16 national master-monks, within which their sari (relics of Buddha or of a Buddhist saint) and belongings are preserved. Usually a small temple protecting each of these stupas was built, and a monk resided for practicing monastic life in it.

According to Sŏnjong's principle that everybody has Buddha's mind, and monks, ordinary or prominent, were seen no less precious than Buddha in the Main Worshipping Hall. The eminent monks, in particular Chinul, the founder of the temple, have been valued even higher than Buddha. Their stupas have been seen as even more important than Buddha's statues.

Stupas themselves are said to have been situated in the spots ideal for Feng-shui (*pungsu* in Korean). For instance, Chinul's stupa, located in the highest spot, has been moved several times between 1477 and 1770 to fit into the idea of Feng-shui, and each time they have tried to move Chinul's stupa into a location protected from wind and water. This means that in the Chosŏn Period they interpreted the fate of Songkwang Temple in connection with the situation of Chinul's stupa. It was indeed in the late Chosŏn Period that filial piety from Confucian ideology was combined with Feng-shui or Taoist ideology into a dominant ideology of maintaining social and political power. In the Confucian society, Chinul's stupa was respected as nothing but a common ancestor which his descendent monks must commemorate.

3. Folk Landscapes

3. Folk Landscapes

Generally speaking, in Korea, foreign religions with sophisticated organizations and doctrines were adopted by the elite, while the indigenous religions with simple organizations and doctrines were cherished by the commoners, in particular, women. Surprisingly, these indigenous religions have survived until today in the cities as well as in the countryside, but they have not evolved into an organized religion like Taoism in China or Shintoism in Japan. They exist simply in the form of folk religion, which includes Shamanism and folk beliefs such as worship of house deity, village deity and natural deity. Herein, the folk landscape is referred to as a cultural landscape which was formed from Shamanism and folk beliefs.

Folk beliefs clearly differ from Shamanism, even though it is sometimes difficult to distinguish these two indigenous religions from each other. Folk beliefs are retreating to the countryside, being retained by housewives and ordinary villagers, while Shamanism by women is rampant all over the country, in the cities or in the countryside. Confucian rituals have penetrated into the folk beliefs on village deity, while those on house deity have been saturated with Shamanistic rituals. The rituals for the village deity are performed by villagers in common, but those for the house deity and the Shamanistic deity are practiced by individual families. The praying and worshipping in Shamanism, by contrast, is often done by individuals in secret.

In Korea, folk beliefs and Shamanism have not only preserved their own characters, but have transformed their appearance through contact with foreign religions. Folk beliefs intermingled largely with Confucianism in the Chosŏn Period, while maintaining their original character. Shamanism has incorporated some of the folk deity, and shamans are often invited to perform rituals for the folk deity. At times, it is also difficult to tell where Buddhism ends and Shamanism begins. Within a single folk landscape, therefore, one may not read a single history of Shamanism or folk beliefs, but multiple histories of indigenous religions.

However, these indigenous religions have been the homes for the dominated common people or women. The people without power tend to copy cultural elements from those with power to overcome the hardship from above. For instance, believers in folk belief in the village deity were active in introducing Confucian elements, while those in Shamanism were willing to borrow something from Buddhism. What they choose to copy is very selective, because they learn something only when it is necessary for their survival. Folk beliefs and Shamanism in Korea have also been not only flexible, but selective, in adopting cultural elements from foreign religions. The Korean folk landscapes, therefore, may reflect some popular ways of resisting the dominant culture or ideology (**Figure 9**).

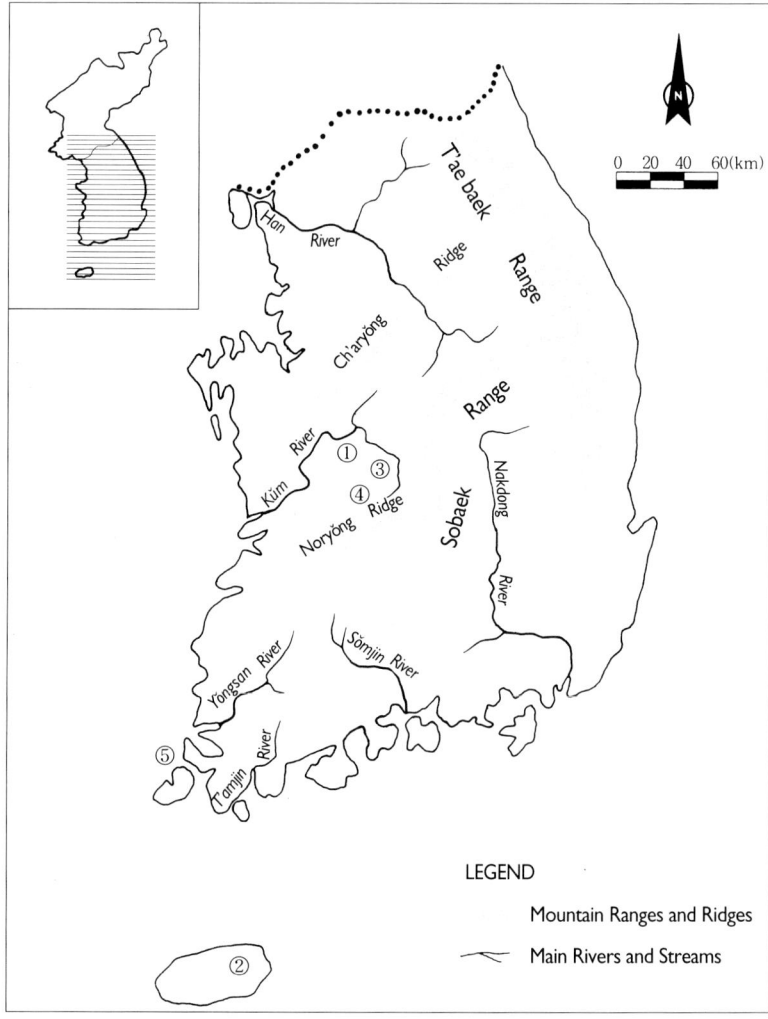

Figure 9. Locations of folk landscapes in Korea:
① Shamanistic halls in Kyeryong Mountain
② Ponhyangdang (main spirit halls) on Cheju Island
③ Sŏndol (standing stones) around Okch'ŏn Town
④ Tolt'ap (pebble-piles) around Kŭmsan Town
⑤ Tangje (village rituals) on the islands in the Southwestern Sea.

1) SHAMANISTIC HALLS IN KYERYONG MOUNTAIN

Korea is one of the important places in the world where Shamanism has been preserved very well up to today. It is hard to estimate the exact number of Korean believers in Shamanism, but it is roughly estimated to be significantly large. About 200,000 shamans registered with the Ministry of Culture and Information in 1990, but the real number of shamans is much higher than this (Koo & Nahm, 1997:126). Many shamans call themselves *posal* (bodhisattvas) these days, and a Buddhist symbol on the gate of a house often means that a shaman lives within. Shamans and their clients usually answer "Buddhism" when asked which religion they believe in. It is not easy to estimate the number of Koreans who claim themselves to be Buddhists but believe in Shamanism.

In Shamanism there is neither church nor congregation, but individual Shamans make contact with deity or evil spirits through ecstatic methods. The shaman is usually a priestess in Shamanism who officiates at rituals. Most shamans are illiterate, and their praying is only based on oral tradition. A shaman has a shrine in which her guardian deity and other instruments for her ritual services are retained. The shrine, usually a small separate building, belongs to an individual shaman. It is sometimes arranged in the corner of the shaman's hall called *tang* when she has no extra space. The shrine is a sacred place, often decorated with flowers, burning incense and fruits.

In Korea today, more than 95% of the shamans practicing ecstasy are females, and an equal proportion of their customers are also women. This tendency for women to occupy Shamanism in monopoly is in direct contrast to the ancient Siberian

Shamanism from which Korean ecstatic tradition descends. The Siberian tradition in which male shamans were more numerous than females seems to have been true in early Korean history. However, as Confucianism became stronger in power and Shamanism became despised as a superstition, male shamans decreased in large number. As women lost their freedom of physical movement and social mobility, some of them became shamans who could then enjoy their own social independence.

Presumably, Shamanism remained alive in Korea due to the interest of women, more than anything else (Covell, 1986:193). These women were barred from taking a leading part in Confucian ceremonies in the Chosŏn Period. However, they were held responsible for maintaining peaceful harmony at home. When instability threatened home, arrangement of *kuts*, or Shamanistic rituals, by housewives was not uncommon. When a *kut* was scheduled, the lofty Confucian scholar-official might scorn the rituals as useless, but he would seldom forbid them, especially when it concerned matters within his own home. Only when attending Shamanistic rituals, women, common or noble, were allowed to remain outside of the Confucian ideal.

The social status of women deteriorated still further to the extent that women could not inherit property. They could not even remarry after being widowed, even if it had been a childhood marriage and never consummated physically. Gradually, upper class women became more and more restricted to the home. They could go outdoors only when covered from the crown of the head to the ankles by long overgarments. *Kut* was an acceptable way for women to socialize by expressing their feelings openly during dancing and singing. At the close of the Chosŏn Dynasty, Shamanism permeated almost every breath that Korean women inhaled.

In Korea, shamans are summoned to perform *kut* for the same reasons as in ancient times. Their main services include appeasing malignant spirits, curing sickness, forecasting the future, and supplicating the spirits for future successes. A shaman is asked to handle spiritual worlds which are believed to be the cause of calamity in a family or an individual. As in ancient times, the spirit of the dead is one of the principal fears to individual Koreans. *Kuts* are held on many occasions related to accidental death, such as drowning. The spirit of an unmarried woman or a man who died as a youth without leaving children is considered the most dangerous.

In Korea, Kyeryong Mountain is known as the most important mountain that shamans either visit for their prayers or for their service. There are many places that allure both shamans and Shamanists. The best places where shamans like to communicate with spirits are mountains with high peaks and deep valleys. In these mountains they usually stay for a long time to strengthen their supernatural ability, and sometimes establish their own halls to provide services to their clients.

In terms of physical geography, indeed, Kyeryong Mountain is distinguished from other mountains. Although Kyeryong Mountain rises as an isolated small mountain (845.1m) in the southeast of the Ch'aryŏng Ridge, it is easily conceivable from a distance because of its mystic outlook. Since a series of peaks form an elongated ridge resembling a dragon with a cock's comb head, the mountain is called Kyeryong Mountain meaning Cock Dragon Mountain (**Photo 12**). It consists primarily of fine-grained granite with porphyry, only partly covered with thin layers of soil and vegetation. There is a lack of plentiful

Photo 12. A series of peaks on Kyeryong Mountain: Following one peak after another like mountain walls, the mountain has attracted human eyes in various aspects since ancient times. There had been other names to describe this mystical-looking mountain, and its specific name, Kyeryong, or Cock Dragon, was not given until the late Chosŏn Period.

water in the stream valleys, which are usually dried up during the dry season. The straight western boundary is formed by a deeply incised valley, which extends from the east of Kongju City to the east of Nonsan City.

V-shaped valleys, terraced and embellished by waterfalls, have cut in five directions. The ridges separating the side valleys are razor-edged and jagged (Lautensach, 1988:358). Gigantic, steep block, streams fall from the heads of the valleys. These peaks of granite stone and waterfalls with poles have been the best places for shamans and Shamanists to communicate with spirits because of the mystic outlook or secluded location. Of these places, the most popular among Shamanists are two peaks and two waterfalls (pot holes): Sambul Peak (Three Buddhas Peak), Yŏnch'ŏn Peak (Continuous Sky Peak), Sutyong Pond (Male Dragon Pond), and Amyong Pond (Female Dragon Pond).

The mountain peak, named Sambul Peak (775.1m), is one of the most holy places in Kyeryong Mountain, because it literally symbolizes the important deities in Shamanism (Kim, 1997:50). It is said that below this mountain peak many women used to come with shamans or by themselves and pray for the birth of a son. Neo-Confucian principles in the Chosŏn Period demanded that women give birth to sons in order to carry on the family life, and women in desperate need of a son relied on Shamanism. The extreme importance of male descendants made the shaman's performance undeniable as a sort of last resort. In this way, Shamanism could exist as an assistant to Confucianism which emphasizes ancestor worship. The deities called *samshin* (three spirits) or *sambul* (three Buddhas) were those which shamans used to resort to in kut for the birth of sons (Covell, 1986:86-88). These deities together represent procreation or pregnancy, and thus are a principal symbol of fertility in Korean Shamanism.

Since Shamanism was influenced by both Taoism and Buddhism, it is not surprising that Taoist-type and Buddhist- type icons exist. At present, there seems to be no purely unadulterated Shamanist representation of a deity. The *samshin* are a meld of Buddhist appearance with a Shamanist concept as directly involved in the birth process (Covell, 1986:86). The Shamanistic concept of *samshin* went through a long history, and acquired both Shamanist and Buddhist elements. Because the *samshin* are depicted as three monks in religious robes, they are often called

"Three Buddhas." In the time of Buddhism and Confucianism with hegemony in power, Shamanism, disguised in Buddhist clothes, appealed to women's desperate need for male descendants. Shamanism was only able to survive the suppression from Buddhism in the Koryŏ Period and Neo-Confucianism in the Chosŏn Period by catering to Buddhism and Confucianism.

Yŏnch'ŏn Peak (738.7m) is another important peak under which many Shamanists come in search of spirits (Kim, 1997:50-51;57-58). This peak is regarded as an excellent spot for Shamanists because from it one can look closely up to Ch'ŏnhwang Peak (the Heavenly Emperor Peak), the highest peak (845.1m), to which they believe the Heavenly Spirit comes down. Below this mountain peak, a small Buddhist hall named Dŭngunam had been established, and now not only Buddhists but also Shamanists visit it. There are many more Buddhist halls scattered in the mountain, and they house Shamanists who would like to spend nights. In general, Shamanists like to pray for spirits, especially at night, because of the mystic atmosphere. The important examples of this type are Kyeryongjŏngsa under Sambul Peak and Kŭmryongam in the valley where the famous temple, Shinwon Temple, lies.

Like Dŭngunam in Kyeryong Mountain, many Buddhist halls inspired by their outlook, including names, are in fact Shamanistic halls where shamans can perform Shamanistic rituals. Before the official ban on Shamanism in 1975, more than one hundred Shamanistic halls occupied the entire mountain in the form of housing, earth caves, stone caves and tents (**Figure 10**). Under the official ban on Shamanism in the modern era, Shamanists had to pretend to be Buddhists to ward off the suspicious eyes of the government.

However, Sutyong Pond and Amyong Pond, the most holy places in Shamanism, are today completely closed to human entry for military reasons. In the valley containing these waterfalls and ponds, since 1983, a headquarters commanding land, sea and air forces was established. Since then, to protect this military base, any human entry has been barred from the valley. Under these circumstances, Shamanists did not give up their minds, but stole their way into these holy places at night in search of spiritual communications (**Figure 11**).

The holy places of Sutyong Pond and Amyong Pond are too important for Shamanists to stop coming and praying. These ponds are believed to be the best spots where shamans can meet the three main spirits at the same time: heaven, land, and water. At night, in fact, the sounds of waterfalls breaking on the rocks, and the dark shades of woods and rocks are qualified enough to orchestrate a mystic atmosphere.

Sutyong Pond and Amyong Pond are ponds with depths of 4-5m, which were formed in the rocky valleys from the erosion by waterfalls. It is said that these names were made from the myth that a male dragon and a female dragon resided separately in these two ponds. However, the division of sex in their names may have been from the overall shape of the ponds. From the air, Sutyong Pond looks like a penis, while Amyong Pond resembles a vagina (Kim, 1997:54).

Before 1983 many women could come to Sutyong Pond and pray for the birth of sons. On the rocks around this dragon pond many names of those who prayed wholeheartedly for their wish were found inscribed. At night, in particular, these ponds were busy with women, shamans or Shamanists, who dedicated foods to spirits and lighted candles. But now under

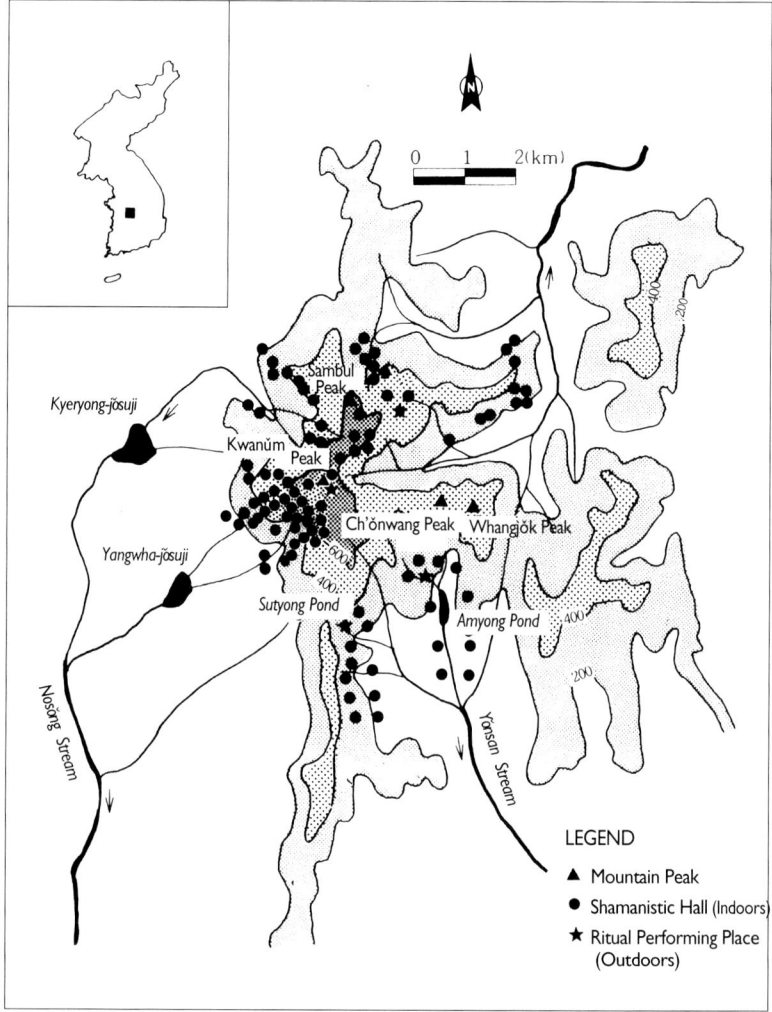

Figure 10. The spatial distribution of Shamanistic halls on Kyeryong Mountain before 1975: The mountain peaks and pot-holes (ponds) were very crucial to the locations of Shamanistic halls before an official ban was imposed on Shamanism on Kyeryong Mountain. (Source: Su-dong Kim, 1997, "The Making of Places on Kyeryong Mountain," Unpublished Master's Thesis, Department of Geography, Korea National University of Education, p. 51.)

3. Folk Landscapes

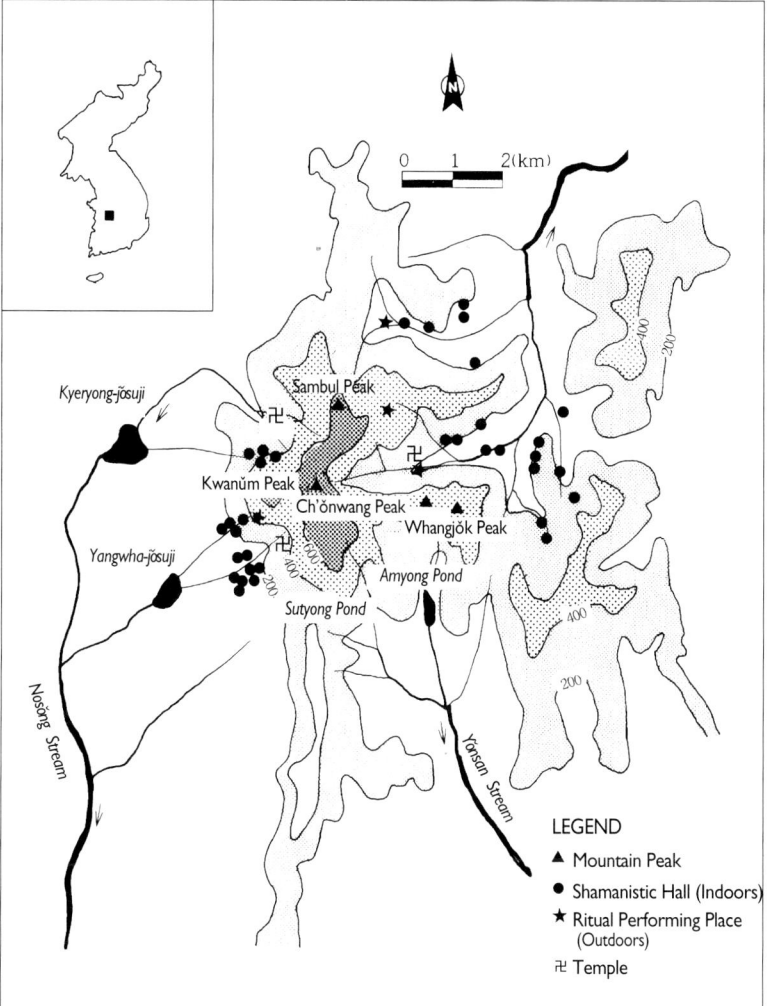

Figure 11. The spatial distribution of Shamanistic halls on Kyeryong Mountain after 1975: After the offical ban was imposed on Shamanism, Shamanistic halls near mountain peaks and pot-holes (ponds) almost disappeared, but those near Buddhist temples managed to survive in the limited locations. (Source: Su-dong Kim, 1997, "The Making of Places on Kyeryong Mountain," Unpublished Master's Thesis, Department of Geography, Korea National University of Education, p. 52.)

the public ban on human entry, only a small number of shamans with strong spiritual needs dare to steal their own way into these ponds.

2) *PONHYANGDANG* (MAIN SPIRIT HALLS) ON CHEJU ISLAND

With less influence from Confucianism, Shamanism and other folk beliefs have been preserved better on Cheju Island than in mainland Korea. Even in village rituals shamans are summoned to pray for villagers. Cheju Island, indeed, can be called a storing house of Korean Shamanism. The native beliefs on Cheju Island synthesized popular features of foreign religions while retaining its basic core, rather than being assimilated into them. It preserved Korea's ancient heritage better than any other area in Korea where influence from foreign faiths was greater.

Sanshin, or the mountain deity, is particularly treated as the main deity in Korean Shamanism. By contrast, *yongwangshin*, or the dragon-king deity, which had once been as important as the *sanshin* is now seldom worshipped in Korean Shamanism. Normally, the dragon king has been thought to inhabit the seas and rivers, and through his powers brings rains and storms (Covell, 1986:57).

On Cheju Island, also a majority of Shamanistic deities belong to the type of *sanshin*, but there still remain quite a number of dragon kings. Very common are the *sanshin* which came down from Halla Mountain, the highest peak. However, in contrast to mainland Korea, more *sanshin*s identified with old women than old men are worshipped as Shamanistic deities. Here, the women did a great deal more physical work than the norm in Korea, and had more independence and freedom of movement. It is, therefore, somewhat natural that female deities had once dominated the sexual divisions of *sanshin*.

On Cheju Island, surrounded by sea, the dragon king remained important and has continued so to the present day (Covell, 1986:67). Owing to its distance from Confucianism on the mainland, people on Cheju Island have always been conscious of the dragon king. The condition of the sea affects the livelihood, and even the lifespan of its inhabitants. Especially in the spring, the dragon's special season, prayers for a big haul of fish are held at port villages on the coast.

In direct contrast to mainland Korea, the shamans on Cheju Island were mostly male. The ancient tradition that male shaman performed rituals or *kut* still survive here due to the stronghold of Shamansim on Cheju Island. Unlike many of those of mainland Korea, shamans on Cheju Island had acquired their knowledge and position through heredity. They did not have individual patrons like those in the large cities, but usually served several villages when summoned.

This type of service by a shaman was called the *tanggol*, or the villages served by a shaman's spirit hall. The shaman usually makes her or his own holy place in one room of her or his dwelling where portraits decorate the space around the altar. He or she also sometimes creates a holy place outdoors, either permanent or temporary.

These two types of holy places are together called *tang*, or spirit hall, and are particularly abundant on Cheju Island. Even within a village, in addition to *ponhyangdang*, or a main spirit hall, there were other spirit halls or *tang*s for families and individuals. It is said that in the Koryŏ Period hundreds of *tang*s and Buddhist temples flourished on Cheju Island, but in the Chosŏn Period only tens of *tang*s survived while Buddhist temples were on the verge of extinction.

Ponhyangdang was the outcome of compromising Shamanism with Confucianism. The name, *ponhyangdang*, literally means the principal one out of many spirit halls within a village. In the Chosŏn Period, the local government did not allow any other spirit halls, except for one, called *ponhyangdang*, within a village, in order to reduce the social power of Shamanism on Cheju Island. During this period, many *tang*s disappeared on western Cheju Island, but those on eastern Cheju Island called the Tongch'on Region survived. *Ponhyandang*s on eastern Cheju Island also continued to survive a series of ordeals in the Chosŏn Period.

In terms of physical geography, eastern Cheju Island is in striking contrast to western Cheju Island (Song, 1988:10-11). On eastern Cheju Island, rainfall is easily saturated into the underground, and thus the scanty run-off on the surface of the earth forms streams very poorly. The bottoms of streams are usually dried up most of the year, and the surface of the earth is covered with thin layers of soil, with depth less than 20cm. The soil is not only minimal in organic contents, but also poor in fertility. Most of eastern Cheju Island, not suitable for farming, was left as pasture land only to be used for ranching. The coastal zone was also not good for fishing, because it received strong winds from the northwest during the winter season. There, only the sea-women called *haenyŏ* were able to dive into the water and catch a variety of sea plants and animals.

Western Cheju Island, by contrast, had physical conditions

which were more suitable for farming and fishing. In the Chosŏn Period, Confucianism penetrated more easily into this region, and lineage villages called *chipsŏngch'on* were more common than on eastern Cheju Island. As Confucianism built up its own social and political power, Shamanism and other folk beliefs yielded their own place to Confucianism. For instance, the village ritual named *p'oje*, Shamanistic in origin, finally changed into a Confucian style, and only men could participate in this ritual. According to the principles of Confucianism, women were excluded from membership in these village rituals.

However, the situation on eastern Cheju Island was quite to the contrary (Song, 1988:16-17). There, in the village ritual named *ponhyangje*, Shamanism rather than Confucianism was still intact, and women were allowed to participate. As the women's role in livelihood was more active here, their social power was not weaker than men. Their social power was strong enough to organize the village ritual for their own.

To perform this village ritual regularly, women gathered in a *ponhyangdang* which was usually made outdoors on Cheju Island. Unlike mainland Korea, where spirit halls usually are indoors, they are commonly found outdoors on Cheju Island. The spirit halls are usually surrounded by walls built with stones in the woods, either near or in the village. Since these spirit halls are hidden in a quiet place, outsiders cannot easily recognize them (**Photo 13**). It is said that in the early 18th century, people could resist the most severe suppression from Confucianism by relocating spirit halls in as many secret places as possible. A guerrilla-like locational strategy was indeed crucial for the survival game by Shamanism under the hegemony of Confucianism in power.

Another strategy of Shamanism to overcome the ordeals from Confucianism was to adapt the concept of deities to the Confucian type. As Confucianism grew stronger in power, the deities worshipped in the *ponhyangdang* gradually changed from natural deities (rocks and trees) into human deities (mostly old women), and then from old women into old men (Ko, 1997:268). On eastern Cheju Island, women were stronger in social power than men, and there had been more deities called *halmang* (grandmother in Cheju Island dialect) than *harŭbang* (grandfather in Cheju Island dialect). The name of deities was usually a combination of a specific name with a generic name, *halmang*, literally meaning grandmother.

Sometimes these human deities are those who existed in real-

Photo 13. The forest surrounding a *ponhyangdang* (main spirit hall) on Cheju Island: Once entering the forest, one can find a holy tree decorated with colorful cloth and low stone walls surrounding it. Even during the village ritual called *ponhyangje*, villagers, mostly women, come here to dedicate food and liquor individually, not in a group.

ity, and their legends have been handed down from generation to generation through oral tradition. The deity of old women on eastern Cheju Island is traced back to ancient times when hunting was the principal means of livlihood. It is said that many of these deities were later replaced by those of old men descending from Halla Mountain (**Photo 14**). Some of the deities from Halla Mountain are said to have come down to villages in order to live with human beings. Some of them also got angry like human beings when food and clothing were not supplied (Ko, 1997:154-155).

The story about the deity of Kimssi Harŭbang (Grandfather Mr. Kim), one of the three most important deities on eastern Cheju Island, implies how and why deities were either replaced

Photo 14. A main crater called Paekrokdam on the summit of Halla Mountain during the winter time: It was made from volcanic activity and has been viewed as a sacred mountain by the people on Cheju Island. Many myths were created in association with this sacred mountain.

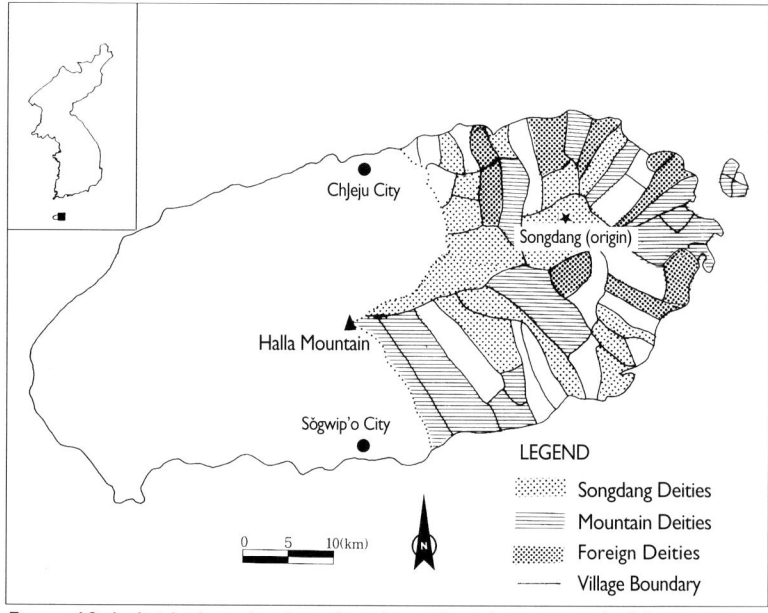

Figure 12. Individual territories of *ponhyangdang* (main spirit halls) on eastern Cheju Island: All of the Songdangshins (Songdang deities) are male deities with the family name Kim, while *sanshins* (mountain spirits) and foreign deities are not. Today many of these deities still remain female without any specific family names.

or relocated in the past. According to oral tradition, the deities changed not only from old women into old men, but also from natives into immigrants. The major duty of deities also turned from hunting into farming and ranching, and their character transformed from Shamanism into Confucianism. All in all, the changes in deities strongly suggest that the villagers continued to adapt themselves to the changing environment, physical as well as social (**Figure 12**).

Originally, they worshipped a deity of an old woman, named Semyŏngju in *ponhyangdang* around Kujwa Town (Ko, 1997:40). It is said that a woman named Kŭmbaekjo moved there from

Photo 15. A *ponhyangdang*, or main spirit hall around Kujwa Town on Cheju Island: The hall was located at the origin of the village deities named Songdangshin, or Kimssi Harŭbang, the sons of a woman named Kŭmbaekjo. Herein, the deity of Kŭmbaekjo is preserved along with that of her husband named Soch'ŏnguk.

Seoul to be married to a man named Soch'ŏnguk who was hunting for his livelihood on Halla Mountain. The ex-wife of Soch'ŏnguk, Semyŏngju, was driven out of the village into the coast, and Kŭmbaekjo later became a new deity for the *ponhyangdang* around Kujwa Town (**Photo 15**).

Kŭmbaekjo's sons received the family name of Kim from the royal court, and opened new villages in other locations on eastern Cheju Island (Ko, 1997:299). Here they also became new deities called Songdangshin, or Kimssi Harŭbang, replacing the deities with the family name of Song. Today villages with *ponhyangdang*, worshipping Grandfather Mr. Kim, occupy the largest part of eastern Cheju Island. There villagers worship these old men as ancestor-deities providing them good farming and ranching.

These deities of Grandfather Mr. Kim are sometimes worshipped together with wives of different origins (Song, 1998:36-37). Some of them are from *sanshin*, dragon kings and Grandmother Mrs. Song, all of which are indigenous deities. This means that villagers were very flexible and practical in the belief to accept other deities when it was necessary for their subsistence. The most important for villagers has not been their deities per se, but their subsistence. Such a resiliency and flexibility underlies the dynamic changes in the deities, and their survival from the repression of Confucianism.

3) *Sŏndol* (Standing Stones) around Okch'ŏn Town

Depending on the histories and environments of villages, the types of deities and rituals vary from one village to another. Many different names are applied to village rituals in different regions: *tangsanje, sanshinje, tangje, sŏnangje, p'oje,* and *pyŏlshinje* (Yun et. al., 1996:122). The village rituals are usually mixed in procedure, but roughly classified into two types: Confucian and Shamanistic. The closer a region or a village maintains its relation to Confucianism, the deeper a penetration of the Confucian type into the village ritual may be.

Geographically speaking, the closer to Seoul, the center of Confucianism, a village is located, the more it contains a Confucian type of village ritual. Villages in the remote locations such as coastal margins or islands are more likely to show less influence on rituals from Confucianism. However, even within a region one can find diverse types of rituals; the Confucian type adjoining the Shamanistic type. Within a village, also common is a ritual in which Confucian and Shamanistic types are mixed.

There are numerous deities in village rituals, and plurality of deities is an important characteristic of Korean village rituals. The more isolated a village is from cities, the more likely it maintains the plurality of deities. Village deities, in reality, vary from natural to human ones: trees, rocks, pebble-piles, high poles, ancestral tablets in shrines, portraits, icons, and pieces of folded Korean paper. The more a village was involved with Confucianism, the more it created human deities.

In general, however, village deities are classified into two types depending on their location: *sangdangshin* (deity in a spirit hall above a village), and *hadangshin* (deity in a spirit hall below a village). *Hadangshin*s are the deities at the village entrances, such as pebble-piles, trees, and road icons or high poles. Those classified into *sangdangshin*s are deities called *sanshin*, or the mountain spirit, behind a village, at the highest location, mountain peak or side. As village rituals have been diminished due to nationwide industrialization, only the *sangdangshin*s without the *hadangshin*s are today worshipped in most villages.

The mountain surrounding a village is usually perceived by villagers as a holy place where the *sanshin* resides. The *sanshin* is believed to guard the whole village. In a certain sense, each locale with a mountain has its local *sanshin*, but no rivalry exists. Each is simultaneously a *sanshin* to that particular location, and one does not dominate the other. Confucianism's ancestor worship reinforced Shamanism's earlier belief in the continued life of the soul as a "spirit" after death. It was also

Photo 16. A road icon, or a totem pole, called *changsŭng*, at a village entrance: It is believed that this type of *hadangshin* had once been the most popular in rural Korea.

Confucianism that drove so many Korean women to depend on the *sanshin* or the *samshin*, which guaranteed them to produce male children necessary for attendance at Confucian family shrines.

The inlets of a village constitute the boundary of the village. To villagers, inside a village is a secure and sacred world, while a world of the profane is formed outside. The two opposite worlds meet each other exactly at the entrances of the village. All misfortunes, disasters and diseases (especially epidemics) from the outside world infiltrated into the village through the entrances. Therefore, villagers tried to block them out with spiritual powers from high poles (road icons), rocks, stones, trees, pebble-piles, pagodas and so on (**Photo 16**). These deities called *hadangshin* not only keep away misfortunes from a village, but also retain good fortunes within a village (Yun et. al., 1996:124).

3. Folk Landscapes

Photo 17. A *sŏndol* (standing stone) as a mountain deity around Okch'ŏn Town: The standing stone is usually found as a *hadangshin* (deity in a spirit hall below a village) at the entrance of a village. It is, however, rarely seen as a *sangdangshin* (deity in a spirit hall below a village) on the mountain behind a village.

In the upper valleys of the *Kŭm* River, in particular around Okch'ŏn Town, village rituals worshipping both *sangdangshin* and *hadangshin* have been preserved relatively well. In a village ritual, people first worship the *sanshin*, and then deities at the entrance of the village. Against the modern trend in Korea within which village rituals have drastically died out, they have survived here in good shape. Confucianism has deeply permeated the procedures of rituals, but natural objects of trees, rocks and stones still dominate the village deities. Among them, those which attract outsider's eyes are stones standing as *hadangshin* at the entrance of the village (**Photo 17**).

These stones, unusual in shape, sometimes stand with dolmens, or *koindol* in Korean, and look to visitors as if they possess mystical spirits. Usually only one or two stones stand at the entrance of the village, but sometimes four or five stones are

Photo 18. A dolmen, called *koindol* in Korean, located in the upper reaches of Kŭm River: Being huge in size and mystical in shape, it causes people to believe it as a supernatural being.

found in all directions encircling the village. It is said that even in ancient times many *sŏndol*s, or standing stones, formed as pairs with dolmens in the upper valleys of the Kŭm River (Yang, 1993:21). Villagers dared neither to relocate nor to touch them because of not only the belief that *sŏndol* possessed spiritual powers but also the fear that they would cause disasters when relocated. In fact, it is said that many *sŏndol*s have been standing there from the beginning. Village deities around Okch'ŏn Town, therefore, can be traced back to animism within which natural objects such as stones were worshipped as if they possessed supernatural spirits.

In the beginning individuals had worshipped them as their own deities, and later villagers came to view them as their common village deities. Today dolmens are sometimes symbolized as turtle rocks or "Seven Dipper Rocks" with spiritual ability to

3. Folk Landscapes

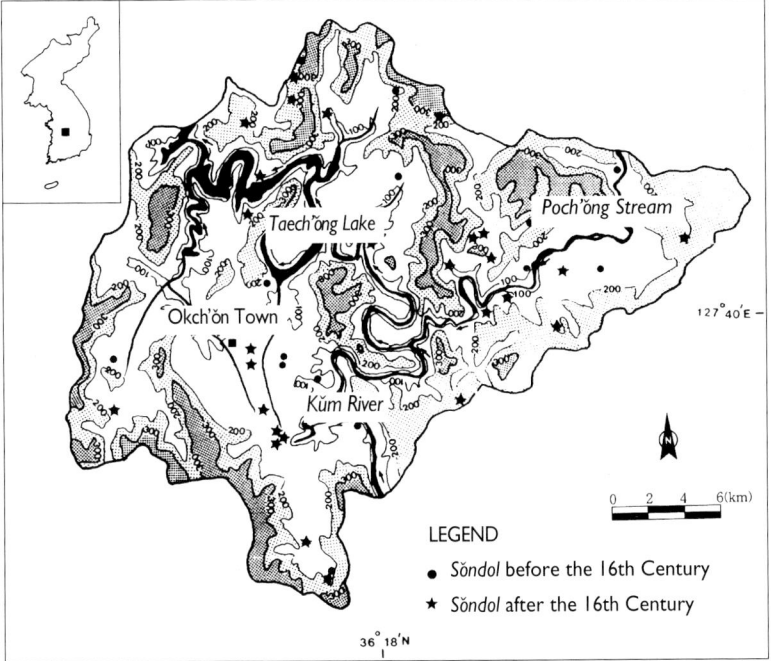

Figure 13. The spatial distribution of sŏndol (standing stones) around Okch'ŏn Town before and after the 16th Century: As sŏndol as a hadangshin (deities in spirit halls below a village) became very popular among villagers after the 16th century. Population growth along with the introduction of paddy-rice cultivation seems to have contributed to the wide spread of sŏndol. (Source: Yong-sik Yang, 1993, "The Distribution Pattern of Folk Landscapes around Okch'ŏn Town," Unpublished Master's Thesis, Department of Geography, Korea National University of Education, p. 88.)

ensure longevity (**Photo 18**). *Sŏndol*s, by contrast, are sometimes symbolized as sexual organs of men or women, and believed to ensure good harvests and male descendants. It seems that since ancient times, neither the basic needs nor the deities have changed.

Surprisingly, these rocks and stones are usually found at locations near streams (**Figure 13**). When a dolmen was identified with a turtle, it was placed with the turtle's head toward the

Photo 19. A male *sŏndol* (standing stone) around Okch'ŏn Town: With a sharp-shaped head, the standing stone's body is wound with rice-straw string, making it a male deity. Located at one side of the road entering the village, it did have a female partner, *sŏndol*, on the other side of the road.

direction in which the stream flowed. Near a dolmen, a *sŏndol* was situated on the hills from which one could look down upon the stream. People transformed the shapes of *sŏndol* artificially to make them look more real. They liked to make heads of male stones more sharp, and those of female stones more round (**Photo 19, 20**). They sometimes made holes in the body of

3. Folk Landscapes

Photo 20. A more typical shape of a male *sŏndol* around Okch'ŏn Town: The stone looks natural and mystical enough to make people believe in its supernatural power.

Photo 21. A female *sŏndol* (standing stone) around Okch'ŏn Town: An archaeologist once speculated that ancient men or women might have inscribed a circle on this stone. They could have imagined that the stone looked like a pregnant woman with her swollen stomach. Then, the circle on it might have been intended to describe a mother's womb within which a baby resided.

stones with the intention to make it look similar to sexual organs of women. A certain female stone with a round body even symbolizes a pregnant woman, and people used to pray for the birth of sons in front of it (**Photo 21**).

It was in the Chosŏn Period that *sŏndol* became the village deities protecting the village from the outside world. From the 16th century when the lineage village called *chipsŏngch'on* became widespread along with paddy-rice farming, village rituals began to be performed. Since then other symbolic meanings, which have something to do with daily lives, have been attached to the *sŏndol*. The *sŏndol* gradually degradated from *sangdangshin* ensuring good harvests and male descendants into *hadangshin* protecting villages from devil spirits or natural disasters such as epidemics and floods. The protection from floods, in particular, was the most important in the villages located near streams and exposed to floods. The names of *sŏndol*, therefore, are often called *sugumagi* or *susalmagi*, literally meaning a thing to block a water inlet or to defend from being killed by floods (Yang, 1993:15-16).

By the late Chosŏn Period, such a trend had already become very popular nationwide in Korea, but with regional variations. Since Confucianism held sway at that time, village rituals were not immune to the influence from Confucianism. One of the dominant trends was the replacement of natural deities by human deities. In villages around Okch'ŏn Town, nonetheless, abundant with *sŏndol* along with dolmens, the transition from natural to human deities was deterred, but the procedures became salient with Confucian elements.

To the preservation of natural deities, of course, its isolated location and physical conditions made an undeniable contribution. The topography of canyons within which the meandering streams crisscrossed in a zigzagging manner made the locations more isolated from the outside world. Once settled inside the canyon, the settlement could not easily be seen from the outside. Into this secluded location, many family groups with social status of *yangban* moved in the 15th century when foreign invasions twice entirely devastated Korea (Yang, 1993: 21-22).

Since then, many more family groups moved into these canyons and settled permanently with the intention of insulating themselves from the outside world. Their residential areas were divided in small scale by narrow valleys of canyons, and one or more lineage groups could not dominate the others. The whole area was relatively homogeneous in social characteristics, which in turn contributed to the universal preservation of *sŏndol* as *hadangshin*.

The village locations near streams, vulnerable to the danger from floods, made more people believe in the spiritual power of *sŏndol*. Because of steep slopes in canyons, the water flowing in the streams could easily spill over the bank and threaten the village with floods during the rainy season. In the Chosŏn Period, the only way for villagers to protect their village from floods may have been the use of manual labor in cooperation. With the common symbol of *sŏndol* at the entrance of the village, they may have wanted to alert villagers all the time to defend themselves from floods in unison. Moreover, the popular belief in Feng-shui about an artificial establishment to bar the village from the water inlets also made *sŏndol* more acceptable to the people.

4) *TOLT'AP* (PEBBLE-PILES) AROUND KŬMSAN TOWN

In the upper valleys of the Kŭm River, *hadangshin*s (deities in spirit halls below a village) appear in the form of *tolt'ap* (pebble-pile) as well as *sŏndol* (standing stone). Especially around Kŭmsan, *tolt'ap*s artificially made into the shape of a cone are easily seen at the entrances of villages. The *tolt'ap*s are sometimes called stone pagodas, and they are found beyond the reaches of the Kŭm River, especially heavily concentrated in the upper valleys of the Kŭm River (**Figure 14**).

Around Kŭmsan Town the size of *tolt'ap* varies from the largest, 2.6m in height and 18m in circumference, to the smallest, 1.3m in height and 4-5m in circumference (Yi, 1990:168). The most common ones are 1.5m in height and 6-10m in circumference. Usually a pair of *tolt'ap*s are built both inside and outside the front boundary of village which faces a stream. Moreover, on top of it or in front of it is placed a *sŏndol*, which makes the *tolt'ap*s look more mystical. The *sŏndol*, if seen from afar, resembles the head of a snake or man's sexual organ (**Photo 22**).

In general, a pair of *tolt'ap*s within a village are perceived as partners in terms of sexuality as well as location: male and female. The pair of terms referring to them are grandfather versus grandmother, man versus woman, husband versus wife, outside versus inside, and large versus small. The idea of a *yin* and *yang*, originated in Taoism, may have influenced the establishment of *tolt'ap*s as a pair. The sexuality of a *tolt'ap* is easily distinguished by its shape and size. If it is a steep cone in shape, large in size, it is more likely to be male. When it is a gentle cone in shape, small in size, it is more likely to be female.

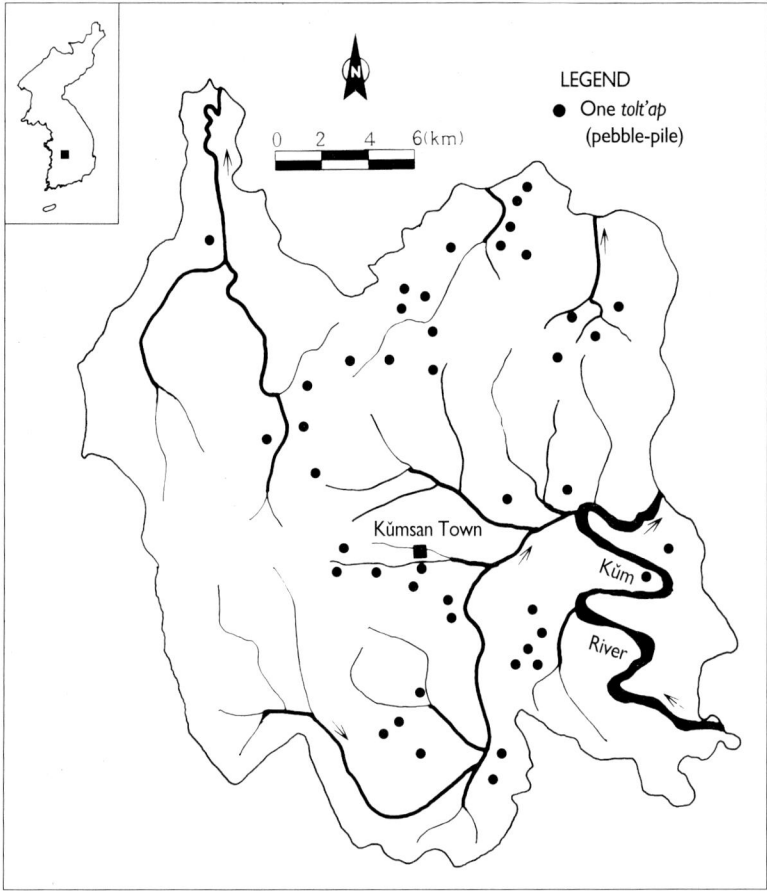

Figure 14. The spatial distribution of tolt'aps (pebble-piles) around Kŭmsan Town (in the upper valley of the Kŭm River): Many tolt'aps are located beside streams, especially branch streams of the Kŭm River. Here, the topography is dominated by the canyons deeply incised by streams meandering in a zigzagging manner. (Adapted and modified from the Appendix in Village Rituals around Kŭmsan Town, 1990, Published by the Institute of Ch'ungch'ŏng Culture, Hannam University, Taejŏn: Seminsa.)

However, the cone-like pebble-pile is totally different from sŏnangdang, or the shrine of a tutelary deity, which is made of small pebbles. The folk landscape of sŏnangdang, round in shape, seems to share its origin with oboe in Mongolia. It is usu-

3. Folk Landscapes

Photo 22. A *tolt'ap*, or pebble-pile, around Kŭmsan Town: The pebble-pile at the entrance of a village is called the Grandfather Pagoda. On the top of it, villagers placed a stone resembling the head of a snake to make it a male deity.

ally found under a tree whose branches are tied up with a colorful cloth. It is also located on the trail passing over a hill or mountain, and travelers would stop and wish for their safe journey in front of it. In terms of function as well as location, the

Photo 23. A *sŏnangdang* with a small pile of pebbles on the trail passing over Mungyŏng Town: The pile is seen on the right-hand side under a tree, while the hall is behind it.

tolt'ap is not the same as *sŏnangdang* (**Photo 23**).

People within a village usually perform the second village ritual, called *t'apje* (pagoda ritual), in front of *tolt'ap* after performing the first village ritual called *sanshinje* (mountain spirit ritual) at the mountain. It is believed that the *t'apshin* (pagoda spirit) resides in *tolt'ap*, while *sanshin*, or the mountain spirit, is in the mountain (Yi, 1990:169).

In the village ritual for the *sanshin*, a few villagers, exclusively male, participate, and the ritual itself is very much like an ancestor worshipping ceremony in Confucianism. After the ritual for the *sanshin* is over, villagers walk around the village dancing and singing behind the leader of a village band, and gather around the pile of pebbles. In the village ritual for the pagoda spirit, all the villagers, female as well as male, are welcome to participate, and the ritual is a mixture of Shamanistic and Buddhistic styles.

Most of the people cannot tell the origin of *tolt'ap* exactly in their village. They do not know when and how the *tolt'ap*s were established there (Yi, 1990:164). What they can recall roughly is only that they were built according to a certain geomancer's or shaman's advice. When a disaster such as an epidemic occurred to the village, the villagers sought a spiritual solution from a shaman or geomancer. Recently, however, in the villagers' view, the most serious disasters are not epidemics, but the accidental deaths of youths who moved out of the village into other places. Upon the villagers' request, the shaman or geomancer would tell them to establish a pair of *tolt'ap*s, and perform a Shamanistic ritual called *kut*.

Interestingly, in addition to Shamanism and Taoism, the elements of Feng-shui and Buddhism were adopted into the village rituals for *tolt'ap*. Those who believe in Feng-shui would go for advice to a geomancer, who would in turn point out the exact locations at which to establish a pair of *tolt'ap*s. In this case, the pair of *tolt'ap*s are believed to compensate for the topographical weakness which the village has in terms of geomancy. As a pebble-pile is really called a pagoda, its position and shape reminds one of a stone pagoda in a temple.

Women, in particular, have been very active, not only in the maintenance, but also in the revival of stone-pagoda rituals around Kŭmsan Town (Yi, 1990:172). They even sometimes lead the performance of the pagoda ritual with a shaman in a village where men have lost their interest in it. In such a village, the village ritual for the pagoda spirit is a mixture of Shamanistic and Buddhistic styles. For example, there is a village where women walk around the pebble-pile with a candle in hand, while chanting a prayer to Amitabha with the wishes that their families and sons would prosper.

The *t'apshin* is not only a *hadangshin*, but also an individual woman's deity. Women would also come to the *tolt'ap* when they felt like praying for their wish. Here they would pray for the delivery of sons and the longevity of their children, the most important in women's prayers. In fact, it is said that many of *tolt'ap*s were built less than tens of years or one hundred years ago.

Villagers also believed that the pagoda spirit in the *tolt'ap* would protect them from the natural disaster of floods. In the upper valley of the Kŭm River, they thought that the defense against the danger from flood was very crucial for their safe life. In piling-up the pebbles to establish a so-called stone pagoda, villagers were willing to supply their labor with their belief in the power of the pagoda spirit. Every member of a household, no matter how young or old, had to participate in the tedious labor of piling up pebbles. At that time, everybody knew that he or she should carry even the smallest stone with a sincere mind to make a firm construction of the stone pagoda.

When the technology of water control was underdeveloped in the past, the natural disaster of floods occurred frequently in the upper valleys of the Kŭm River during the rainy season in summer. Because streams flowed through canyons with steep valleys, flooding could easily break out and threaten the fortunes and lives of villagers.

The topography around Kŭmsan Town was once characterized by high mountains over 500m above sea level. Kŭmsan Town is situated in a small basin, which is surrounded by high mountains in all directions like a folding screen: Taesŏng Mountain (705m), Kuksa Peak (668m), Sŏngju Mountain (624m) to the east; Taedun Mountain (878m) to the west; Sŏdae Mountain (910m) to the north; Chinak Mountain (747m), Tŏkgi Peak (558m), and Ki Peak (537m) to the south. Therefore, the farther one goes into the valleys, the deeper and narrower the valleys become and one feels like being shut up inside the valleys.

Moreover, the area around Kŭmsan Town receives more rainfall than the vicinity areas mainly due to its topographical conditions. As the rain clouds are usually blocked by the high mountains, rainfall tends to be much heavier here than in other areas without high mountains. Around here the average annual rainfall records around 1,300mm, which is more than 1,159m, the national average. With heavy rainfall and thin soil on the steep slopes of the valleys, this area is really vunerable to flooding even in the deep valleys.

There, villagers had to build dikes together along the streams with stones in order to protect the paddy-rice fields and villages from flooding. Nonetheless, to carry stones with hands and build dikes from them with human muscles was a painstaking job which required cooperative labor from all the villagers. The dikes, if not firm in construction, also easily fell down when a severe flood attacked them. Piling up pebbles, therefore, may have been an extension of building dikes along streams to protect villages from flooding.

5) *TANGJE* (VILLAGE RITUALS) ON THE ISLANDS IN THE TADOHAE (SOUTHWESTERN SEA)

To the southwestern sea with many islands, large and small in size, is given a special name of "Tadohae," or Sea with Numerous Islands. This group of islands, once called by Westerners "the Korea Archipelago," lie partly off the large islands and partly in the outer expanses of bays on the coast (Lautensach, 1988:364). The islands lie quite close together and often flock together in groups to form an inner ring with a width up to 35km. Separated by expanses of sea without islands about 20km in width, there finally follows an outer ring, consisting of sporadic small islands. The outermost of the latter Sohŭksan Island lies far out into the Yellow Sea, 126km from the closest point on the mainland.

In Shinan County alone, there are 830 islands: 111 inhabited ones and 719 uninhabited ones. On these islands can be seen a variety of village rituals with different names and styles. The name of village rituals vary from island to island, depending on the distance from mainland: *sanshinje* (the ritual for *sanshin* or the mountain spirit), *tangje* (the ritual at *tang* or a spirit hall), *yongwangje* (the ritual for *yongwang* or the dragon king).

The style of rituals also tends to transit from Confucian into Shamanistic on the islands. The farther one travels from the mainland into the sea, the more likely one can observe Shamanistic rituals. Village deities are multiple not only in numbers but also in kinds, with some remnants of ancient origins. On an island, plural deities within a village really co-exist in harmony with one another: animistic, Shamanistic and Confucian deities.

The Tadohae in Shinan County stretches from the sea near the

3. Folk Landscapes

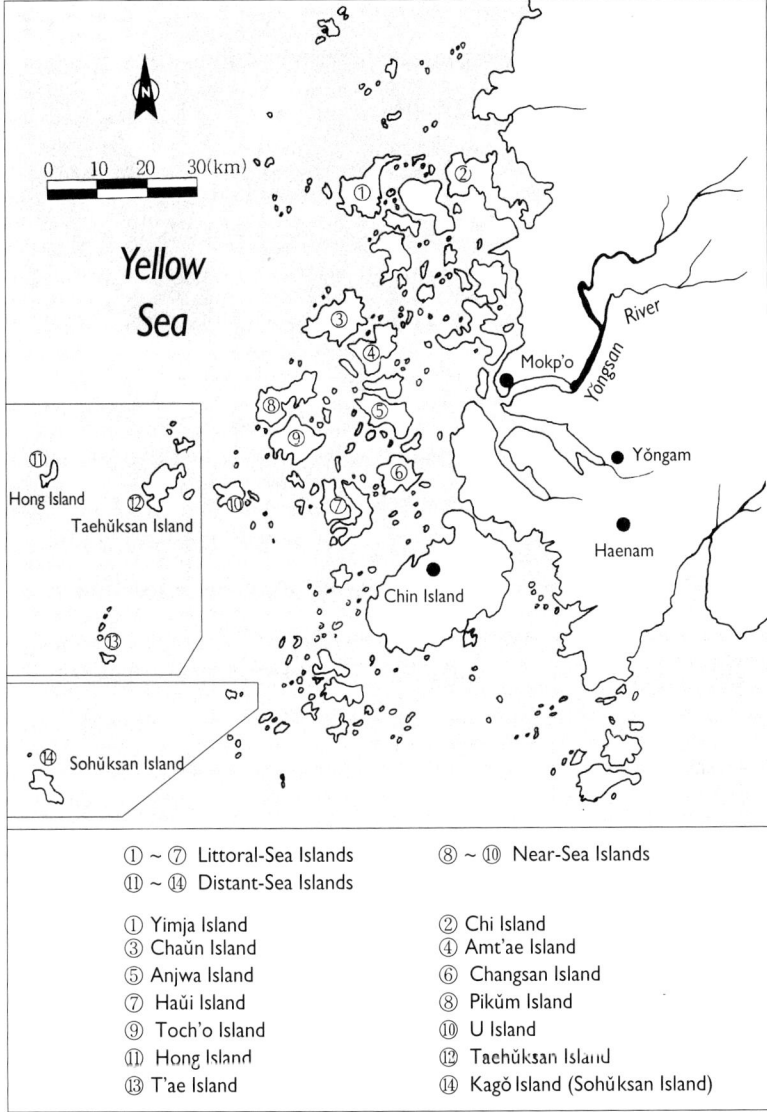

| ① ~ ⑦ Littoral-Sea Islands | ⑧ ~ ⑩ Near-Sea Islands |
| ⑪ ~ ⑭ Distant-Sea Islands | |

① Yimja Island
③ Chaŭn Island
⑤ Anjwa Island
⑦ Haŭi Island
⑨ Toch'o Island
⑪ Hong Island
⑬ T'ae Island

② Chi Island
④ Amt'ae Island
⑥ Changsan Island
⑧ Pikŭm Island
⑩ U Island
⑫ Taehŭksan Island
⑭ Kagŏ Island (Sohŭksan Island)

Figure 15. The spatial division of islands in the Southwestern Sea called Tadohae: Based on the distance from the mainland, islands can be divided into three rings, such as littoral-, near-, and distant-sea islands. The number of islands decreases substantially as one moves farther into the sea. The islands in the distant sea, in reality, are located much farther out than indicated on the map.

mainland into the sea far from the mainland. According to the distance from the mainland, the islands in the southwestern sea are classified into three groups: islands in the littoral sea, in the near sea, and in the distant sea. The large islands in the littoral sea are Yimja Island, Chi Island, Chaŭn Island, Haŭi Island, Anjwa Island, Changsan Island, and Amt'ae Island. Those in the near sea are Pikŭm Island, Toch'o Island, and U Island, while those in the distant sea are Hŭksan Island, Hong Island, T'ae Island, and Kagŏlsland (Sohŭksan Island) (**Figure 15**).

On the islands in the littoral sea, farming is more important than fishing to maintain people's livelihood. Fishing is simply subservient to farming in the way of people's life, and people on the islands visit the mainland by boat without any difficulty, if necessary. As cultural contact through transportation and communication was frequent between these islands and the mainland, village rituals on the islands are not much different from those on the mainland. The ceremonies common in agricultural villages, such as trampling on the ground around a village, playing farmer's music, and pulling ropes, are also found on these islands (Ch'oe, 1990:26).

On these islands, moreover, *sanshin*s in the hall are worshipped as *sangdangshin*s (deities in spirit halls above a village) along with trees and stones as *hadangshin*s (deities in spirit halls below a village). The procedures in rituals also reflect the strong influence from Confucianism. The way in which foods are arranged on the table and ritual prayers are read are replicas of Confucian rituals on ancestor worship. Due to its proximity to the mainland, village rituals on the islands in the littoral sea could not easily retain insular characteristics. It is probable that ancient types of village rituals have been largely assimilated

3. Folk Landscapes

into those from the mainland.

By contrast, fishing becomes more important on the islands in the near and distant seas, where natural conditions hinder the development of farming. The important islands in the near sea are Pikŭm Island, Toch'o Island, and U Island, transitional in their livelihoods between islands in the littoral sea and those in the distant sea. These islands are located at the passageway to the distant sea, one of the major fishing grounds in Korea. There are factories refitting fishing boats and ships and the seasonal markets on fisheries called *p'ashi*. On these islands, farming is nothing but a subsidiary activity even when it is possible, and it is totally unthinkable in general.

In the distant sea, Hŭksan Island, Hong Island, T'ae Island, and Kagŏ Island (Sohŭksan Island) are the important islands where most inhabitants are engaged in fishing. In the past these islands served as the main ports for international sea transportation from southern Korea to southern China. Now they are used as bases for fishing in the distant sea, the Yellow Sea and the East Chinese Sea.

The changes in the kinds of village deities and styles of village rituals from island to island are gradual, and sometimes overlapping on the islands between the near sea and distant sea. Because the islands are situated in proximity to one another, it is easy to travel by boat either from the mainland or from one island to another. Moving into the distant sea, people with small boats could safely continue to visit islands, one after another, as if the islands were stepping stones on the water.

Among village deities on the islands in the near sea, the most common are trees and stones, which are called grandfather and grandmother. These deities, animistic by nature, are also common on the mainland along with the names of grandfather and grandmother. These deities are placed either at the same locations altogether or at different locations separately. When they are placed in separation, the deity of the grandmother is often at the higher location, with that of the grandfather at the lower location.

Usually, villagers at first would dedicate the ritual to the deity of the grandmother, and then to the deity of the grandfather. For instance, in a village on Chi Island named T'andong, the deity of the grandmother is a *sŏndol*, or standing stone, 40cm in height and 30cm in width, wrapped up with Korean paper on the slope of Kimang Mountain on Saok Island, and that of the grandfather is a tree in the middle of the field in front of the village (Ch'oe, 1990:45-50). It is speculated that the way of treating female deities more importantly than male deities may have been derived from the ancient tradition, originated in Southeast Asia.

On the islands in the near and distant seas, a variety of animistic deities are even worshipped in addition to human and natural deities. Animal deities such as the horse and mouse are often worshipped as village deities, which cannot be seen on the mainland. In particular, the habit of worshipping the mouse as a village deity is widespread on the islands in the near and distant seas. It is suggested that the Shamanistic ritual for the deity of the mouse may be the remnants of animism from ancient times, which had already disappeared completely on the mainland.

On Pikŭm Island, for instance, there is a village named Wŏlp'ori where the mouse spirit is worshipped as *sangdangshin*, along with the *sanshin*, the grandmother spirit and the grandfa-

3. Folk Landscapes

ther spirit. In this village, four kinds of human spirits who died from misfortune are also worshipped as *hadangshin*s, or deities in spirit halls below a village. These human spirits are the ghosts from those who once lived in reality and died by accident. They are called the ghosts from those who died as the disabled, bachelor, beggar and the hanged.

Because of its distance from the mainland, the cultural contact between these islands and the mainland was very much limited. On these islands, ancient types of village rituals are sometimes found, and they may have originated in the Koryŏ Period. On the island of Toch'o Island, for example, in a village named Koranri, a horse whose body is made of bamboo is worshipped as the village deity (Ch'oe, 1990:65-71). The deity of the horse, originated in the Koryŏ Period, has a head which is woven with straws and wrapped with paper, and on the paper the nose and eyes are drawn in Chinese ink to make it appear real.

On the islands in the distant sea, almost every village performs the ritual for *yongwangshin*, or the deity of the dragon king, in separation from the ritual for the deity of the *sanshin* or the grandmother spirit. The special name *kaetje* or *tŭkje* had been given to this type of village ritual peculiar to Tadohae (Ch'oe, 1990:20). In some villages, the *sanshin* is no longer the main deity, and *yongwangshin*, or the deity of the dragon king, is worshipped as the main deity. In Korea, the legendary deity of the dragon king is believed to secure good fishing and a safe journey on the sea.

The types of village deities as well as the styles of village rituals are also exclusively Shamanistic by nature. The deity of the dragon king is usually in the shape of a small straw man, and other village deities are identified with hemp cloth, cotton cloth, cotton thread, white clothes and white Korean paper (called paper money), which are neither animistic nor Confucian deities. Each of these deities were given a variety of Shamanistic names, and shamans are called on by villagers to perform the village rituals for these deities.

In the ritual for *yongwang*, villagers come together on the coast in front of the village. An individual woman from each household brings to the coast the table with foods on it, and prays to *yongwangshin*, which is represented by a straw man. Women feed the straw man with foods and liquors, while praying for their husbands' good haul in the fishery and safe journey on the sea. Then men take the straw man on a boat to the sea and float it away farther into the sea. This type of ritual is also found in the rituals for the sea deity in the Ryukyu Islands, southern China and Southeast Asia.

4. LINGUISTIC LANDSCAPES

4. Linguistic Landscapes

Many linguists consider the Korean language as belonging to the Tungusic branch of the Altaic language family, which includes Turkish, Mongolian, and Tungus, or Tungus-Manchu, but the similarities between Korean and other Altaic languages are not striking. Although the Korean language displays some important Altaic linguistic features, its linguistic affiliation with them has yet to be proven precisely. Korean and Japanese are often regarded as closely related and are sometimes included in the Altaic group.

Korean dialects have traditionally been classified into eight groups, corresponding to the eight provinces, called To in the Chosŏn Period: Hamgyŏng Province, P'yŏngan Province, Kyŏnggi Province, Ch'ungch'ŏng Province, Chŏlla Province, Kyŏngsang Province, Cheju Province, and Kangwon Province dialects (Koo & Nahm, 1997:3). Depending on the linguistic affiliation, these dialects in Korea can be roughly merged into two groups: northern and southern (Ch'oe,1986-b:383-384). The northern dialect is spoken in the entire parts of Hamgyŏng Province, P'yŏngan Province and Kyŏnggi Province, and the

4. Linguistic Landscapes

northern parts of Ch'ungch'ŏng Province and Kangwon Province. The southern dialect is used in the entire parts of Kyŏngsang Province and Chŏlla Province, and the southern parts of Ch'ungch'ŏng Province and Kangwon Province.

Today, the standard language of Korea is generally defined as the dialect spoken by the middle-class living in Seoul and its vicinity, that is Kyŏnggi Province. Seoul has been the capital city for more than six hundred years since the Chosŏn Dynasty began in 1392. From 918 to 1392, Kaesŏng City in the northern part of Kyŏnggi Province served as the capital of the Koryŏ Dynasty for less than five hundred years. As these two cities lie within the boundary of Kyŏnggi Province, the Kyŏnggi Province dialect has been the source of standard language in Korea for more than one thousand years.

In the period of the Unified Shilla Kingdom (668-892), however, the capital was located in contemporary Kyŏngju City. Before the Shilla Kingdom destroyed the Paekje Kingdom (660) and the Koguryŏ Kingdom (668) with military assistance from Tang China, these three kingdoms divided the Korean Peninsula into three parts for more than six hundred years. The core in the territory of the Shilla Kingdom was contemporary Kyŏngsang Province with her capital in contemporary Kyŏngju City. The core in the territory of the Paekje Kingdom was contemporary Ch'ungch'ŏng Province and Chŏlla Province with her capital in contemporary Kongju City and Puyŏ Town. The Koguryŏ Kingdom occupied not only Kyŏnggi Province, Kangwon Province, Hamgyŏng Province and P'yŏngan Province, but also Manchuria in China.

The northern dialect, therefore, developed from the ancient language in the territory of the Koguryŏ Kingdom, while the southern dialect from those in the territories of the Shilla and Paekje Kingdoms. As the Kyŏnggi Province dialect has been the source of Korean standard language for more than one thousand years, the influence from it on both northern and southern dialects has been paramount. The closer to Kaesŏng City or Seoul the location of a dialect lies, the more it receives influence from the standard language. In the remote locations, distant from the capital cities, the relics of ancient language have sometimes survived in the form of a "linguistic island" up to today. In southern Korea, in particular, the linguistic contrast between Kyŏngsang and Chŏlla Province dialects is still striking, and these dialects are partly remnants from the Three Kingdoms Period.

On the other hand, Koreans did not have their own writing system corresponding with their own spoken language until 1446. The Korean alphabet was created by a royal commission of linguists and philologists during the reign of King Sejong (1418-1450). *Hangŭl*, or the Korean alphabet, is alphabetical in which symbols represent sound units or phonemes of the language. Even after the Korean writing system was invented, public documents continued to be written in Chinese during the Chosŏn Period. Under Japanese colonialism (1910-1945), public documents were recorded in both Japanese and Chinese. Until 1945, therefore, on public records place and personal names were written in Chinese characters, the ideograms, which could not represent every sound unit of the Korean language exactly.

To adopt Chinese characters was based on their similarities with place names in terms of either meaning or sound when they were spoken in Korean. A place name consisting of two

4. Linguistic Landscapes

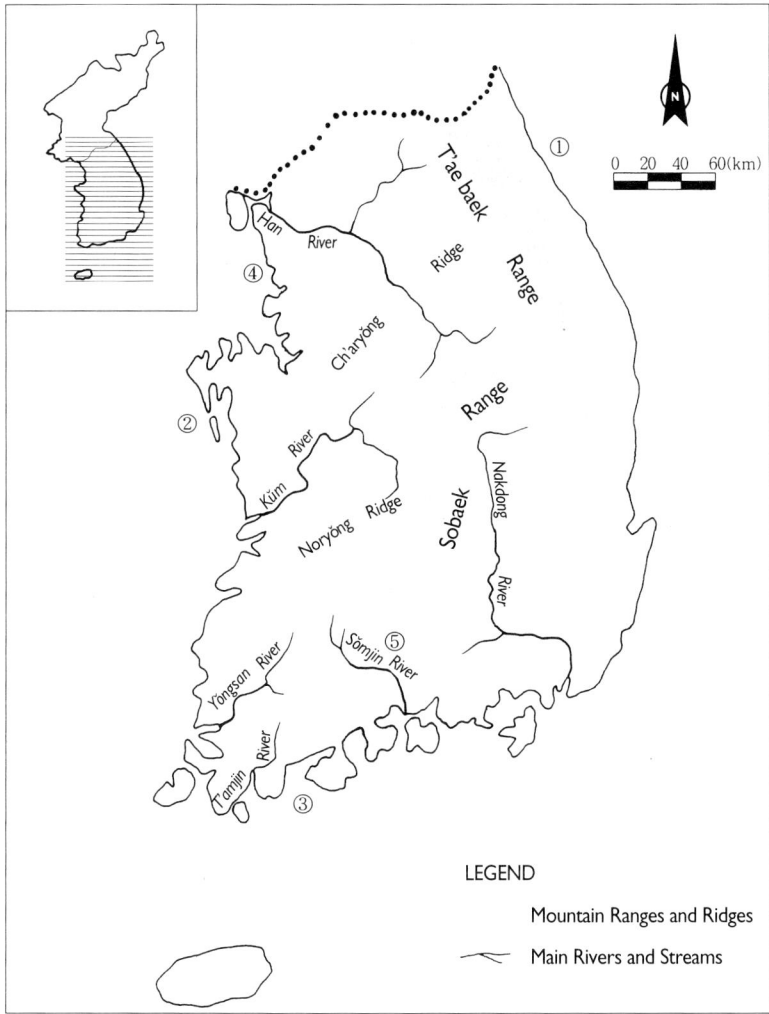

Figure 16. Locations of linguistic landscapes in Korea:
① Isoglosses on the East Coast
② Isoglosses on the West Coast
③ Linguistic islands on the Southwest Coast
④ Place names in Kyŏnggi Bay
⑤ Place names in Chiri Mountain

letters was often found, and within it the former one was written in Chinese imitating sound with the latter representing meaning. Therefore, in order to learn the original sounds and meanings, one ought to unveil the hidden history of place names in relation to how they have been changed in the use of Chinese characters. There are also place names written in Chinese for which the original Korean names have been completely substituted. These place names, however, would often mean no more than they sound in Chinese (**Figure 16**).

1) Isoglosses on the East Coast

Many different dialectic regions can be divided on the basis of vocabulary, grammar, pronunciation and tones. The borders of dialectic regions are called isoglosses or isoglotic lines, and no two isoglosses are duplicates. Isoglosses typically cluster together, and these "bundles" serve as the most satisfactory dividing lines among dialects. As a result, dialectic boundaries are never sharp, in keeping with the general character of cultural borders. Rather than a dividing line, they form a zone within which isoglosses crisscross one another.

One often encounters a core-periphery pattern, in which the dominance of a dialect diminishes away from the center of the dialectic region, through an outlying zone of mixing different dialects. Indeed, dialect terms often overlap considerably, making it difficult to draw isoglosses. Linguistic or dialectic "islands," separated from the main body of a dialect, often further complicate the drawing of borders.

The isoglosses between northern and southern dialects in Korea run from east to west across the territories of Kangwon

4. Linguistic Landscapes

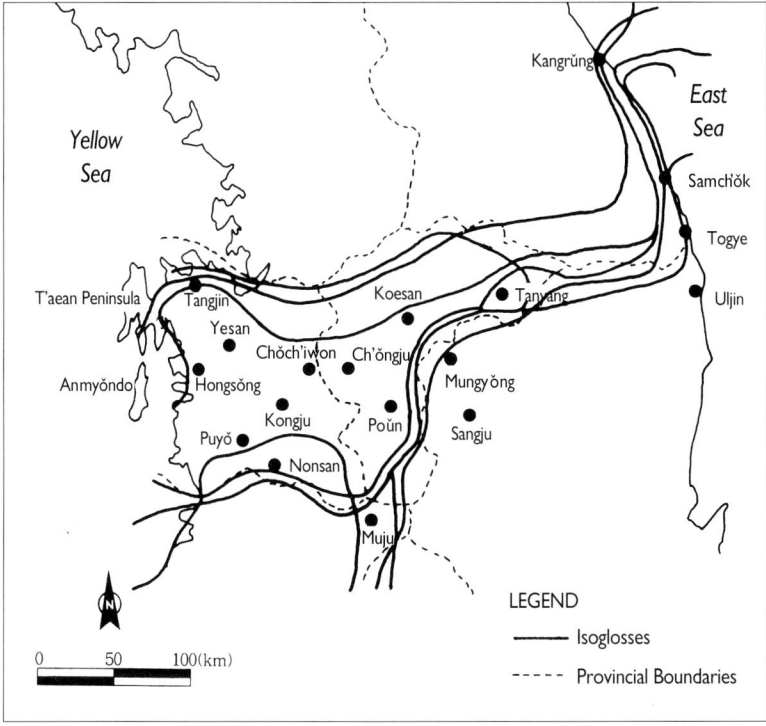

Figure 17. Isoglosses based on vocabulary: The range of isoglosses becomes wider as one moves from the east coast to the west coast. On the east coast, isoglosses run between Kangrŭng City and Samch'ŏk City where a hybrid sub-dialect called Kangrŭng sat'uri is spoken. (Source: Hak-gŭn Ch'oe, 1986, Studies on Korean Dialectics, Vol.2, Seoul: Osongsa, p. 506.)

Province and Ch'ungch'ŏng Province. They crisscross one another to form bundles especially on the east and west coasts. On the east coast, the isoglosses concentrate on the zone between Kangrŭng City and Samch'ŏk City, where different dialects are spoken simultaneously (**Figure 17**). More than three dialects of Kyŏngsang Province, Kyŏnggi Province and Hamgyŏng Province can be often heard in one place, and sometimes even hybrid ones. When hearing them, one cannot tell exactly what kind of dialect they belong to, and sometimes call them the "Kangrŭng City sub-dialect," the hybrid between the Kyŏngsang Province and Kyŏnggi Province dialects.

The hybrid dialect can be heard clearly from Kangrŭng City down south to Samch'ŏk City. In the dialectic zone between Kangrŭng City and Samch'ŏk City, more people call *mogi* in standard Korean (a mosquito in English) as *mogu* rather than *mogi*, while all the people pronounce *nabi* the same as in standard Korean (a butterfly in English) (Ch'oe, 1986-b:396-397). People also call *maru* (wooden veranda) in standard Korean either *maru, marung* or *mari*. The different pronunciations of one word, even if they are not so clear as in Samch'ŏk City, can also be heard farther south down to Uljin, which lies within the territory of Kyŏngsang Province.

The pronunciation of the Kangrŭng City sub-dialect indicates the stronger influence from the Kyŏngsang Province dialect than the Kyŏnggi Province dialect (Ch'oe, 1986-b:406-409). In this sub-dialect, the consonants (k, b, s) tend to be retained in the middle of words. In the Kyŏngsang Province dialect, all the consonants (k, b, s) are retained completely in the middle of words, but only partially in the Kangrŭng City sub-dialect. While the consonants of b and s are not always retained, the consonant of k is never omitted in the middle of words.

They say *horŏmi* (widow) in standard Korean as *hoburemi* and *pŏngŏri* (mute) as *pŏbŏri*, but pronounce *kuwosŏ* (bake) and *tŏwosŏ* (hot) the same as in standard Korean. They say *maŭl* (village) as *mashil*, but pronounce *kaŭl* (autumn) as *kal* and *puŏk* (kitchen) as *pŏkŭ*. To the farther north from Kyŏngsang Province, it is more likely that the consonants of b and s tend to be omitted from words. By contrast, they always retain the consonant of k, and pronounce *morae* (sand) as *molgemi* or *molge*, and *pawi* (rock) as *panggu* in the same way as in Kyŏngsang Province.

In Kyŏngsang Province, people pronounce *ssal* (rice) as *sal* and *ssak* (bud) as *sak*, but *koch'u* (hot pepper) as *kkoch'u* and *tuggŏbi* (toad) as *ttuggŏbi*. The fortis (hard) pronunciation of these front words can be heard even around Kangrŭng City well beyond the north of Samch'ŏk City. However, it is surprising that *ssal* and *ssak* are not pronounced as *sal* and *sak*, but as *ssal* and *ssak* in the speaking of the Kangrŭng City sub-dialect (Ch'oe, 1986-b:410-413).

In the Kangrŭng City sub-dialect, there still remain old vocabularies which can never be found in the Kyŏngsang Province dialect. Linguists generally argue that vocabularies have the strongest tendency of resisting change. Around Samch'ŏk City, a majority of vocabularies have already been assimilated into the Kyŏngsang Province dialect, but there still remain a minority of vocabularies that are not used in the Kyŏngsang Province dialect (Ch'oe, 1986-b:415). For instance, the term of *chaenggi* (plow) in standard Korean is said as *pogure* in the north of Samch'ŏk City, but as *chaenggi* in the south of Samch'ŏk City. The term of *pyŏ* (paddy) in standard Korean is called as *pyŏ* or *pe* in the north of Samch'ŏk City, but as *narak* in the south of Samch'ŏk City. This phenomenon suggests that the Kangrŭng City sub-dialect, once an independent dialect, has been assimilated into the Kyŏngsang Province dialect for quite a long time with less influence from the Kyŏnggi Province dialect.

By contrast, the influence from the Kyŏnggi Province dialect is strongly felt in the realm of grammar (Ch'oe, 1986:415-418). Linguists suggest that it is the easiest for those who speak dialects to learn grammar from the standard language. It seems that those who speak the Kangrŭng City sub-dialect could also easily adopt the grammar from standard Korean. In the dialectic zone between Kangŭng City and Samch'ŏk City, a variety of unusual words such as the interrogative end-form are used at the end of speech asking a question.

These words are also the hybrids within which elements in both Kyŏngsang Province and Kyŏnggi Province dialects are intermingled. Even when listening to them carefully, they sound as if they belong to an independent dialect, totally different from the Kyŏngsang Province dialect. The speech around Kangrŭng City reflects less influence from the Kyŏngsang Province dialect in grammar than in pronunciation and vocabulary.

The most important factors in the formation of hybrid dialect on the east coast were the topography and geopolitical location. The east coast lies on the eastern rim of the Korean Peninsula against the natural barrier of the T'aebaek Range, and it is difficult to cross over the T'aebaek Range from Seoul. The movement between north and south along the coastal plains was much easier than between east and west across the high mountains. By way of the coastal routes, the dialect in Kyŏngsang Province was easily introduced from south to north into Kangwon Province.

The T'aebaek Range (literally meaning the Big White Mountain Range), called the backbone of the Korean Peninsula, begins south of Yŏnghŭng Bay, and follows the east coast, repeating its gentle curvature (Lautensach, 1988:309-310). It extends further south down to the wide structural valley from P'ohang City through Kyŏngju City to T'aegu City with a length of 380km. The T'aebaek Range contains the crest, the steep eastern slope and the highest parts of the more gentle western slope

4. Linguistic Landscapes

of the Main Korean Tilt Block. The contrast between the steep eastern slope and the much more gradual western slope is the basic feature of the relief on the T'aebaek Range.

Taegwan Pass (865m), or the pass over the drainage divide from Kangŭng City to Seoul, is only 18km from the East Sea. To the west of the pass the road stays above an elevation of 560m for a stretch that is just as long. Whereas to the east of the pass, the road winds its way up extraordinarily steep slopes, to the west of the pass it leads through fairly gentle slopes. For this reason, the east of Taegwan Pass, called Yŏngdongjibang, was cut off in connection with Seoul and even with the west of Taegwan Pass, called Yŏngsŏjibang.

To the east of Taegwan Pass, ridges often extend out into the immediate vicinity of the coast. Two such ridges, together with the main ridge, enclose the granitic basin of KangrŭngCity. The brownish-yellow, weathered hills on its floor are separated by alluvial plains that become broader and broader toward the coast. Between Uljin Town and Kangnŭng City the coast is almost exclusively a cliff-lined coast dissected by shallow embayments. Even sizable valleys approach the coast with rather narrow alluvial bottoms (Lautensach, 1988:313).

These alluvial plains end toward the sea with short bars, which occasionally leave only a very narrow opening for the rivers. Above the cliffs there are elevated marine terraces with marine deposits at various elevations up to 150m. Along the transportation routes connecting these coastal plains via the terraces and the beach platforms, possibly used from ancient times, people have moved back and forth to exchange linguistic elements with one another.

2) Isoglosses on the West Coast

The isoglosses crossing the Korean Peninsula from east to west are merged onto a narrow zone in the interior, and the zone becomes wider as they get closer from the interior to the west coast. In the interior, the Sobaek Range, running from T'aebaek Mountain (1,567m) through Sobaek Mountain (1,421m) to Songni Mountain (1,058m), acts as a natural boundary against which the northern dialect confronts with the southern dialect (Ch'oe, 1986-b:450-451). This mountain range certainly served as a natural barrier to deter the diffusion of language. Toward the west of Songni Mountain, at the foothill of which Poŭn Town is situated, the isoglosses crisscross each other to form bundles (**Figure 18**).

The T'aebaek Range stretches southwards from the massive Hwangryong Mountain (1,268m) in the north. After a slightly lower section there follows Kŭmgang Mountain, or Diamond Mountain, which rises to 1,638m at Piro Peak. The drainage divide drops to an extremely low elevation in the vicinity of the passes, and a little bit southward it rises again to the highest peak in the entire range, Sŏrak Mountain (1,708m).

In the west of Taegwan Pass, the marvelous Odae Mountain rises to 1,563m, Kyebang Mountain to 1,577m, and Parwang Mountain to 1,458m. Farther to the southeast the divide drops again to 651m, and the mountains become higher to the west crowning the divide between the Han River and the Nakdong River: Hambaek Mountain (1,573m) and T'aebaek Mountain (1,561m). In these summit massifs the Sobaek Range branches off from the T'aebaek Range in a southwesterly direction.

The mountains within the range between T'aebaek Mountain

4. Linguistic Landscapes

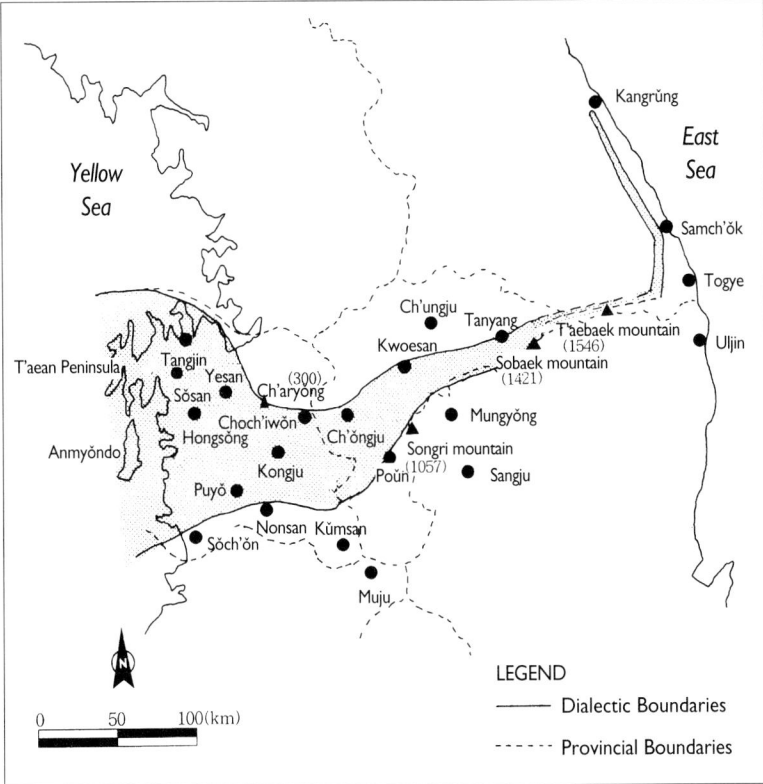

Figure 18. The linguistic boundary between northern and southern dialects in Korea: The overall pattern of boundary appears as a zone except between T'aebaek Mountain and Sobaek Mountain. Here it is almost like a line, and to the west from Sobaek Mountain, the zone becomes wider and wider, and finally becomes widest on the west coast. (Source: Hak-gŭn Ch'oe, 1986, *Studies on Korean Dialectics*, Vol.2, Seoul: Osongsa, p. 508.)

(1,567m) and Sobaek Mountain (1,421m) served as "absorbing barriers" against the diffusion of language, whereas those within the range between Sobaek Mountain (1,421m) and Songni Mountain (1,058m) were "permeable barriers." Across the range between Sobaek Mountain and Songni Mountain people could walk back and forth beyond the traditional passes: Chuk Pass,

Cho Pass, and Yihwa Pass. Through these passes, accordingly, the Kyŏngsang Province dialect could penetrate into the territory of South and North Ch'ungch'ŏng Provinces.

The farther west one travels from the line connecting Sobaek Mountain with Songni Mountain, the less influence from the Kyŏngsang Province dialect one can feel. Moreover, if traveling further toward the west from there, one can also feel more influence from the Chŏlla Province dialect. In terms of tone, one can feel something similar to the Kyŏngsang Province dialect in the speech around Chuk Pass and Yŏnp'ung Town, in contrast to the Chŏlla Province dialect around Poŭn Town and Ch'ŏngju City (Ch'oe, 1986-b:451). Around Tanyang Town and Kwoesan Town, however, one can also feel something in between, whose tone is not certain to tell to which dialect, Kyŏngsang Province or Chŏlla Province, it belongs.

To the west of Poŭn Town and Ch'ŏngju City, the hybrid, usually called the Ch'ungch'ŏng Province dialect, between the Kyŏnggi Province dialect and the Chŏlla Province dialect is widely spoken with many variations. When traveling through there, one may well be perplexed at the irregular changes in folk speech. The dialect tends to draw out sounds and "round" its vowels, in comparison to the smooth and metered Seoul dialect, or the clipped Pusan City dialect.

A series of isoglosses on the west coast really form a wide zone which stretches from Asan Bay to the Kŭm River. Isoglosses which were drawn according to the pronunciation of vowels roughly converge into three lines: Ch'ŏngju City-Choch'iwon Town-Tangjin Town-Sŏsan City-Anmyŏndo Town; Ch'ŏngju City-Choch'iwon Town-Yesan Town-Hongsŏng Town; and Poŭn Town-Muju Town-Kŭmsan Town-Nonsan City-Sŏch'ŏn

4. Linguistic Landscapes

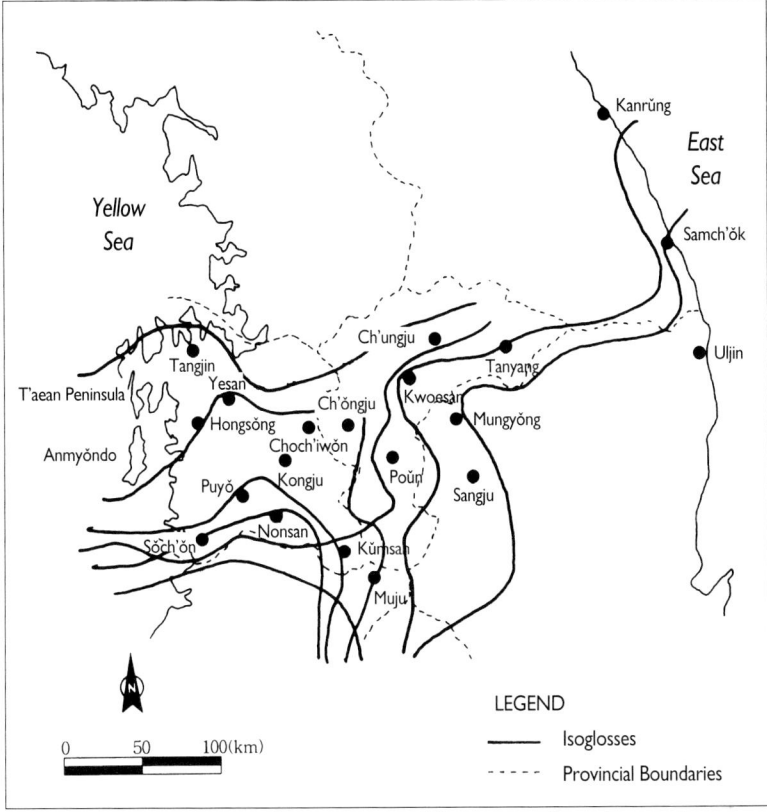

Figure 19. Isoglosses based on grammar: The range of isoglosses drawn on the basis of grammar is much wider on the west coast than that on the basis of vocabulary. The isoglosses run even farther into the territories of North Chŏlla Province and North Kyŏngsang Province. (Source: Hak-gŭn Ch'oe, 1986, *Studies on Korean Dialectics*, Vol.2, Seoul: Osongsa, p. 507.)

Town (**Figure 19**). For instance, people around Tangjin Town pronounce *chŏgori* (jacket) as *chŏguri*, but *nabi* (butterfly) as standard Korean. As on the east coast, the consonants of k, b and s are also either retained or omitted irregularly in the middle of words.

In the Ch'ungch'ŏng Province dialect, some ancient vocabularies are also preserved from the period of the Three Kingdoms. Here, people call *morae* (sand) in standard Korean, as *mosae*, which is believed to be the vocabulary from the Paekje Kingdom (Ch'oe, 1986-b:488). Indeed, Ch'ungch'ŏng Province was once within the territory of the Paekje Kingdom, and her capitals, both Kongju City and Puyŏ Town, were situated on the west coast. By contrast, in Kyŏngsang Province where the Shilla language once dominated, it is spoken as *molgae* or *morae*.

The relics of the ancient Paekje language, in fact, are better preserved on the rim of the west coast around the T'aean Peninsula, which has been relatively isolated from the outside world. The delicate crenulation of the ingression coast with lots of small bays and peninsulas produces many small isolated places. In order to reach from one point to another, one often in the past had to follow a long and winding road.

Kyŏnggi Bay and, in particular, its southeastern tip, the estuary of Ansŏng Stream near Asan City, separate off the secondary peninsula that is named the T'aean Peninsula after a town on it. From the north, the west and the south, delicately crenulated ingression bays cut into the peninsula. Attached to its main body like a bunch of grapes is the tertiary peninsula of Anmyŏndo, which is interrupted in two places by narrow tidal channels. Moreover, a host of bays filled with flats carve it up into little quarternary peninsulas. The extreme southwestern tip of the T'aean Peninsula, for its part, projects out another 10km like a peninsula.

The T'aean Peninsula ends in the east at Sapgyo Stream, and there a north-south trending mountain scarp, called Kaya Mountain, rises like a wall to more than 450m in several places. The peninsula, at the extreme northwestern location, was secluded by the mountain scarp from the main road to Seoul. It was, therefore, difficult for the Kyŏnggi Province dialect to be diffused into the peninsula.

In comparison with the Kyŏnggi Province dialect, the Ch'ungch'ŏng Province dialect is characterized by its unique end-form of speech. Its pronunciation, vocabulary and tone are too greatly assimilated into the Kyŏnggi Province dialect to produce its own characteristics. On the west coast in South and North Ch'ungch'ŏng Provinces, the end-form of *yu* is particularly used widely in interrogative speech.

In the north it is spoken only as an interrogative end-form, but in the south it is also used as an affirmative or imperative end-form. Around Puyŏ Town, Taech'ŏn City, Sŏch'ŏn Town and Nonsan City at the extreme south of South and North Ch'ungch'ŏng Provinces, the end-forms of *ti* and *kke* from the Chŏlla Province dialect can be heard in addition to *yu* . Traveling from north to south on the west coast, one can hear the end-form of speech changing from *yo* through *yu* to *ti* or *kke* (Ch'oe, 1986-b: 488-491).

The geographical factors which have influenced the transition in the usage of the end-form, *yu,* are the Ch'aryŏng Ridge and the Kyŏngbu Railroad or Honam Railroad. Around Chŏnan City and Onyang City which lie in the north of the Ch'aryŏng Ridge, the more popular end-form of interrogative speech is still *yo,* standard Korean, rather than *yu*. After crossing over the Ch'aryŏng Ridge, one can hear the usage of the end-form, *yu,* more often. The farther south one travels from Tangjin Town, Sŏsan City and Anmyŏndo Town through Yesan Town and Hongsŏng Town to Ch'ŏngyang Town and Kongju City, the more often one can hear it. The Ch'aryŏng Ridge, as a permeable barrier, has contributed only to the formation of the end-form distinctive to the Ch'ungch'ŏng Province dialect.

The Sobaek Range does not have a pronounced western foot, and only the Ch'aryŏng Ridge stretches to the west coast. The Ch'aryŏng Ridge crosses the Namhan River downstream from City and extends out to the Yellow Sea near Taech'ŏn City. This ridge is named after Ch'aryŏng Pass, on the traditional overland route from Seoul to Naju City. In its northern part, it is composed mainly of gneiss, rising up to 700m at the highest, and elsewhere hills dominate (Lautensach, 1988:350;357). Toward the south, the hills are increasingly interspersed with alluvial plains, and merged into marsh areas along the lower courses of rivers. In general, the topography on the west coast is dominated by hill country that generally does not exceed an elevation of 200m.

However, in Taejŏn City and Choch'iwon Town with main railroad stations are found "linguistic islands" where the end-form of *yo* in standard Korean rather than *yu* is more generally spoken (Ch'oe, 1986-b:49). In addition to *yo*, the end-forms of *ya* or *yŏ*, which sound like somewhere between *yo* and *yu*, are also used. As Taejŏn City and Choch'iwon Town served as transportation centers with railroad stations, they became the popular destinations where many people from Seoul would come and go.

3) LINGUISTIC ISLANDS ON THE SOUTHWEST COAST

On the southwest coast between Hamp'yŏng Bay on the Yellow Sea and Kwangyang Bay on the Korean Strait, peninsulas, large islands and bays follow each other closely, so that there is no room for a straight stretch of coast between them. Nowhere else is the horizontal crenulation as deep and pronounced as here (Lautensach, 1988:362). The Haenam Peninsula is 40km long, and the Kohŭng Peninsula and Yŏsu Peninsula are only slightly shorter. In between there are large bays separating them, and the most important are Sunch'ŏn Bay, Posŏng Bay and Kwangyang Bay. Large islands, such as Chindo and Wando, are often separated from the mainland only by narrow sounds, which take the place of the peninsulas.

In general, neither in cultural nor physical geography is a fundamental difference between the island realm and the part of the mainland directly adjacent. Evergreen vegetational elements are conspicuous in the landscape, which is simultaneously an indication of a special climate. The small green element, however, is restricted to the lowest altitudinal zone. Natural fishing and shipping are more important here and there due to the immense interpenetration of land and sea. But, in general, the keystone of the economy on the southwest coast remains agriculture.

In the diffusion of language, the sea between the peninsulas and islands served either as natural barriers or as natural routes, depending on the situation at that time. Some linguistic elements were diffused easily by way of the sea route, while others were not. Some places were more accessible to linguistic diffusion than others, and the latter ones often appear as "linguistic islands" with much preservation of old language. Usually, people on the coast viewed the peninsula, instead of the island, as an island-like place which was difficult to enter.

Some islands, in reality, do not show any linguistic difference from the mainland in terms of speech. As many islands are connected to the mainland at low tide, there is no fundamental difference between the large islands and the mainland coast. Besides, it was also easy to reach many small islands from the mainland through the sea routes. The distance between these islands was so small that the ordinary people could easily travel from one island to another. In the process of linguistic diffusion from the mainland toward islands, the sea sometimes served as natural routes rather than natural barriers.

On the southwest coast, the Kyŏnggi Province dialect was diffused in two directions, first from north to south and then from west to east (Yi, 1994:110-112). In the first stage, the primary receivers of the Kyŏnggi Province dialect were the ports, cities and islands on the west side of the southwest coast which were close in contact with the Kyŏnggi Province dialect. In the second stage, from there, the Kyŏnggi Province dialect was diffused to the secondary receivers on the east side of the southwest coast. In the third stage, from these secondary receivers, it was diffused to the tertiary receivers in the adjacent interior on the southwest coast. The islands and peninsulas untouched by the process of diffusion had to remain as linguistic islands (**Figure 20**).

On the west side of the southwest coast, bays and peninsulas were small, and islands were adjacent to each other. The sea waters between them, therefore, were often used as diffusion routes in the first stage of diffusion. Today, here, the islands, peninsulas and mainland are altogether homogeneous in terms of speech. The dialect spoken in the large islands of Chindo and Wando is not so much different from small islands in the vicinity and adjacent mainland around Haenam Town (**Figure 20**).

There, *salgang*, or a traditional kitchen shelf made of bamboo pieces, is pronounced as *sarang* which can be heard nowhere

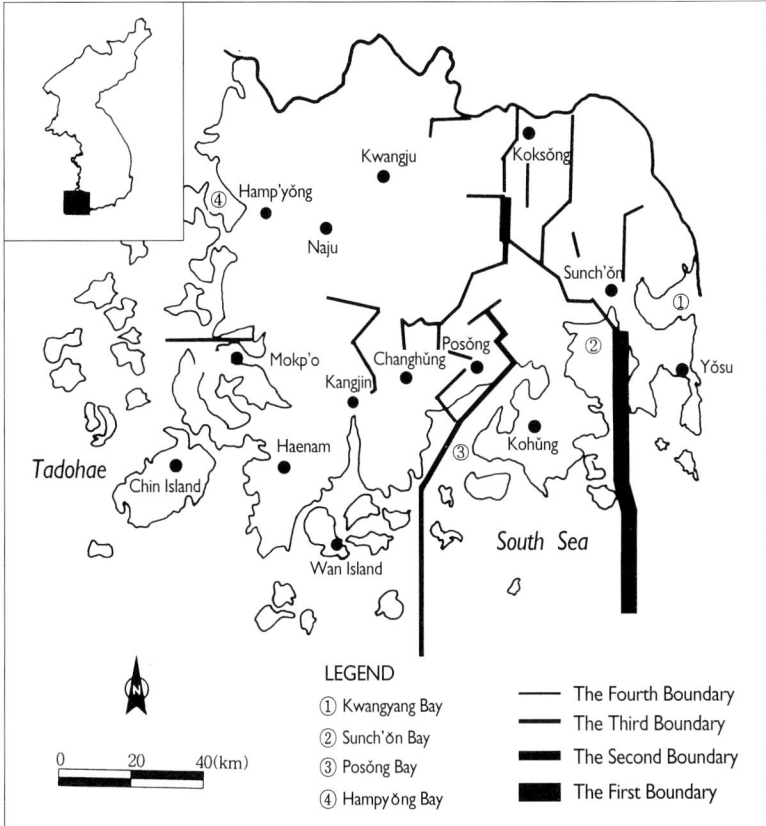

Figure 20. Dialectic boundaries on the Southwest Coast: In the South Cholla Province, particularly on the Southwest Coast, dialectic boundaries run mainly from north to south. On the coast, Sunch'ŏn Bay serves as the primary boundary, and Kohŭng Peninsula remains as a "linguistic island." (Source: Ki-gap Yi, 1944, *A Lingustic Geography of South Cholla Province*, Series in Korean Language Study, No. I, The Asssociation Korean Language Studies, Seoul: T'apch'ulp'ansa, p. 134.)

but on the coast of Kyŏnggi and Hwanghae Provinces. It seems that the pronunciation of *sarang* was adopted from there first on the islands, from which it was in turn diffused to peninsulas and other areas on the mainland. In this case, islands are not the last, but the first receivers of linguistic diffusion, and peninsulas served as bridges to link the islands with the mainland (Yi, 1994:30).

By contrast, on the east side of the southwest coast, two large peninsulas are separated by large bays, which in turn serve as natural barriers. In Sunch'ŏn Bay between the Kohŭng Peninsula and the Yŏsu Peninsula, there are few islands to stop by on the way along the sea routes. In Posŏng Bay between the Kohŭng Peninsula and the Kangjin Peninsula, the situation is almost the same as in Sunch'ŏn Bay. As a result, the diffusion in the second stage, from west to east, began to slow down as soon as it arrived at Changhŭng Town. From Changhŭng Town to the east, the sea waters as natural barriers either retarded or blocked the diffusion process of the Kyŏnggi Province dialect.

The Kohŭng Peninsula, in particular, because of its size and insularity, was the main barrier against linguistic diffusion. It serves as a main divide beyond which two kinds of speech differ from each other in terms of vocabulary and pronunciation (**Figure 20**). On the coast, exclusively to the east of the Kohŭng Peninsula, people pronounce *yŏwida* in standard Korean (to become thin in English), as *yaburŭda* or *yaurŭda* (Yi, 1994:41). This pronunciation can hardly be heard in the Kohŭng Peninsula itself or on the coast to the west of it. Against this linguistic element, the Kohŭng Peninsula served as an absorbing barrier only to block its diffusion to the west of it.

When making a journey on the sea routes, people often kept on moving forward without stopping at the Kohŭng Peninsula. They may have found it more convenient to keep on sailing on the sea simply by dropping by islands one after another as if they were stepping stones. Some linguistic elements were transported along the sea routes even without landing on the Kohŭng Peninsula.

There are, indeed, certain kinds of speech that are not spoken in the Kohŭng Peninsula, but in its surrounding coastal areas. For example, the verb word *ttulta* (to punch), in standard Korean, is pronounced as *ttulbuda* extensively on the coast except on the Kohŭng Peninsula (Yi, 1994:87-88). This pronunciation can even be heard on Chin Island and its adjacent mainland around Haenam Town, which are considerably distant from the Kohŭng Peninsula.

The Kohŭng Peninsula, today, represents an excellent case of a linguistic island, preserving many words of ancient pronunciation and vocabularies which can never be heard elsewhere. In the Kohŭng Peninsula, some vocabularies are too deviated from standard Korean to be recognized easily (Yi, 1994:139). There *hap'um* (yawning), *ikda* (to ripen) and *puddumak* (a kitchen range) are respectively pronounced as *hak'im*, *ssackda* and *pudduk*. The vocabulary of *komurae* (a solid wood rake) is particularly pronounced as *tanggirae*, totally different from standard Korean.

The coastal line there is too widely crenulated to walk along when traveling into the Kohŭng Peninsula. In order to enter there from the coast, people may have found it more convenient to sail across Posŏng Bay rather than to walk along the coastal line. But, as it was unthinkable for the ordinary folk to sail across Posŏng Bay which is deep and wide, the Kohŭng Peninsula could not but rejoice in its island-like location, isolated from the outside world.

4) Place Names in Kyŏnggi Bay

Between the Hwanghae Peninsula in the north and the T'aean Peninsula in the south, the coast of the mainland recedes almost 100km toward the northeast, and here Kyŏnggi Bay and Asan Bay spread out. The coast of the mainland is dissected by a number of funnel seas, considerable in size, into which rivers and streams flow. The largest ones lie at two ends of this stretch of coast, the estuaries of the Han River in Kyŏnggi Bay and Ansŏng Stream in Asan Bay (**Figure 21**).

Only below Seoul does an uninterrupted flood plain follow the Han River for 35km, and then it merges into tidal flats. Just below the mouth of the Imjin River this tidal bed is already 3km wide, and in the north of Kanghwa Island it increases to 9km. A narrow arm still resembling a river, named Yŏmha, separates the large island of Kanghwa (280km) from the Kimp'o Peninsula. Northwest of Kanghwa Island lies the actual estuary, which is divided again into several branches by the Kyodong and Sŏkmo Islands (Lautensach, 1988:285).

The hill country, seldom higher than 200m, but quite extensive along the coast, extends eastward to the Namhan River, and westward into the small peninsulas. But, even on the island of Kanghwado there are still mountains as high as 468m. Only in the innermost tips of bays, small areas with coastal marshes have developed. Nowhere on the Yellow Sea coast than here is the tidal range greater, and thus the tidal flats are wider. Tremendous areas of continuous mud and sand flats extend from the estuary of the Han River out to the islands closer to the mainland. Sandbanks extend from there out to the outer edge of Kyŏnggi Bay. The deposition of sands and muds, which were

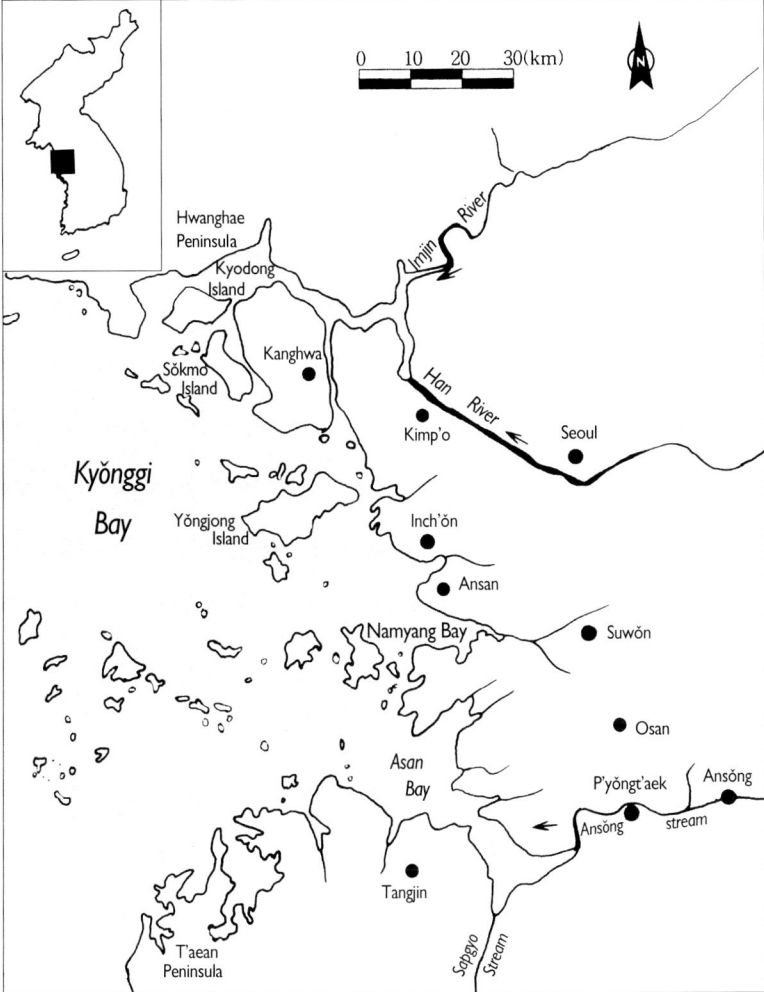

Figure 21. The coastal lines around Kyŏnggi Bay: On the coast, the deposition of sands and muds, which were transported by river flows and tidal currents, produced many promontory landforms, protruding into the sea from the land.

transported by river flows and tidal currents, eventually produced a peculiar landform protruding into the sea from the mainland.

Whether it is made from the extension of hills or the deposition of sands and muds, Kyŏnggi Bay is under the natural conditions ideal for the landform of a promontory to be developed. This type of landform, protruding into the sea from the mainland, can be observed repeatedly on the coast in Kyŏnggi Bay, in particular on Kanghwa Island. The promontory landform is usually called *kot* in Korean and written in Chinese as 岬 (kap), and there are many variations of the place name, which was originally named after the promontory (Lee, 1998:182-183).

On the coast in Kyŏnggi Bay, there still remain today many relics of place names in Chinese as well as in Korean which were first composed in association with a promontory landform (Ch'oe, 1987:5-27). The place names in Korean with the generic names, such as *kot, kkot, kuji, kkuji, koji* and *kkoji*, are, in fact, those which are named after a promontory landform. Even the place names in Chinese with the generic names, such as 花 (*hwa*) and 華 (*hwa*), are the same as the former ones in Korean.

The oldest Chinese words representing the spoken word *kot* or *koji* were 古尸 (*kosi*) and 古次 (*koch'a*), the simple description of sounds. In the United Shilla Kingdom, 口 (*ku*) in Chinese was used more often than 古尸 (*kosi*) or 古次 (*koch'a*) in writing the word *kot* in Chinese. Interestingly enough, the Chinese word 口 (*ku*) is still in use as the generic name for place in association with a promontory landform. However, all in all, these Chinese words did not convey any meaning in written form.

Kanghwa Island has the old name, 甲比古次 (*kapbigoch'a*) which was transformed into 穴口 (*hyŏlgu*) by the Koguryŏ Kingdom (Kim, 1980:161). Then, it was written as 海口 (*haegu*) by the United Shilla Kingdom and 列口 (*yŏlgu*) by the Koryŏ Kingdom. It was no later than in the Chosŏn Period that the island was called 江華 (*kanghwa*) in Chinese. In such a series of Chinese words that have been used in alternative terms, one can see the sequence in change from 古次 (*koch'a*) through 口 (*ku*) to 華 (*hwa*) to describe an island with many promontories.

In the Chosŏn Period, it was written in Chinese as 串 (*kot*), the marvelous invention in Korea that had never been known in China. At that time, this word sounded the same as *kot*, and meant both the verb *kotda* (to stick in) and the noun *koch'aengi* (spit). Today the words of *kotda* and *koch'aengi* are respectively pronounced as *kkoch'aengi* and *kkotda*. As the pronunciation changed from *kot* into *kkot*, the Chinese word 串 (*kot*) was replaced by 花 (*hwa*) which sounded like *hwa* meaning *kkot* (flower).

The selection of the word 花 (*hwa*) was based only on how it sounds when reading the meaning in Korean. People probably preferred to use the word 花 (*hwa*) because it has the better meaning of flower. Later on, the word 花 (*hwa*) was gradually replaced by 華 (*hwa*) which had the sound of *hwa* and meant *pitnada* (to be glorious). People may have adopted the word 華 (*hwa*) because it has a better meaning than 花 (*hwa*) while it has the same sound with 花 (*hwa*).

Now, in Korea, the words 花 (*hwa*) and 華 (*hwa*) are the most common as the generic name of the place with a promontory landform. Kanghwa (江華) County and Hwasŏng (華城) County in Kyŏnggi Bay are the best examples whose names were associated with a promontory landform. One ought to be careful about its original meaning when confronting the Chinese characters of 花 (*hwa*) or 華 (*hwa*) in the place name. To begin with, they were not supposed to convey the meaning "flower" or "being glorious" but a promontory landform. Even in such place names as 梨花 (*yihwa*) (pear blossom), 菊花 (*kuk'hwa*) (chrysanthemum), 梅花 (*maehwa*) (ume flower), 蓮花 (*yŏnhwa*) (lotus flower), they have nothing to do with any kinds of flower, but something to do with a promontory landform (Ch'oe, 1987:11). People's intention to beautify their own place is hidden in the continuous transformation of the place name for a promontory landform.

Particularly in Kanghwa Island, a variety of names referring to promontory both in Korean and Chinese are found. There old and new versions of generic names in Chinese as well as in Korean are still in use side by side: *kot, kkot, kuji, kkuji, koji, kkoji,* 串 (*kot*), 花 (*hwa*), 華 (*hwa*), 古地 (*koji*), and 古支 (*koji*). In addition to these words, other types of place names are also found in relation with promontory: *kojan* and *kkotbat*.

The former, *kojan*, is often written in different forms of Chinese such as 古棧 (*kojan*), 高棧 (*kojan*), 古蓋 (*kojan*), and 高蓋 (*kojan*), which indicate nothing special. Nonetheless, these two words may have originated from the place name *kojian* or *kojan*, which are composed of *koji* or *kot* (promontory) and *an* (inside). This word was, therefore, originally supposed to mean the inside (*an*) of a promontory (*koji* or *kot*) (Ch'oe, 1987:22). It is repeatedly found in the names of villages located inside the promontory, and all the versions of *kojan* are in relation with promontory. There is also a village on Kanghwa Island called 高陵里 (*korŭngri*) with dual Chinese names, 古棧 (*kojan*) and 串內洞 (*kotnaedong*), and the latter, in particular, literally means the inside of a promontory (Ch'oe, 1987:23).

The latter, *kkotbat*, on the other hand, is written in Chinese as 花田 (*hwajŏn*) which literally means a "flower garden" in English. The place names, written as 花田 (*hwajŏn*) in Chinese, are repeatedly found in the villages located outside the promontory landform. Certainly, the place name *kkotbat*, whose old form is *kojibat* or *kotbat*, is also in relation with the promontory. Its original meaning is the outside of the promontory because it is composed of two words: the noun of *koji* or *kot* (promontory) and the preposition of *pat* (outside).

The Chinese words, 花 (*hwa*) and 田 (*jŏn*), respectively sound *hwa* and *chŏn*, and mean *kkot* (flower) and *pat* (garden) in Korean. In the beginning, while writing it as 花田 (*hwajŏn*) in Chinese, people read it as *kotbat* or *kojibat* in Korean which was later transformed into *kkotbat*. The word, then, gradually lost the phonetic meaning, the outside of the promontory, and picked up the literary meaning, the flower garden. Now very few people living in the villages with the name of 花田 (*hwajŏn*) know that it originally meant the outside of the promontory. People may have intentionally kept on erasing the phonetic meaning in their memory, with the idea that the literal meaning, "flower garden," was better than the phonetic meaning, the outside of the promontory.

5) PLACE NAMES ON CHIRI MOUNTAIN

The language and literature in Korea have been greatly influenced by China. According to the Korean Great Dictionary, compiled by the Korean Language Society, the Korean vocabulary of Chinese origin accounts for more than half (54%) of the words in use today (Koo & Nahm, 1997:103). Nearly all the technical terms in law, economy, social science and natural science are of Chinese origin. Such a peculiar phenomenon is because of the long predominance of Chinese learning, and the public policy of approving Chinese as a written language until the Chosŏn Period.

Moreover, the place names in public use such as those of administrative areas had to be written in Chinese. The important physical features of big rivers and high mountains were also given Chinese names. In the beginning, the government translated the Korean names into Chinese on the basis of sound or meaning, but later replaced them completely with Chinese names whose sounds were identical with meanings. The United Shilla and Koryŏ Kingdoms, in particular, liked to endow the mountains with names which symbolized Buddhism. In the long run, Korean place names have been in the process of turning into Chinese.

In spite of the general trend in place names being Chinese, there still remain many names of physical features with Korean connotation, such as Chiri Mountain. There has never been clear agreement upon the primitive sense of Chiri Mountain which now has various forms in Chinese: 地理山, 地利山, 智異山, and 智理山. Many linguists and historians are too ambivalent about these names to tell the real meaning behind them. There are only a few laymen who insist on interpreting the original meaning from 地利山 (chirisan) in relation with Buddhism.

The oldest term naming Chiri Mountain in Chinese is 頭流 (turyu) Mountain and 方丈 (pangjang) Mountain, and among them the former provides the key to unveil the original meaning of Chiri Mountain. Although it is no longer in use today, the name, 頭流 (turyu) Mountain, was mentioned in the poem written by a prominent Confucian scholar, named Sik Cho (1501-1572), in the Chosŏn Period (Pae, 1994:14).

According to the recent research by Korean linguists, the

name, 頭流 (*turyu*) Mountain, may have been borrowed from Chinese to depict the sounds of *Turu* Mountain, the Korean word meaning a round mountain. The word *turu* is now used mostly as an adverb meaning "widely," but once in the past had the modern connotation, *tunggŭlda* (round) as an adjective. The term, *san* (mountain in English), is still in common use, meaning a mountain, and thus Turyu Mountain was at first nothing but an onomatopoeic (sound imitating) Chinese word of Turu Mountain (a round mountain).

Many Korean linguists insist that the pronunciation, *turu*, was finally changed from *turi*, *tŭri* and *tiri* into *chiri* by the inhabitants in Chiri Mountain (Pae, 1994:16-17). The various forms in Chinese (地理山, 地利山, 智異山, and 智理山) must, then, be the representatives of the recent pronunciation of Chiri Mountain. Unlike other important mountains as Paekdu Mountain, T'aebaek Mountain, Sobaek Mountain and Songni Mountain, only Chiri Mountain has resisted being Chinese. Its peculiar topography dominated with many round mountains and winding valleys in the long distance made a considerable contribution to the persistence of the Korean name, Chiri Mountain.

For a distance of 280km, the Sobaek Range, or the Small White Mountain Range, runs diagonally through southern Korea. Now it maintains a southwesterly, and then a more purely southerly direction to form a natural boundary between Kyŏngsang Province and Chŏlla Province. The first section of the range, culminating in Kukmang Peak (1,421m), extends to Chuk Pass (689m). The latter is followed by a granite part of the range stretching almost westward as far as the passes, named Hanŭl Pass or Yihwa Pass. Here, the range is again crossed by structural valleys, in which the divide drops down to 519m and 548m, respectively (Lautensach, 1988:343).

The next section stretches almost toward the south and remains much lower in elevation. The highest peak is Songni Mountain (1,057m), and then comes exactly in the middle of the whole range, the extremely deeply incised Ch'up'ung Pass, which is now utilized by the Korean trunk line between Seoul and Pusan City. Directly beyond this pass the range rises again to 1,111m in Hwanghak Mountain. This more than 100km long section of the Sobaek Range reaches a height of 1,290m at the peak of Taedŏk Mountain and even 1,594m at the ridge of Tŏkyu Mountain. Then the range rises to the highest elevation (1,915m) in the gigantic massif of Chiri Mountain, only to drop immediately thereafter to below 30m in the gorge of the Sŏmjin River.

As the widest and by far the highest part of the Sobaek Range, Chiri Mountain does, after all, have a large number of individual valleys. Its backbone forms a west-east stretching ridge only 25km long, along which the drainage divide between the Nam River and the Sŏmjin River runs. It culminates in the west in Nogodan (1,507m); in the middle, the pyramid of Panya Peak (1,751m) lies just off it to the north; and in the east it ends in a peak (1,682m).

A transverse ridge branching off from the latter toward the north contains the very steep summit pyramid of Ch'ŏnhwang Peak (1,915m), splintry, jagged, dissected by steep ravines, and towering far above everything else. Other transverse ridges run both northward to the Nam River valley and southward to the Sŏmjin River valley. The mountains are composed of hard black and white gneiss, diorites, which weather to a grayish blue color in round shape (Lautensach, 1988:346). Into these ridges also the individual streams and rivers dissect a number of elongated rounding valleys.

There are other place names in Chiri Mountain which have been resistant to being Chinese, but imbued people with fantastic imagination and false image: Paemsagol, P'iagol, and Nogodan. All of these are believed to have been from indigenous place names characterizing physical features. However, their original meanings do not unveil themselves, when believing in the popular knowledge concerning their names. The popular knowledge is often based on the oral tradition which was painted with myths. In order to explore their origins correctly, one ought to have ample knowledge about the language and the topography around Chiri Mountain. The name, Paemsagol, refers to an elongated valley extending from the ridge of Nogodan toward the northeast. The word, *paem* in Korean means a snake in English, and *sa* recalls a snake because its sound is the same with 蛇 (*sa*) in Chinese. The word, *gol*, is a common vocabulary usage pointing to a valley in Korea. For this reason, people tend to imagine that the name, Paemsagol may have been from the fact that the valley is full of snakes.

But, in reality, there is no place name such as Paemsagol which consists of two words, Korean and Chinese, in juxtaposition, with the same meaning. The word, *sa*, may have been a Korean word meaning something other than a snake, because the Korean word, *paem* meaning a snake, is in front of it. Along the valley there are many more place names with the initial word as *paem* in Korean meaning a snake (Pae, 1994:32-34). These names, even with initial words, *paemsa*, appear repeatedly in the names of pond, rock, pass, road, village, and so on.

These names, then, may have been made after the elongated winding valley which reminds one of a snake. Otherwise, there must have been plenty of snakes living in the valley when the place names were first made.

Today the valley name, P'iagol, too, renders a meaning totally different from what was originally meant to be. It is now known to the public that the valley was occupied by communist guerrillas during the Korean War (1950-1952). At that time, the combat with them was furious, and the valley stream was filled with the blood of the killed. In association with history concerned with this war, people tend to think of the word, *p'i* meaning blood in English, as the origin of the place name, P'iagol (Pae, 1994:25).

However, it is not true at all from the viewpoint of Korean linguists. According to them the name, P'iagol, may have been from the word, P'ibatgol (P'ibattgol in standard Korean), which means the field where the "Deccan grasses" grow. The vocabulary, *p'ibattgol*, is composed of three words, *p'i* (a Deccan grass), *batt* (field) and *gol* (valley or village). In the vicinity, a village with a similar name in Kurye (求禮) County is also found. It is called P'igol, P'iatgol or P'iyagol in Korean, but written as 稷田 (*chikjŏn*) in Chinese, indicating the field with Deccan grasses. The famous valley name, P'iagol, then, may have been from the village name, characterizing the field where the Deccan grasses grow in numbers (Pae, 1994:26).

The name of a peak, called Nogodan (1,507m), one of the highest in Chiri Mountain, has been so much modified that the original meaning cannot be understood. Now it directly conveys the meaning of old grandmother when written as 老姑 (*nogo*) in Chinese. The peak picked up its name with the generic

4. Linguistic Landscapes

Photo 24. The peak called Nogodan on Chiri Mountain: It is said that the national shrine for a female deity called Mago or Sŏndosŏngmo was still there until the Koryŏ Period. Now only a pebble-pile, recently built with the name Nogodan on it, testifies to the legendary past.

word, 壇 (tan), meaning the altar, because the Shilla Kingdom used to perform a ritual for a *sanshin*, or the mountain spirit, in Chiri Mountain (**Photo 24**). The Shilla Kingdom thought of Chiri Mountain so highly that she might worship the *sanshin* as the mother of her royal founder, named Pakhyŏkhgŏse (Yi, 1992:16). The latter one called 麻姑 (*mago*) or 仙桃聖母 (*sŏndosŏngmo*) in Chinese is often identified with the old grandmother, written as 老姑 (*nogo*) in Chinese (**Photo 25, 26**).

The name, Nogo Mountain, also appears on and on in the mountain peaks around the country. Linguists argue that the Chinese name, Nogo Mountain, may have been the translation from the Korean Halmibong, in which the word *halmi* in Korean sounds like a grandmother, and the word *bong* in Chinese

Photo 25. The shrine for the female deity called Mago or Sŏndosŏngmo on Chiri Mountain: As the deity's status deteriorated radically in the Chosŏn Period, the shrine was relocated in the remote spot within the territory of Hwaŏm Temple in the western valley of Chiri Mountain.

Photo 26. A front view of Hwaŏm Temple with the Main Worshipping Hall, pagoda, lantern and stairway.

means a peak (Pae, 1994:91-92). Nonetheless, the latter could have been identical with the ancient word, *halmi*, which has been transformed into the modern word, *hanmoe*, characterizing a high and large peak. All the mountains, called Halmibong, in fact, have in common the topography characterized by high and large peaks

5. RURAL LANDSCAPES

5. Rural Landscapes

Casual travel in the Korean countryside immediately reveals that clusters of homes, large or small, can be nestled in foothills or dispersed on open plains and so on. In many of the regions with rice farming, the dotlike distribution of the cultivated area makes hamlets appear the natural form of settlement. In the rice farming areas, too, the rural landscape is dominated by irrigation facilities such as reservoirs, canals and ditches. Even in densely populated areas, the villages are frequently no larger than hamlets, but they are located only in short distances from each other. Only in southern Korea, densely crowded and irregularly clustered settlements, called farm villages, are the rule. Dispersed settlements are confined primarily to the pioneer region with dry farming in the mountainous environment.

In Korea, the villages, hamlets or farm villages, were themselves often clusters of households of affinal kin. In these lineage villages, the vast majority of residents are related to the father's side. There social relations accord with the patrilineal principle and hierarchy based on Neo-Confucianism. Still today in the rural landscapes, one can feel the kinship primacy through impressive graveyards that are nestled in the most auspicious spots of villages. Graves are a palpable reminder that lineages are tied to locales, the places where the ancestors are buried, and periodically the group of mourners must gather.

During the Chosŏn Period, in villages where a single *yangban* lineage dominated numerically, the village organization and life tended to follow the lines of hierarchy of Korean patrilineal ideology. By the Chosŏn Period, *yangban* families or patrilineages were ideally those which could claim ancestors who passed the state examinations called *kwagŏ* and served in official positions. The primary lineages and aged seniors tended to dominate, and much of the social life was caught up in the more formal excercise of Neo-Confucian ideology such as filial piety.

Many villages, however, were composed entirely of commoners, and others still of a mixture of commoner and *yangban* lineages. In villages where a single *yangban* lineage did not dominate, social ties were far more egalitarian, and Neo-Confucian ideologies concerned with gender and age hierarchies did not exert an absolute control over social life. Instead, mutual cooperation in economic activities, and more informal and even unruly social exchange in leisure activities guided the tenure of social life.

Until the late Chosŏn Period, the indoctrination of Neo-Confucianism reached as far as the countryside, with its imprints on the rural landscapes. The interplay between culture and power was so complex that Neo-Confucianism, in particular, its patrilineal ideology, caused an enormous transformation of rural landscapes. The strict adherence to Neo-Confucianism meant the observance of filial piety, the practice of ancestor worship, or the seclusion and subordination of women. In *yangban*-dominated villages one can more frequently find the rural landscapes symbolizing these cultural values. For instance, near the *yangban* lineage villages there are often the pavilions, the splendid architecture, tile-roofed with no side walls.

Regardless of their social origins, *yangban*-dominated or commoner-dominated, Korean villages share in common certain visible characteristics, which show some regional variations. In a *yangban* lineage village, there are more houses, which are larger in size with tiled-roofs, but the floor plan of the houses tends to be the same within a certain range of area. Under the floors of the rooms run the flues for *ondol*, or the Korean traditional floor heating system, which is operated from the kitchen. Even the simplest house has a *maru*, or a wooden veranda, usually made of wooden boards, extending along outside rooms at the level of the floors.

Moreover, in many villages trees are planted in the surrounding spots, usually in the front, so that they cannot be seen from outside. On the coast the planted trees are often lined up to protect the village from the sandy wind from the sea. The artificial woods, consisting of trees planted with intention, would bring the villagers protection and convenience in daily life. They are also treated as sacred places and are inscribed with meanings and symbols from the ideology of Feng-shui. In the late Chosŏn Period, Feng-shui nearly became a popular belief influencing the selection of village sites and the tending of village landscapes (**Figure 22**).

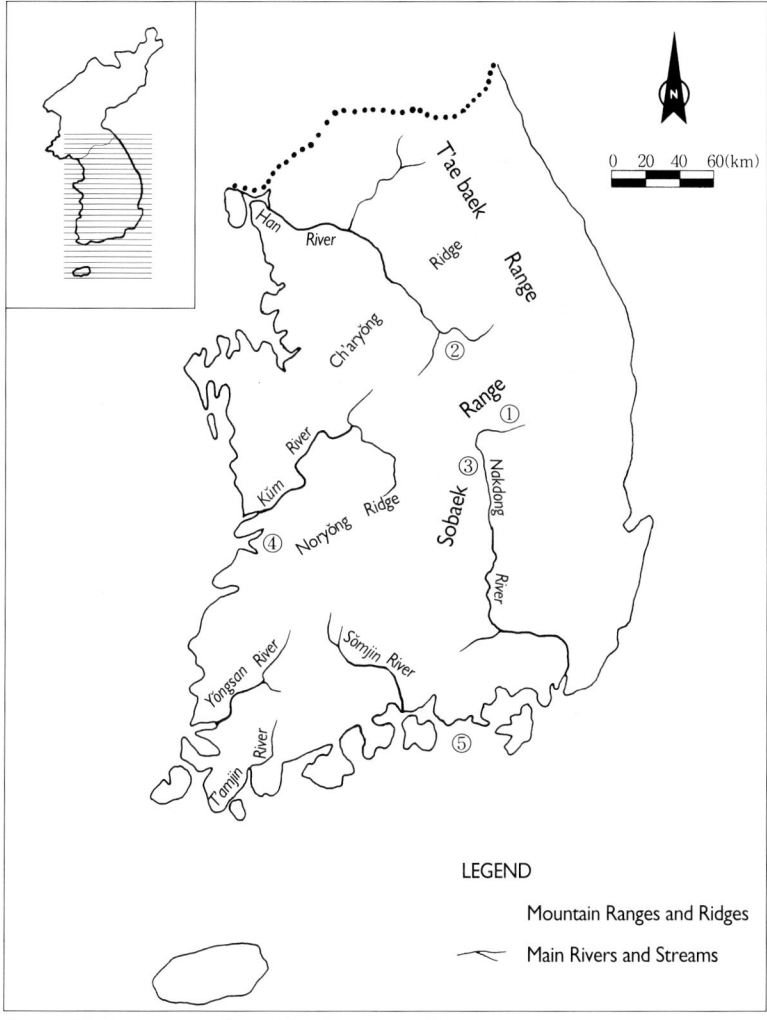

Figure 22. Locations of rural landscapes in Korea:
  ① *Yangban* lineage villages around Andong City
  ② *Chŏngja* (pavilions) in the upper reaches of the Namhan River
  ③ Folk housing on the west bank of the Nakdong River
  ④ Irrigation networks on the Honam Plain
  ⑤ Village forests on the South Coast.

1) YANGBAN LINEAGE VILLAGES AROUND ANDONG CITY

Confucian rituals at the village or inter-village level were performed by family and lineage groups. The honored at family rituals were their parents, their grandparents and their grandparents' parents, and so on who had died. The lineage or segments of the lineage commemorated remote ancestors who were the apex of a pyramid of descendants that could number from dozens to thousands. In *yangban* lineage villages, such rituals were usually held once a year at a *sadang*, or an ancestral hall with spiritual tablets, and at a graveyard with a *chaeshil*, or a ritual preparation hall. The higher the social status became, the stronger the power of the family or lineage group grew and the larger the physical size of the *sadang* or *chaeshil* became, and the more ornate its decoration of them became.

In *yangban* villages, monuments were also erected to commemorate the contributions of those who exemplified the Confucian values: filial sons, loyal subjects, and faithful wives or widows. Usually these monuments were the inscribed stone tablets that were several feet tall. Some monuments had little pavilions built to house them within. The decision to build such a monument was usually not a private one or even family business. Only with the permission from the government, local or central, could a monument be erected.

Around Andong City, one can see more *yangban* lineage villages with these landscape elements than in any other area. In addition to ancestral hall, ritual preparation hall, and monuments for filial sons, loyal subjects and faithful wives, other Confucian buildings were erected there for the *yangban*'s life: *chŏngja* (a pavilion), *chŏngsa* (a Confucian convent), *sau* (a Confucian shrine), and *sŏwon* (a private Confucian academy).

The pavilion, which was erected at a spot outside a village suited to enjoyment of the beautiful scenery, was also used as the private space for teaching and learning. The Confucian convent was also the private space in a village where teaching and learning was done. The Confucian shrine was the public space in a village where spiritual tablets of eminent scholar-officials were preserved and worshipped. The Confucian private academy was the public space outside a village where teaching and learning of Neo-Confucianism was done along with worshipping of eminent Confucian scholars.

Contemporary Andong City and its surrounding county have historically been a stronghold of Neo-Confucianism, which has deeply influenced all aspects of people's lives (Yim, 1997:18-19). In the low hills of Andong County, *yangban*'s tile-roofed manor houses once stood proudly among commoner's thatched-roof houses. Andong City and County are, in fact, the ancestral home of many *yangban* families which not only influenced the local areas around Andong City but also the whole country. The greatest Confucian scholar of Korea was produced from there, T'oe-gye, or Hwang Yi (1501-1570) and numerous government servants. Perhaps the best known of these was Sŏng-ryong Ryu, prime minister during the disastrous Imjin War of the 1590s and a student of Hwang Yi.

Prior to the *Chosŏn* Period, the *yangban* families were not concentrated so much in the areas around Andong City. Among them only a few were *yangban* families native to the areas around Andong City, and all the rest were immigrants from other areas who were mostly the relatives of those from the areas around Andong City. In the 15th and 16th centuries, most of them migrated and settled where their wives' families or mothers' families lived. The ancestors of the Kosŏng Yi, Uisŏng Kim, Hŭnghae Pae, Ch'ŏngju Chŏng, and Yŏngyang Nam families are those who migrated into the areas around Andong City at that time (Chŏng, 1997:61). Marriage with the prominent *yangban* families from the areas around Andong City provided them, as strangers, with social as well as material conditions to settle down there.

Since then, Andong Kim, Hahoe Ryu, Uisŏng Kim and Andong Kwon have been the most prominent *yangban* families around Andong City, and all of them except for the Uisŏng Kim family were from areas around Andong City. These three families were promoted from the local officials called *hyangri* to the *yangban* class in the late Koryŏ Period. The two families, Andong Kim and Andong Kwon, in particular, took their strongholds around Andong City in the early Koryŏ Period.

Even today the *yangban* lineage villages, established by these families, can still be seen in the architectural forms. In the small village named Ch'ŏnjŏnri, for example, there is a *yangban* house that belongs to the clan-head of the Uisŏng Kim family. Around 1650, this traditional post-and-beam house was built in squares around two courtyards and had several additional buildings. This house gives a good idea of traditional *yangban* architecture from the Chosŏn Period, like the Andong Kim family's head house in Mukgye Village, and the Hahoe Ryu family's houses in Hahoe Village.

In the famous Hahoe Village, situated on a defensive side of a meandering river, the Ryu family took its roots about 600 years ago (**Figure 23**). In the late 1500s, this family produced two brothers of outstanding merit, Un-ryong Ryu and Sŏng-ryong

5. Rural Landscapes

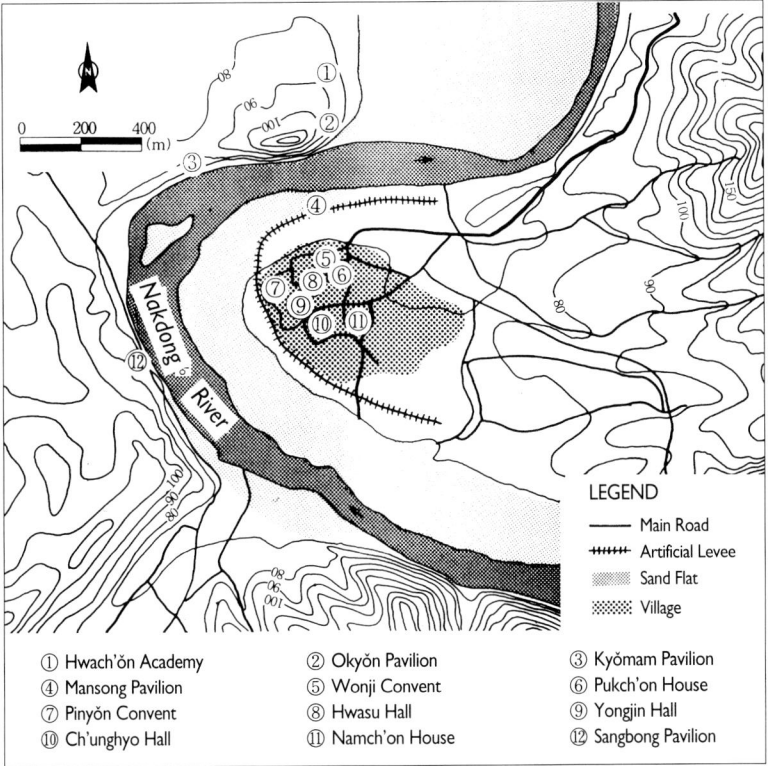

Figure 23. The site and layout of Hahoe Village: Three pavilions and one private Confucian academy were erected on the erosional side of the river. On the depositional side, by contrast, *yangban* houses and halls were clustered inside the artificial levee.

Ryu. Here, the former's manor called Yangjindang and the latter's called Ch'unghyodang still remain (Yim, 1992:71-84). Yangjindang which has been *chongga*, or the clan-head house, in the center of the village is a sturdy post-and-beam, tile-roofed *yangban* house about 400 years old. Ch'unghyodang, nearly as old as the former, is located only a short stroll away. Surrounding the two *yangban* manor houses were the much smaller farmer's houses. A majority of houses in the village today are

Photo 27. An aerial view on Hahoe Village and its surroundings: The river meanders in a zigzagging manner, and the village is situated on the defensive side of the river.

still small and thatched with hay, as they were centuries ago (**Photo 28, 29**).

Opposite to Hahoe Village is a precipice called Puyongdae, which literally means Lotus Bluff in English. A wide sand flat at this curve in the river lies in front of a pavilion and traditional-style house. About three kilometers from the village is the splendid architecture of Pyoungsan Academy, a private Confucian academy, which was erected in honor of Sŏng-ryong Ryu who served as the prime minister during the disastrous Hideyoshi Invasions. Inside dormitories flank the courtyard, and to its front is a narrow, unwalled pavilion, an excellent example of a clean-lined open structure.

Three local men, named Sŏnpyŏng Kim, Haeng Kwon, and Kil Chang, around Andong City, assisted King T'aejo, the founder of the Koryŏ Dynasty, to win the decisive battle over

5. Rural Landscapes

Photo 28. Yangjindang, the clan-head house in Hahoe Village: The house is one of the two mansions that dominate the scene in the village, and it was first built by Un-ryong Ryu, the elder brother of Sŏng-ryong Ryu.

Photo 29. Ch'unghyodang, the clan-head house in Hahoe Village: The house is the other important mansion in the village, which was first built by Sŏng-ryong Ryu, the famous wartime premier during the Hideyoshi Invasions.

the Later Paekje troops (Chŏng, 1997:60). This victory led to the eventual unification of the peninsula under the Koryŏ king. For their military contribution to the Koryŏ Dynasty, each man was raised to the rank of general and given a family name: Kim, Kwon, or Chang. Among them Kim and Kwon are still the most prominent *yangban* families around Andong City. In the center of Andong City, a small memorial shrine called T'aesamyo was built in 1542 as a symbol of loyalty, devotion and patriotism to honor these three local men.

In the Chosŏn Period, the members of these families continued to pass *kwagŏ*, or the state examination, and to work for the royal court in Seoul. Although they stayed in Seoul during their time in the civil service, they still owned their lands and houses in the areas around Andong City, where they could return in time of retirement. While they were in the civil service in Seoul, they also married into families from those other than the areas around Andong City. For the members of families who were married to them, the areas around Andong City may have been the place to retire from their public life, because there relatives could offer the social and economic assistance for them to settle down.

In terms of the inheritance rule, the primogeniture was not yet firmly established, but daughters were treated equally with sons in dividing the parent's property. Until the early Chosŏn Period, daughters quite often succeeded their fathers' households, and inherited lands when there were no sons. As male-dominance in the inheritance rule, in particular primogeniture, became the social norm, the son-in-law who lived with his wife's parents inherited their property.

Moreover, there was plenty of uncultivated land around

Andong City, waiting to be reclaimed. In the mountain valleys running southwards from T'aebaek Mountain and Sobaek Mountain, there remained the lands covered with forests where immigrant *yangban* families could pioneer and settle. According to Neo-Confucianism, the valley where a stream flows in a quiet and gentle manner, but not too far distant from the profane world, is the most ideal human shelter (Kŭm, 1995:262-269). The *yangban* families around Andong City, being pious in the belief of Neo-Confucianism, may have ardently sought to find shelters under such physical conditions.

In the practical sense, they also viewed these valleys, somewhat secluded from outside worlds, as suited to hide from political turmoil as well as civil wars. Because streams in these valleys never dried up all the year round, these valleys were endowed with stable conditions for the cultivation of paddy-rice along with transplanting. It is historically known that *yangban* families around Andong City were the first innovators in paddy-rice cultivation, adopting the method of transplanting from southern China in the 15th and 16th centuries (Chŏng, 1997:66). They also began barley cultivation after the harvest of paddy-rice, making double-cropping possible within a year. As a result, the increasing productivity of agricultural land could absorb the growing population of the *yangban* class at the maximum level.

2) CHŎNGJAS (PAVILIONS) IN THE UPPER REACHES OF THE NAMHAN RIVER

In their architecture, *chŏngja*s, or pavilions, closely resemble tile-roofed houses. Picturesquely set into nature at particularly

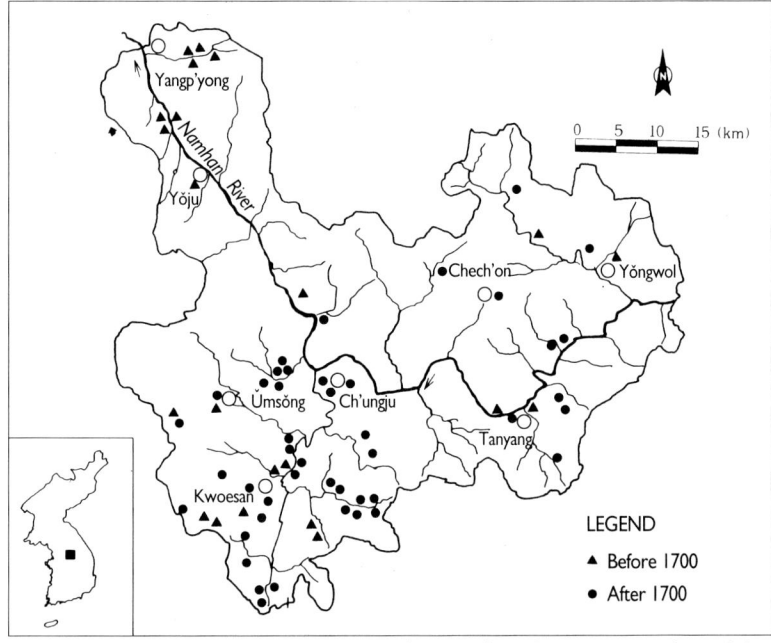

Figure 24. The spatial spread of chŏngja (pavilion) in the upper reaches of the Namhan River before and after the 18th century: In the early stage of diffusion, chŏngjas (pavilions) were erected mostly along the main stream of the Namhan River. It is after the 18th century that more chŏngjas were built around Kwoesan Town than in any other area. (Source: Ch'i-gyu Nam, 1997, "The Meaning of Pavilion as a Place," Unpublished Master's Thesis, Department of Geography, Korea National University of Education, p. 16.)

attractive scenic spots in the vicinity of villages, their serene and stately presence dominates a cliff, a river valley or an isolated hill. They have no side walls, however, so that the eye can roam freely to all sides. The main supporting pillars are very thick tree trunks, suited to the weight of the mighty roof. In Korea, from the 16th century, the *yangban* class began to erect many pavilions along the streams or rivers for various purposes. As a result, one can now find many types of pavilions easily wherever *yangban* families lived in the past.

Photo 30. A pavilion situated on a cliff: Such a pavilion, without walls, was generally built as a platform from which to look down upon the scenery as a panorama.

In the tributary of the Namhan River, in particular, it seems that the *yangban* families competed with one another to build as many pavilions as possible (**Figure 24**). There one can find various types of pavilions standing either outside or inside the village. If they are outside the village, the pavilions are generally located on the cliffs or on the hills where one can look down upon the flowing streams or rivers (Nam, 1997:31-38). When they are within the village, however, the pavilions are often situated in the middle of houses where one cannot see the streams or rivers (**Photo 30, 31**).

The Namhan River, literally meaning the South Han River, is the longest branch of the Han River, whose system drains the

Photo 31. A pavilion situated in the village: Such a pavilion was normally built as a monument by which villagers could commemorate their common ancestors.

western slope of the T'aebaek Range, or the Main Korean Range. The Kwangju and Ch'aryŏng Ridges and the Sobaek Range extending westwards from the T'aebaek Range form intermontane basins, narrow and deep valleys, and forested hills. Through the valleys between these ridges and ranges flow the branches of the Han River such as the Pukhan, Soyang, Hongch'ŏn and Namhan Rivers.

The Namhan River originates from Odae Mountain (1,563m) in the T'aebaek Range and describes an enormous curve toward the south as far as Tanyang Town, with the northwest course beginning at Ch'ungju City. Near Yŏngwol, the P'yŏngch'ang

River flows into the Namhan River, which joins downstream from Kangch'ŏnri with the Hoengsŏng River and finally 40km upstream from Seoul merges with the Pukhan River, literally meaning the North Han River.

All the branches of the Han River meander strongly in granite gneiss. For most of their length, they are entrenched into the dip of the tilt block in the form of V-shaped valleys and gorges with rock terraces, running along above them at various levels (Lautensach, 1988:283). The Han River still flows in such a canyon as far as Changuri, 30km above Seoul.

As compared with other branches such as the Pukhan River, the Namhan River flows through lower mountains and hills, and produces many beautiful scenic sites that are easier to visit. Tanyang County, Ch'ungju City and Kwoesan County are those which lie in the tributaries of the Namhan River with beautiful scenery along the streams or rivers. To these counties, in the Chosŏn Period, the ferry boats and merchant ships used to frequently sail back and forth from Seoul along the Han River. It is said that it took less than a day for boat or ship to get there from Seoul. For this reason, many *yangban* men found these counties ideal for shelter while not in civil service.

Until the 16th century, the *yangban* men usually gathered in the pavilion to compose poems together or discuss political and living matters while enjoying the scenery. From the 16th century, the *yangban* men began to utilize pavilions for other purposes than enjoying the scenery and meeting with friends (Nam, 1997:10). They often secluded themselves in the pavilion to concentrate on studying by themselves or teaching the village students about Neo-Confucianism. In the 19th century, *yangban* families erected pavilions in honor of their ancestors who became the eminent Neo-Confucian scholars or the high-ranked officials.

In general, the pavilions on the cliffs or hills were erected to enjoy the scenery, whereas those in the stream valleys were to learn and teach Neo-Confucianism. The former buildings appear in the architectural forms that are typical to the genuine pavilions without side walls. The pavilions of Kwanranjŏng (1456) in Chech'ŏn City, Samdojŏng (1776) in Tanyang County, and Suwoljŏng (1565) and Kosanjŏng (1595) in Kwoesan County are of this type (Nam, 1997:31-32). The latter buildings are often with side walls within which one or two rooms are arranged with the Korean traditional heating system called *ondol*. In the tributaries of the Namhan River only a few pavilions of this type remain today, and T'aksajŏng (1560) in Chech'ŏn City is one of them.

The pavilions in honor of ancestors in the family were generally located at the entrance or in the rear of a village where they could easily be seen. These pavilions, by contrast, are irregular in architectural forms, sometimes even with side walls. In the counties of Tanyang, Ch'ungju and Kwoesan, and in particular Kwoesan County, the pavilions of this type were erected in large numbers in the 19th and 20th centuries (**Figure 24**). The pavilions of Pukgajŏng (1813) in Ch'ungju Town, and Yilgajŏng (1913), Mosŏnjŏng (1940) and Hansajŏng (1959) in Kwoesan County, even though they were located outside villages, belong to this type (Nam, 1997:37). The pavilions of Samyŏnjŏng (1859) in Ch'ungju City and P'ungp'ajŏng (1901) in Kwoesan County, were typical of those erected inside villages in honor of ancestors.

Once the *yangban* men erected a pavilion, they offered it a specific name with a certain meaning, and composed poems to create a special sense of place around it. The name of the pavilion was written in Chinese on the front board to be hung facing outside under the roof, so that one could see it from outside. The poems were also written in Chinese on the boards hung facing inside under the ceiling. With these names and poems on the pavilions, the *yangban* men eventually created their own authoritative place so that they could make friends with one another, being segregated from commoners. By inscribing ancestor's intentions in the names or poems, they also wanted to turn the pavilions into symbolic places to demonstrate their own social prestige in comparison to other family members.

The right to enjoy the scenery from the pavilion and the opportunity to share leisure life with friends in the pavilion was enjoyed only by the *yangban* men in the Chosŏn Period. The pavilion, then, was not only the material landscape, but also the symbolic landscape which the fellow *yangban* men shared in common at that time. They sometimes attached their personal emotions and memories to the pavilion to inscribe a particular sense of place that should never be forgotten.

Those who visited the pavilion would be confronted with the Chinese name on the front board, which sometimes required some knowledge in classical Chinese to interpret the symbolic meaning behind it. One would read the poems that were often full of metaphor, and interpret the emotions, imaginations, experiences and meanings embedded in them, only if one understood classical Chinese very well. Most of the time the natural phenomena mentioned in them were not simply the natural per se, but the metaphor of a human mind that was borrowed from classical Chinese.

Understanding knowledge of classical Chinese as the representation of social power was the privilege restricted only to the *yangban* men in the Chosŏn Period. All in all, the elements of knowledge, power and landscape were interwoven to create a symbolic place which secured and maintained the authority of the *yangban* men.

The natural phenomena such as the mountain, river, wind, clouds, rain, moon, fog and snow were the topics to be used in the composition of names and poems. The pavilions of Samdojŏng (1776) in Tanyang County, and Suwoljŏng (1565) and Kosanjŏng (1596) in Kwoesan County reflect names from natural phenomena (Nam, 1997:50-53). The poems on the pavilions were also lauding the beautiful scenery around them, while borrowing the expressions from classical Chinese. In the naming of the pavilions on the cliffs or hills to enjoy the scenery, in particular, these topics were very much loved.

Personal names, preferably pseudonyms, however, were often used for the names of pavilions in the village to commemorate the ancestors. For example, the names of Mohyŏnjŏng (1817) in Ch'ungju City, and Mosŏnjŏng (1940s), Hansajŏng (1959) and Koeŭmjŏng (1600s) in Kwoesan County have something to do with an ancestor's pseudonym or biography (Nam, 1997:54-55). On the board inside the pavilion the ancestor's personal history in classical Chinese was also written. With this common cultural landscape in mind, men of the same lineage shared feelings of belonging and group identity superior to other lineages. Such pavilions, imbued with Neo-Confucian ideology, in particular filial piety, served as symbolic places to bind a lineage group together socially.

3) Folk Housing on the West Bank of the Nakdong River

In the past, the folk housing in Korea was a one-story building, wooden or half-timbered. The most common and primitive was the straw-roofed hut, and only the wealthy family could dwell in a house with a tiled roof. The timbers were usually cut from red pine logs which were often somewhat crooked. The main uprights rested on foundation stones dug into the ground and were connected by cross beams and tie beams, the latter of which bore the roof. The spaces in between were filled with sticks tied together with straw rope; wickerwork was spread between the sticks, and finally the outer walls were plastered with mud.

Under the floors of the rooms ran the flues for *ondol*, or the Korean traditional heating system, which is operated from the kitchen. The fireplace for this universal, very practical Korean traditional heating system was built into the large and low kitchen stove. It is believed that this heating system was diffused from Manchuria into the Korean Peninsula at a very early time in history. Once introduced into northern Korea, it gradually spread into southern Korea, and is now used almost everywhere in Korea except on Cheju Island where winter is not so cold.

Since the heating system was started up whenever the kitchen stove was used, the rooms connected to it were unbearably hot in summer. Koreans then preferred to sleep in the open on their verandas, called *maru* in Korean. Even the simplest house had a veranda extending along outside the rooms at the level of the floors, and like them, it was never stepped on with

Photo 32. A *yangban* house with a *maru* (veranda) installed into a guest room called *sarangch'ae*: In the guest room, the *ondol* as a heating system was combined with the *maru* as a cooling system. The *maru* was installed on the second floor which had been boosted up from the ground.

shoes.

In the simplest cases, it consisted of earth piled up and paved on top. Usually, however, it was made of wooden boards that were kept clean, like the mud floors covered with oiled paper in the rooms. In larger houses the veranda was supplanted or supplemented by a *taech'ŏng*, or large veranda, and covered by the roof like the living room.

It is suggested that a *maru* was first used in southern Korea, and then gradually spread northward. Except in the extreme north where summer is rather cool, the *maru*, or the veranda, can be seen today in various forms all over Korea. Somewhere in the middle of the Korean Peninsula, these two systems, the *ondol* and *maru*, were adopted together into a house to overcome cold winter and hot summer (Shin, 1995 : 84 - 89). It is really a Korean invention that the *ondol* and *maru* were combined under the same roof (**Photo 32**).

Traditional houses in Korea are about the same in terms of construction methods and building materials, but in terms of floor plan they are significantly different. The spatial functions differ from one region to another, and these differences may be attributed to cultural diffusion as well as local climatic conditions. Once the ancient people settled in Korea, many regional and local diffusions and adaptations evolved over thousands of years. It is the floor plan that strikingly shows the regional and local contrasts in Korean folk housing (Chang, 1996 : 36 - 39). The regional types of folk housing can be recognized easily based on the floor plan, especially the combination of *maru* and *ondol*.

The houses consist of rooms called *kan*s which have standard sizes varying between 3 x 3 and 5 x 5m in different parts of the country. The distance between the main posts, which stick out of the clay walls on the outside, is determined by these measurements. Inside, several *kan*s are sometimes joined to form a single room by leaving out partitions between them. The simplest houses consist of two or three *kan*s lined up next to each other, resulting in a longish rectangular floor plan, which resembles the Chinese numerical letter "一."

This is the basic form that can be seen quite often in southern Korea, and in other areas there appear many of its modifications. In the simplest case of a "一" shaped house, *puŏk* (kitchen), *anbang* (wife's room), *maru* (veranda) and *kŏnnŏbang* (room across a *maru*) are horizontally placed to form a straight line. In addition, a *t'oetmaru* (a narrow veranda) which is connected to a

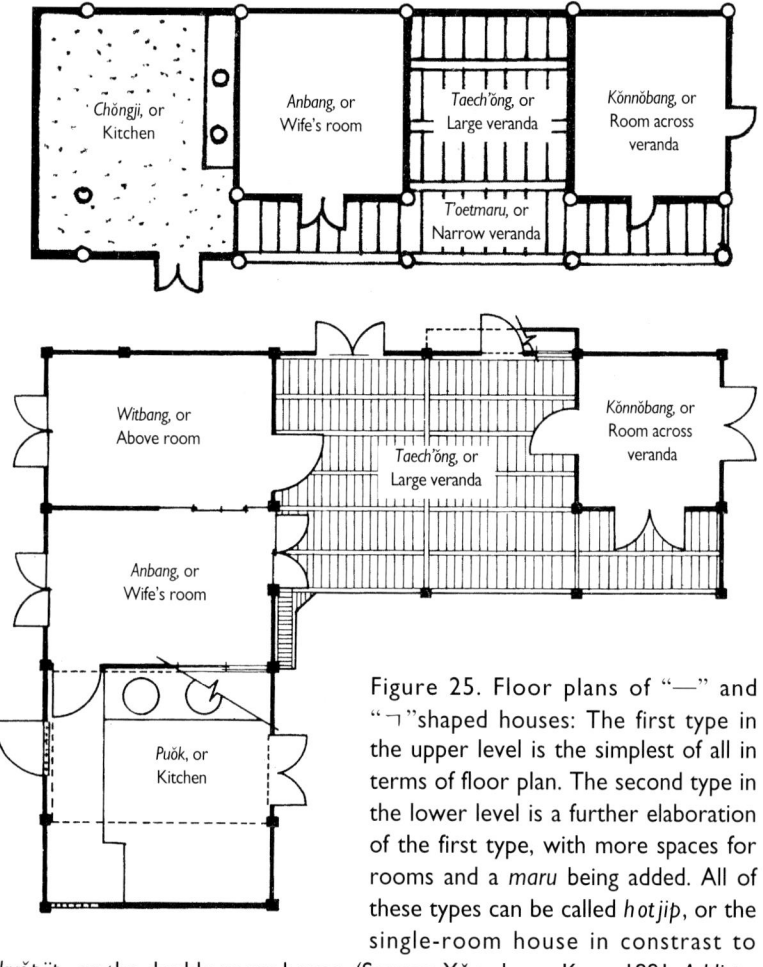

Figure 25. Floor plans of "—" and "ㄱ"shaped houses: The first type in the upper level is the simplest of all in terms of floor plan. The second type in the lower level is a further elaboration of the first type, with more spaces for rooms and a *maru* being added. All of these types can be called *hotjip*, or the single-room house in constrast to *kyŏpjip*, or the double-room house. (Source: Yŏng-hwan Kang, 1991, *A History of Housing Culture in Korea*, Seoul: Kimundang, p. 138; Kwang-ŏn Kim, 1988, *An Ethnography of Korean Housing*, Daewo Academic Series in Human and Social Sciences, No. 29, Seoul: Taewonsa, p. 247.)

taech'ŏng (a large veranda) is placed in front of the rooms (**Figure 25**). This long and narrow wooden floor forms a corridor running in front of rooms, which is utilized as a summer living space. Such a peculiar form of veranda is only to be seen in

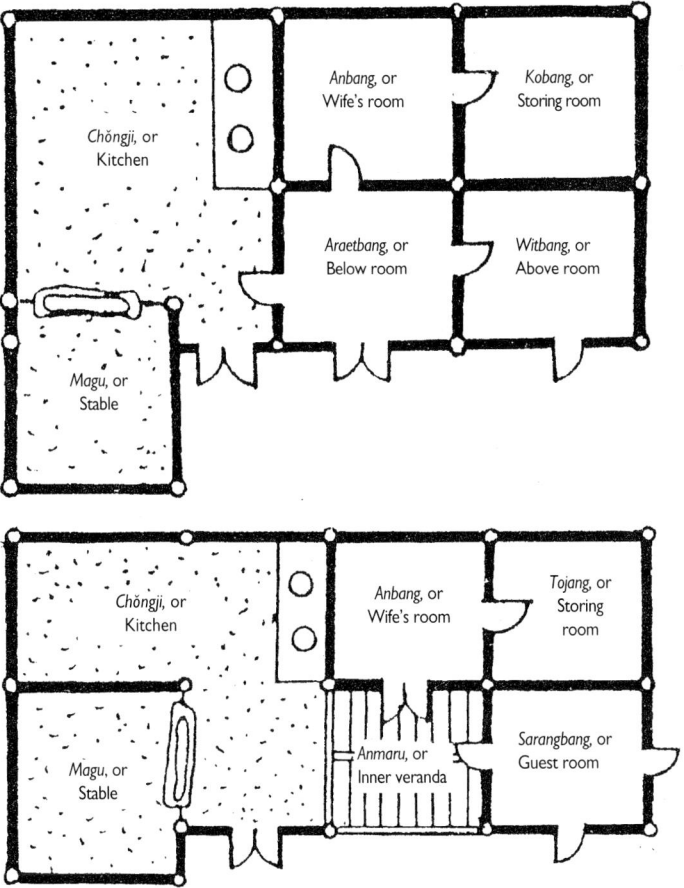

Figure 26. Floor plans of a *kyŏpjip* (double- room house): Like the *hotjip* (single-room house), there are also many variations of the *kyŏpjip* (double-room house). The first type in the upper level shows the simplest pattern of floor plan without a *maru*. The second type in the lower level is a primary modification of the first type, installed with a *maru*. (Yŏng-hwan Kang, 1991, *A History of Housing Culture in Korea*, Seoul: Kimundang, pp.123-124.)

southern Korea where the notoriously hot and humid summer is relatively long.

At the ends of the rectangle, additional *kan* can be attached on one or both sides, so it forms a shape resembling the Korean letter in alphabet "ㄱ" or "ㄷ." These modified forms can frequently be seen in the middle part of Korea such as *Kyŏnggi* Province. In the "ㄱ" shaped house, the kitchen, *anbang* and *witbang* (room above the *anbang*) are built on a straight line. A veranda, as a wooden floor, is located perpendicular to the *witbang* and the *kŏnnŏbang* (room facing the *anbang* across a *maru*) at the end (**Figure 25**).

Moreover, within the entire length of the house, two *kan*s may be arranged behind one another in pairs, forming a double-room house called *kyŏpjip* in Korean, similar to the Chinese character 田 (*chŏn*) (**Figure 26**). The houses with this floor plan, which are believed to be ancient in origin, can still be seen widely in northern Korea and mountainous areas in middle Korea (Chang, 1996:108). In this type, exterior wall space is minimized by placing the four *ondol* rooms in the shape of 田 (*chŏn*) to reduce heat loss in cold winter.

In particular, there exists an *ondol*-heated room, called *chŏngjugan*, beside the earthen-floored kitchen. The two spaces are separated by a change in the ground level rather than a more typical side wall. This room called *chŏngjugan* is a useful space where the family may have meals or do simple household work (Chang, 1996:117). The heat from the kitchen also warms the attached cow barn and the treadmill during the severely cold winters. Hence the cow barn and treadmill are placed with other rooms under the same roof to form a special type of "strewn farmstead."

On the west bank of the Nakdong River one can find a variety of house types, northern or southern, and even the mixed ones (Shin, 1995:159-168). In the areas around Mungyŏng City, Sangju city and Sŏnsan Town, all of the regional types of floor

5. Rural Landscapes

Photo 33. A folk house in the shape of "一" with a *maru* around Mungyŏng City: On the west bank of the Nakdong River, a variety of folk housing floor plans appear, and the "一" shaped house is one of the most common types.

plans, such as "一," "ㄱ" and 田, coexist in harmony without anyone being dominant (**Photo 33**). The northern and intermediate types frequently interrupt the continuous distribution of southern types, and the mixed type does appear between them once in a while. On the east bank of the Nakdong River, by contrast, the "田" shaped house called *kyŏpjip* predominates the areas around P'unggi Town, Yŏngju City and Andong City (Shin, 1995:146-159). In terms of folk housing culture, therefore, these areas should be recognized as the melting pot rather than the transitional zone.

Until it was possible to sail up and down along the Nakdong River, the areas around Mungyŏng City, Sangju City and Sŏnsan Town were situated in the crossroads between north and south or between east and west. The Nakdong River, with its length of 526km, is the longest river of the peninsula, and was navigable from the mouth upstream to Sangju City. There, cultural elements were easily introduced from the south by way of water routes on the Nakdong River.

From there towards Seoul in the north, people had to travel on foot or horseback beyond the passes over the Sobaek Range called Cho Pass or Yihwa Pass. These passes, however, were very busy with many travelers until the Chosŏn Period, because Yŏngnamdaero, or the main road from Sangju County to Seoul, was running across them. Those from the east bank of the Nakdong River also used to travel along this road to reach Seoul.

As people from the north and south or east and west were intermingled, the cultures carried by them were mixed to give birth to a hybrid culture. In the folk housing, for instance, the southern elements were freely married with northern or intermediate ones. In case of the *kyŏpjip*, it is not enclosed as much as it is on the east bank of the Nakdong River, and is partly open to the outside world. Here, a long and narrow veranda called a *t'oetmaru* is often placed in front of the rooms.

A *yangban* house with the special name of Yangjindang in Sangju County is also basically of the *kyŏpjip* type, but with some adoption from southern elements (Shin, 1995:170-174). When first built in 1555, the *taech'ŏng* was arranged between *ondol* rooms, and in connection with this large veranda was the *t'oetmaru* in front of the rooms. Unlike on the east bank of the Nakdong River, the verandas are not enclosed by doors, but open to the courtyard, and from there latticed wooden doors lead into rooms. The doors open on iron hinges and are thus not sliding doors in contrast with those in Japan.

4) IRRIGATION NETWORKS ON THE HONAM PLAIN

The Honam Plain is situated at the southwestern rim of the Korean Peninsula. It is the largest plain in Korea with an area of 3,604 km². Its topography consists of a coast and its adjacent coastal flats, flood plains along free meanders and their surrounding hills, and a series of springs and streams along mountain slopes. The Mangyŏng and Tongjin Rivers are the two main streams on the Honam Plain, all of which originate in the Noryŏng Ridge. The Noryŏng Ridge largely determines the axis of the Honam Plain as a parallelogram. This mountain ridge, extending from north-northeast to south-southwest, separates the plain area in the west from the mountainous area in the east.

Here and there on the coastal flats and flood plains, in particular, marshes and swamps developed where cultivation was almost impossible. Until the late Chosŏn Period, only a small portion of these lowlands were cultivated wherever water control was possible with the drainage and irrigation system, small in size. In general, weirs called *po* were built across streams in the lower valleys to trap runoff (Ryu, 1987:93). The amount of water available from reservoirs or tanks was often insufficient even for irrigation in the upper valleys. Thus, in the lower valleys, there was always a shortage of water. The weir, commonly adopted and used by that time, was not capable of solving the water shortage in the lowlands (**Figure 27**).

Only with the construction of irrigation and drainage facilities during Japanese colonialism, these barren lowlands were reclaimed into paddy-rice fields (**Photo 34**). Through Japanese colonialism the Honam Plain emerged as the major rice belt in

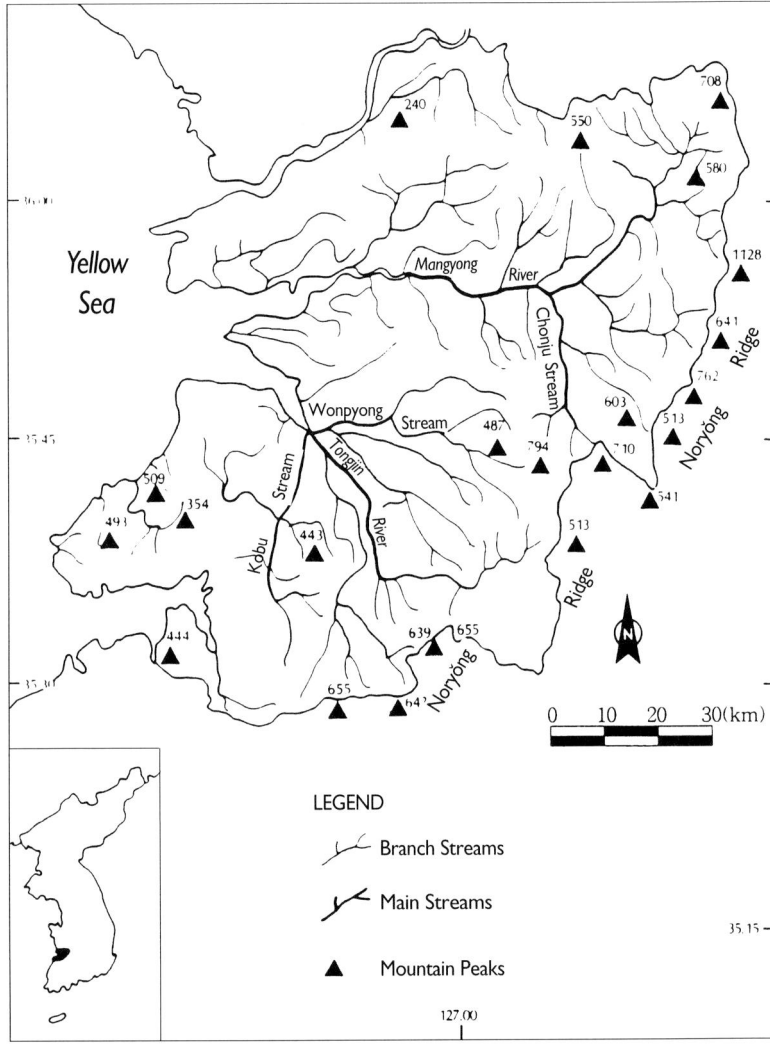

Figure 27. Drainage Systems on the Honam Plain: The plain consists of two river basins, Mangyŏng and Tongjin, tilting toward the Yellow Sea. The watershed between these rivers is sometimes not clear because hill country dominates the topography on the plain. (Source: Je-Hun Ryu, 1987, "Institutionalization and Cultural Adaptaton on the Honam Plain of South Korea: 1789-1982," Unpublished Ph.D. Dissertation, Department of Geography, The University of Texas at Austin, p. 29.)

5. Rural Landscapes

Photo 34. The extensive paddy-rice fields on the Honam Plain: The plain boasts of its immense flat land, unusual in Korea, and there one can observe the sun rising and setting beyond the horizon.

Korea at the same time with the improvement of irrigation networks. In the valleys of the Mankyŏng and Tongjin Rivers separately, a single unit of irrigation system, large in size, evolved during Japanese colonialism. The Japanese landlords introduced reservoirs made of steel and cement, canals dug by machines and lined with foot-powered wheels, and electric pumps and water gates. Moreover, under the strong support from Japanese colonial power, irrigation associations were the public agencies capable of mobilizing the capital and labor necessary to handle the capital-intensive and large irrigation projects.

Until 1920, the main emphasis was on the rehabilitation of existing irrigation facilities which had fallen into disrepair (Ryu, 1987:152). In the 1920s, upon the growing demand for rice in

Japan, the Japanese colonial government encouraged irrigation subsidies and low-interest loans for direct investments enabled irrigation associations to construct large irrigation facilities. Some of these capital-intensive projects on the Honam Plain were even technologically superior to those in contemporary Japan.

In the Mankyŏng River Valley, the first irrigation association in Korea, called the Okgu-Sŏbu Irrigation Association, was organized by Korean farmers in 1908. By the early 1910s, four more irrigation associations were organized there: the Yimik,

Photo 35. An old irrigation canal called Tokjuhang-suro on the Honam Plain: The canal was originally constructed in the late Chosŏn Period by a queen's family named Min, and later enlarged by the Japanese under the colonial rule. It is said that the canal was cut into the hill near Samrye Town when it was first constructed.

Yimik-Nambu, Chŏnik and Yimok Irrigation Associations. These institutions, however, were all organized under the leadership of Japanese landlords. The Yimik Irrigation Association was established in 1909 with the main task to rehabilitate the ancient reservoir called Hwangdŭngje. In 1910, the Chŏnik Irrigation Association was organized to improve the capability of irrigation canals called Tokjuhang-suro which were first constructed in the late Chosŏn Period (**Photo 35**).

Both the Yimik-Nambu Irrigation Association and the Yimok Irrigation Association were respectively established in 1909 and 1911 to extend two irrigation canals of Tokjuhang-suro into the lower valley. There in the past, without these additional canals, irrigation water had to be stored in canals and ditches during the non-irrigation season, and after irrigation the water had to be drained to the Mangyŏng River. The extended canals now reached the Hwangdŭngje, where additional water flowing into these canals could be stored (**Figure 28**).

However, in 1920, these two irrigation associations merged into a single organization, called the Yikok Irrigation Association, in order to increase the scale of economy in management (Ryu, 1987:155). One goal of this merged irrigation association was to construct the huge reservoirs called Taea-jŏsuji and Kangch'ŏn-jŏsuji behind concrete dams in the mountain valley of the Mangyŏng River. These dams were built farther upstream than the canals of Tokjuhang-suro, which could no longer serve as the source of irrigation water. A second task of the Yikok Irrigation Association was to extend the canals farther downstream toward the coastal flats. Through these extended canals, called Taea-gansŏn, the irrigation water was conveyed from the Taea-jŏsuji down to the coastal flats. Here, a Japanese company

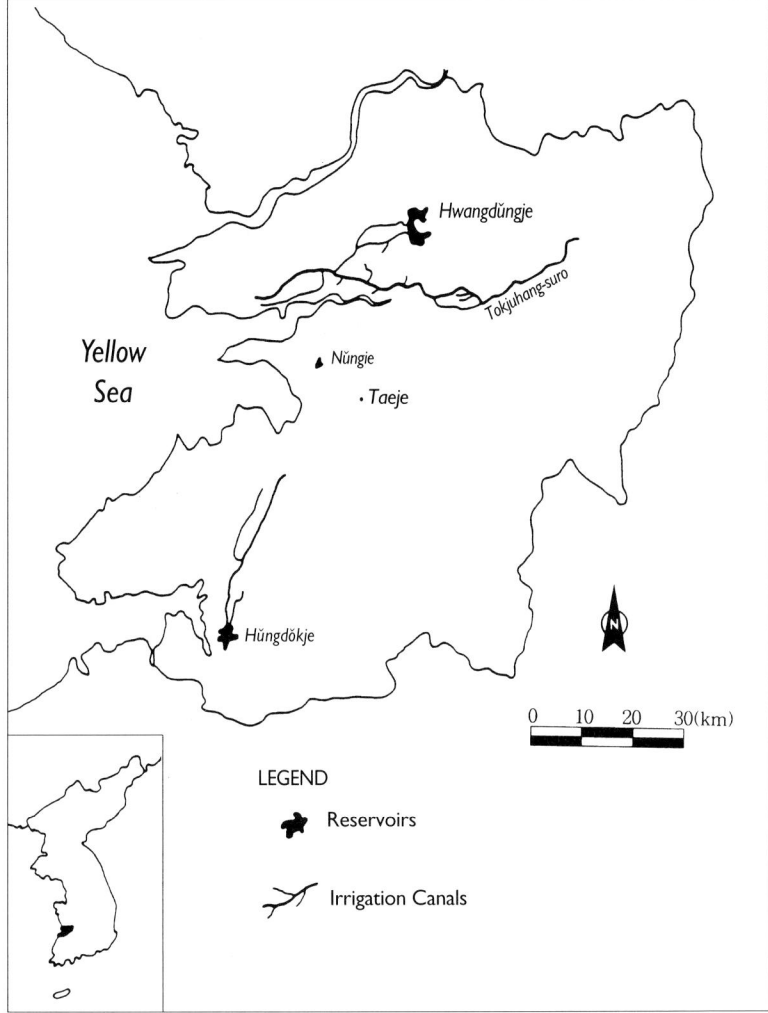

Figure 28. Irrigation networks on the Honam Plain before 1920: In the early stage of irrigation improvement, the Mangyŏng River Valley was much more advanced than the Tongjin River Valley. (Source: Je-Hun Ryu, 1987, "Institutionalization and Cultural Adaptaton on the Honam Plain of South Korea: 1789-1982," Unpublished Ph.D. Dissertation, Department of Geography, The University of Texas at Austin, p. 154.)

5. Rural Landscapes

began a series of large reclamation projects using industrial technology.

Finally, the canals from the Taea-jŏsuji encompassed the lower Mangyŏng River Valley to merge a single unified irrigation system. The Tokjuhang-suro became a part of the extended canals of Taea-gansŏn. With the plentiful water supply, the Hwangdŭngje became unimportant in storing and feeding irrigation water to the lowlands, and was later drained and reclaimed into paddy fields. In 1940, the Okgu-Sŏbu, Yimik and Chŏnik Irrigation Associations merged with the Yikok Irrigation Association (Ryu, 1987:157). From this merging process emerged a single irrigation association, called the Chŏnbuk Irrigation Association, governing the entire Mangyŏng River Valley.

The development and the incorporation of large irrigation systems came later in the Tongjin River Valley than in the Mangyŏng River Valley. Here, several important branch streams such as Kobu, Wonp'yŏng, Tuwol and Shinp'yŏng flow directly into the sea without merging into the main river, called Tongjingang. The terrain was too level to develop a trellis drainage network, and flood plains were drained by shallow streams. Irrigation water from the local streams, runoffs and springs, therefore, was scarcer in volume than in the Mangyŏng River Valley. These unfavorable natural conditions required that a greater amount of capital and a higher level of technology be applied to the development of large irrigation systems (Ryu, 1987:159).

In 1916, the first irrigation association, called the Kobu Irrigation Association, was organized in the valley of Kobu Stream by a mixed group of Korean and Japanese landlords.

Upstream, an ancient reservoir called Nulje was in a state of disrepair for a long time. The Kobu Irrigation Association originally planned to rehabilitate this reservoir, but later changed its plan to build a new reservoir called Hŭngdŏkje farther upstream that was larger than the old reservoir. In 1924, under political and financial support from the provincial government, Japanese landlords organized the Tongjin Irrigation Association, the first Japanese-led irrigation association in the Tongjin River Valley.

In 1927, the Tongjin Irrigation Association constructed the huge reservoir called Sŏmjinje with electric water-gates behind a steel and concrete dam in the valley of the Sŏmjin River. From here, stored water was channeled through a siphon into the adjacent Tongjin River. Once the water was diverted into the Tongjin River, it stayed in the river channel until the water was diverted into two main canals called Kimje-gansŏn and Chŏngŭp-gansŏn. Both of them flowed down to the coastal flats: the Kimje-gansŏn in the north and the Chŏngŭp-gansŏn in the south (**Figure 29**).

Moreover, the level of these main canals was designed to be higher than surrounding fields and streams so that irrigation water could be dispersed by gravity flow. This was an innovative change from other irrigation systems such as those in the Mangyŏng River Valley where canals were nothing but simple modifications of natural streams. As in the MangyŏngRiver Valley, this irrigation improvement benefited Japanese landlords in the lowlands where a series of reclamation projects on the marshes and swamps became feasible.

In 1930, the Kimje-gansŏn was extended to reach a traditional reservoir called Nŭngje, which formerly received its water from

5. Rural Landscapes

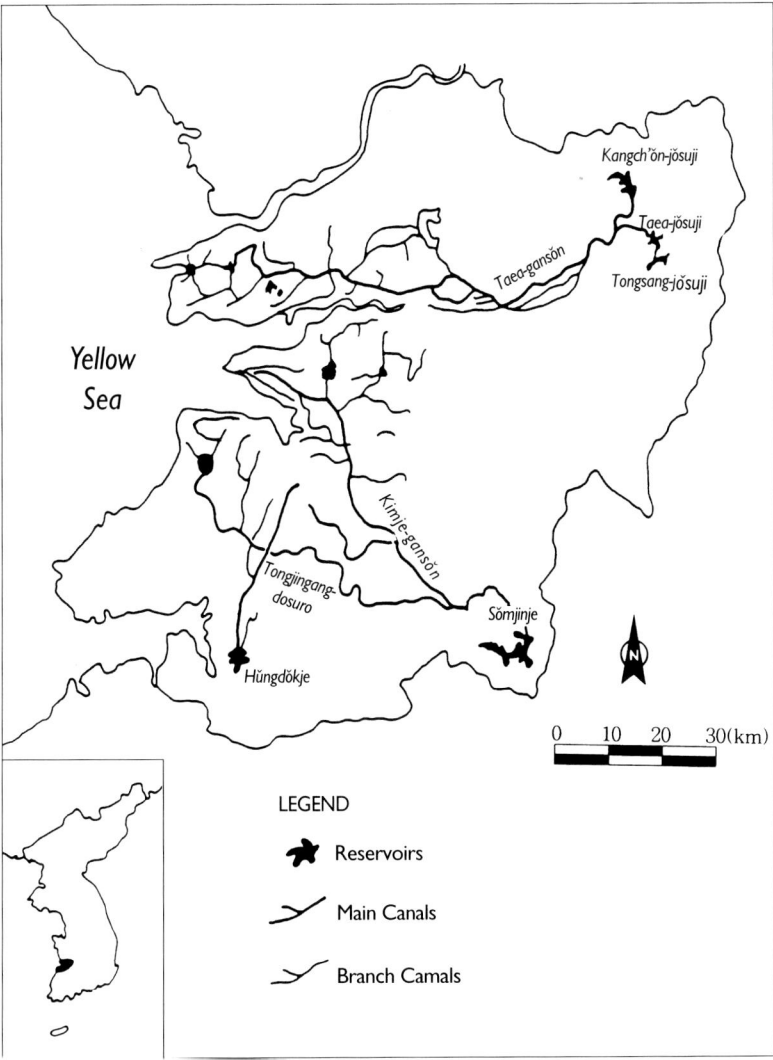

Figure 29. Irrigation networks on the Honam Plain in the 1980s: After 1927, the Tongjin River Valley overshadowed the Mangyŏng River Valley in the development and incorporation of irrigation systems, large in scale. (Source: Je-Hun Ryu, 1987, "Institutionalization and Cultural Adaptaton on the Honam Plain of South Korea: 1789-1982," Unpublished Ph.D. Dissertation, Department of Geography, The University of Texas at Austin, p. 212.)

Photo 36. A traditional reservoir called Nŭngje on the Honam Plain: The reservoir, enlarged threefold in 1930, contributed to the conversion of dry fields into paddy-rice fields in the hilly areas.

natural runoff and stream flow (Ryu, 1987:162). This reservoir had been a large traditional reservoir on the Honam Plain until the late Chosŏn Period. The capacity of this reservoir was enlarged threefold, and the extended canal called Ch'ŏngha-gansŏn conveyed the water from Kimje-gansŏn by a pumping station up to the reservoir during the non-irrigation season. The enlarged reservoir stored this irrigation water, and channeled it down the diversion branch canals in connection with the reservoir during the irrigation seasons (**Photo 36**).

Prior to the enlargement of the Nŭngje, there were ten tanks in the upper and middle reaches of the stream, and four weirs in the lower reaches of the stream (Ryu, 1987:163). Each small irrigation system functioned relatively independently from others, and each irrigation community took care of its own tank or weir within its territory. However, the introduction of a large irrigation system made these scattered tanks and weirs useless. Canals dispatched irrigation water from the reservoir upstream into the upper reaches of the stream. This large irrigation system also made irrigation more reliable in the lowlands where, by then, farmers had striven to tap natural water flows from upstream with little success and frequently suffered from droughts.

After the liberation from Japanese colonialism, the technology and administration of irrigation systems on the Honam Plain remained with little change until the mid-1960s. In the Mangyŏng River Valley, a subsidiary reservoir called Tongsang-jŏsuji was built in 1966 to supplement the water storage of the Taea-jŏsuji. In the Tongjin River Valley, by contrast, instead of a subsidiary reservoir being built, the Sŏmjinje was enlarged threefold in 1965. In order to expand the irrigated area, the Tongjin Irrigation Association constructed a subsidiary reservoir called Paeksanje in 1964 across the upper valley, and extended the Kimje-gansŏn to the reservoir (**Figure 29**).

In 1969, a third main canal called Tongjingang-dosuro was added to the two existing main canals, Kimje-gansŏn and Chŏngŭp-gansŏn (**Figure 29**). This new main canal carried irrigation water directly from Sŏmjinje downslope to the margins of the coastal flats where a large-scale reclamation project was launched in 1962 (Ryu, 1987:213-214). The government initiated this project to reclaim the tidal lands between Kyehwa Island and the coastal flats, and created paddy fields of 669 acres. By 1974, this project could accommodate 1,992 farm households as new migrants.

5) VILLAGE FORESTS ON THE SOUTH COAST

From ancient times, it seems that Koreans highly esteemed the value of forests in a symbolic sense as well as in a practical sense. In Kyŏngju City which was the ancient capital of the Shilla Kingdom, a sacred forest called Kyerim is still preserved in the form of a grove of gnarled old hardwood trees, mostly Chinese elm (Nilsen,1997:438). A legend called Kyerimyusa relates to the forest and the founding of the Kyŏngju Kim family. According to this legend, this forest has been known as the birth place of the Kyŏngju Kim family with the name, Kyerim, or Chicken Forest (**Photo 37**).

One night in A.D. 65, King T'alhae whose family name was

Photo 37. Kyerim, or the Chicken Forest, in Kyŏngju City: In this sacred forest, the Chosŏn Dynasty erected a Confucian-style shrine to commemorate the coming of Alji Kim, the founder of the royal family called Kim in the Shilla Kingdom.

Sŏk heard an imploring cock's crow from this grove, and he sent his prime minister to investigate. The official found a golden box hanging from a branch of a tree with a white chicken sitting underneath. Brought to the palace and opened, an infant boy was in the box. Pleased at this unexpected and unusual event, the king named the boy Alji, or Young Child in the Shilla language, and gave him the family name Kim, the Chinese character for "gold." Alji who became the head of the Kyŏngju Kim family never reigned as king, though many of his descendants continued to be kings after the Pak family.

Even today in Korea, village rituals, Shamanistic or Confucian in style, are often performed in the sacred forests, mostly artificial. Some village rituals are still performed in the forests with many trees, artificially planted near the village. In the commoner villages where different lineage groups lived together, village rituals were often performed in Shamanistic style. In the Chosŏn Period, however, many forests were artificially made near villages to fulfill the ideological meanings from Feng-shui. The planting and taming of trees, based on the doctrines of Feng-shui, were very popular in the *yangban* lineage villages. Here, in the forests, both the village rituals and the ancestor worshipping ceremonies were often performed in Confucian style.

The species of trees were often dependent upon the symbolic meaning that people wanted to realize. Pinus densiflora were more preferable in the forests by those who believed in Feng-shui or Confucianism, whereas Zelkova serrata and Seltis sinensis were preferred by those who believed in Shamanism (Kim, 1991:73). Other important species being planted in the village forests were Pinus thunbergii, Alnus japonica, Ulmus macrocarpa, Ginkgo biloba, Abies hollophylla, Pinus rigida and Carpinus tscholoskii. Among them, all except for the Pinus and Abies species, are deciduous trees thriving in the temperate climate.

In the practical sense, the forests certainly offer benefits to the villagers as they protect the villages from the wind. When the village lies near the sea or river, there rises a practical need to protect the villagers against the sandy wind from the water body. This may be the actual cause that more artificial forests can be found around the villages either on the coast or on the river side. In these locations, villagers often ardently planted and carefully tamed a series of trees in the form of a grove in order to prevent not only the wind from intruding, but also the stranger from peering into the village.

In the late Chosŏn Period, moreover, it seems that the ideology of Feng-shui added symbolic meaning to this practical need of artificial forests around villages. The village forests, originated in the ideology of Feng-shui, can be found all over Korea. Even in the towns and cities, the custom on the making of artificial forests, conforming to the doctrines of Feng-shui, were very popular throughout the Chosŏn Period. Here, still today, the remnants or relics of artificial forests can be traced in the field excursion by means of physical evidences from the old maps. It is said that they planted trees there in order to compensate for the weakness or annihilate the excessiveness on a certain spot from the viewpoint of Feng-shui. They believed that the forests could serve both physical and symbolic protectors to secure both their fortune and safety.

There were three basic doctrines in Feng-shui that everyone had to consider in times of locating and landscaping a settlement. Each of them separately tells how to deal with each of the most important physical elements: wind, water and topography. The first one called *changp'ung-ron* is literally the *discussion on how to block the wind*; the second one called *tŭksu-ron* is *the discussion on how to acquire water;* the third one called *hyŏngguk-ron* is *the discussion on how to interpret the topography*. Being faithful to each doctrine, they often wanted to secure an ideal spot for their settlement by artificially making the forest.

In Kosŏng County of South Kyŏngsang Province, the artificial forest called Usansup in front of Usan Village was intentionally made and willfully maintained, according to the symbolic interpretation of topography surrounding the village (Kim, 1991:169; 309-310). Based on the third doctrine of Feng-shui called *hyŏngguk-ron*, villagers imagined that the topography of the mountain in the rear of the village resembled a cow lying down, and thus named the mountain as Usan, or cow mountain. The name of Usansup, then, literally means nothing but the forest of cow mountain.

With this folk belief in mind, they finally seized the idea of digging a pond in front of the village, symbolizing a bowl for the cow's meals. Then, they planted trees, such as Pinus densiflora, Zelkova serrata and Chionanthus retusus on the bank of the pond so that villagers could not see the pond directly. In the past these trees were lined up in two rows to form a very thick forest. Up to today, however, a row of trees has perished while only one row has survived. This type of man-made topography in a symbolic sense, they believed, was the physical condition necessary for the villagers to make their living, not only healthy, but also happy.

In general, village forests consist of one or more species of trees, which form only a single layer. Because villagers had to plant and tame trees for a long time, they selected species that could grow very well under the physical conditions in Korea. In the Chosŏn Period, pine and zelkova trees were the species that Koreans much preferred in making artificial village forests. In particular, red pine trees were widely planted all over Korea due to their superb adaptability to the physical environment. Koreans also praised highly the characteristic of pine trees to stay green all the year round, and suggested it as a virtue that human beings had to retain. As a result, many village forests, especially near streams, were simply made of pine trees, and, if more, a few other species.

On the south coast, however, one can often find village forests where a variety of tree species form a vegetation community of multiple layers. As one approaches from the north to the south coast, one can observe the pine trees losing their niches as dominant species, while zelkova and other trees are emerging as dominant species. Once in a while, even evergreen trees, such as the Camellia japonica and Torreya nucifera, appear in the middle of these trees, even though they are not dominant species. In Korea, therefore, this is the only place on the mainland where one can feel an atmosphere somewhat close to a sub-tropical landscape (Lautensach, 1998:369).

The south coast is, with the exception of Cheju Island, the only region in Korea in which the mean temperatures of the coldest month lie above 0°C everywhere at low elevations. Within the region, the east is milder than the west in January on the average, and the islands have a higher mean temperature in winter than the nearby mainland. More important for plant growth is the fact that the average minimum January temperatures seldom fall below -3°C, and the absolute minimum temperatures nowhere reach -15°C. Summer, by contrast, is hot, befitting the southern location. The annual range exceeds the 25 °C limit only in the north of the south coast, and this is an extremely low figure by Korean standards (Lautensach, 1998:367-368).

Due to such climatic conditions, the evergreen element gains importance in the vegetation on the south coast. However, on the northern margin of the south coast all the summergreen plants are not replaced by evergreens all at once at a sharp boundary. The evergreen element is restricted to the lowest altitudinal zone, which has a relatively small expanse between mountains.

In the zone of intensive cultivation at the lowest altitude, which is devoted to annual field crops, summergreen deciduous trees thrive along with bamboo trees. Here, the destruction of the natural forests has been just as extensive as elsewhere. The secondary vegetations have replaced virgin forests, the evergreen vegetation elements, which are sensitive to cold. As a result, the lowest zone consists of mixed forest with summergreen and evergreen species.

An artificial forest in a fishing village in Namhae County represents exactly this type of mixed forest with multiple layers (Kim, 1991:130-132). The forest called Ŏburim lies at the estuary from which fishermen sail back and forth in the sea (Figure 30). Roughly, it is a very thick forest consisting of many trees in two layers: 2,000 tall trees and 1,200 short trees, almost enclosing the village inlet against the estuary. Seltis sinensis, Aphananthe aspera, Quercus acutissima and Ulmus davidiana are the species forming the higher layer. Elaeagnus typica,

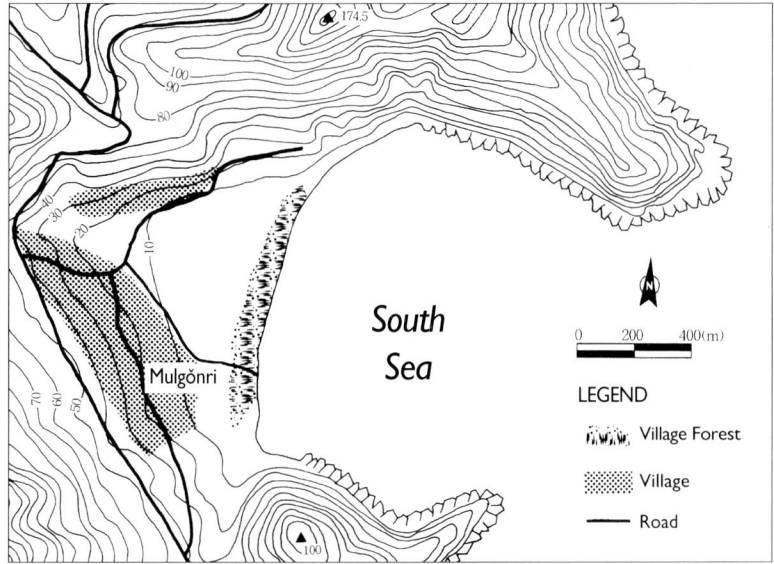

Figure 30. The village forest called Ŏburim on the south coast: Isolated at the remote southernmost tip of Namhae Island, the village named Mulgŏnri has been successful in the preservation of its own village forest.

Camellia japonica, Lespedeza bicolor and Pourthiaea villosa are those forming the lower layer (**Photo 38**).

Looking down from the top of the village, the forest, with the sea water shining in the background, yields a wonderful panorama, with its crest up to 10-15m high, and the length more than 500m. Short evergreen trees intermingled with tall summergreen trees form an exotic- and nice-looking vegetation community.

It is said that villagers began to plant a variety of trees there about 300 years ago, in order to protect the village from the tide, wind and sand. Since then, villagers have symbolized this artificial forest as a sacred place where the village deity dwells. Here, villagers provided an altar under a tree to annually dedicate vil-

5. Rural Landscapes

Photo 38. The village forest called Ŏburim on the south coast: The forest consists of many trees forming mutiple layers and being mixed in species. The trees were planted and tamed rigorously along the coastal line to form a narrow forest zone.

lage rituals to this deity in common. They strongly believe that any kind of disaster could occur to the village if the village forest was destroyed. When a violent storm took many lives from the village in the 19th century, they believed, it was because a part of the sacred forest had been cut down.

6. Urban Landscapes

6. Urban Landscapes

Historically, Korea has experienced three distinct developmental stages of urbanization: dynastic urbanization before 1910; early modern and colonial urbanization from 1910 to 1945; and rapid modern urbanization after 1945. Each stage is characterized by its own urban forms, city functions and networks, population structure, and city size and location. Until the late 19th century, however, Korea had remained as an agricultural society, and the urbanization rate was very low. After the Japanese annexation in 1910, urban growth was more rapid than before 1910, but restricted only to the cities of Japanese colonial interests.

After the liberation from Japanese colonialism, the explosive industrialization accelerated the modern urban growth all over the country. At present, therefore, owing to its sheer size, the modern form now dominates the overall image of urban landscape in every city, and even in the old cities. By and large, the dynastic and colonial forms have been so deeply buried in the extensive covers of modern urban forms that they cannot be seen at first glance.

The old Korean cities usually include the settlements whose

names end with the words, chu, sŏng, won and ch'ŏn. All travel documents from the end of the 19th century agree that in their overall impression they do not differ much from large villages. During the Chosŏn Period, in every city, however, houses were more closely packed together than in the villages, because many of them were surrounded by walls. Larger cities, in particular, were surrounded by high walls of rectangular squared stones, and long stretches of these stone ramparts often still remain. This maze of houses in the city, then, was crisscrossed by narrow, crooked streets.

The only impressive buildings were the seats of the county and provincial governors and the temples to Confucius. A Confucian temple called *hyanggyo*, or the local Confucian school, was founded in each county-seat by the Chosŏn Dynasty. Buddhist temples were lacking in the cities due to the hostile attitude of this dynasty toward Buddhism. In the cities that were former capitals, such as Seoul, Kaesŏng, P'yŏngyang, Kyŏngju and Puyŏ, there were additionally the old royal palaces and other historical monuments. Since they were not constructed of stone, however, many of these old palaces have fallen victim to fires.

In the formation of urban landscape, the Chosŏn Dynasty imposed the iconographies in association with Confucianism and Feng-shui that symbolized the royal authority. Environments became transformed into urban landscapes, when people simply altered them physically and they brought the environment in line with a particular model. On to the construction of walls, public buildings, Confucian temples, shrines, altars, forests, mounds and streets, the dynasty pursued to project their own world views centering around Confucian ideology. Even through the names of these cultural landscapes including streets, the dynasty sought to convey its own ideas, beliefs, wishes, imaginations and intentions. Sometimes, hidden in the modern landscapes, they may be the texts on the old history, waiting for the real interpretation.

This interpretation, then, must be based on the interrelationship between four concepts: ideology, political power, landscape and place. Here, ideology is a set of beliefs about how social life is or should be organized. Politics includes styles of maneuvering and mobilizing power within particular political structures as well as the modes of restructuring power relations. Place is defined as a specific locality, which is characterized in a significant way by its landscapes. The larger old cities in Korea, such as Seoul, Chŏnju and Kyŏngju, are characterized by a number of different landscapes, which have been created and modified over time as a part of the cultural and political changes taking place there.

During Japanese colonialism, the Japanese who settled in Korea were for the most part townspeople, and their energies were concentrated first and foremost on the cities. In the larger cities, particularly in Seoul, the Japanese deliberately usurped and transformed the dynastic symbols of royal authority to achieve political legitimacy. The Japanese policy of creating new symbols went hand in hand with a policy of undermining the old symbols. The palaces of the kings became the museums, public parks, zoos, botanical gardens, and residences of government agents. The streets, once straightened and widened, were sometimes renamed after those in Japan. By replacing the old with the new iconography, the Japanese intended to imbue Koreans with the authority of Japanese imperial coloni- alism (**Figure 31**).

6. Urban Landscapes

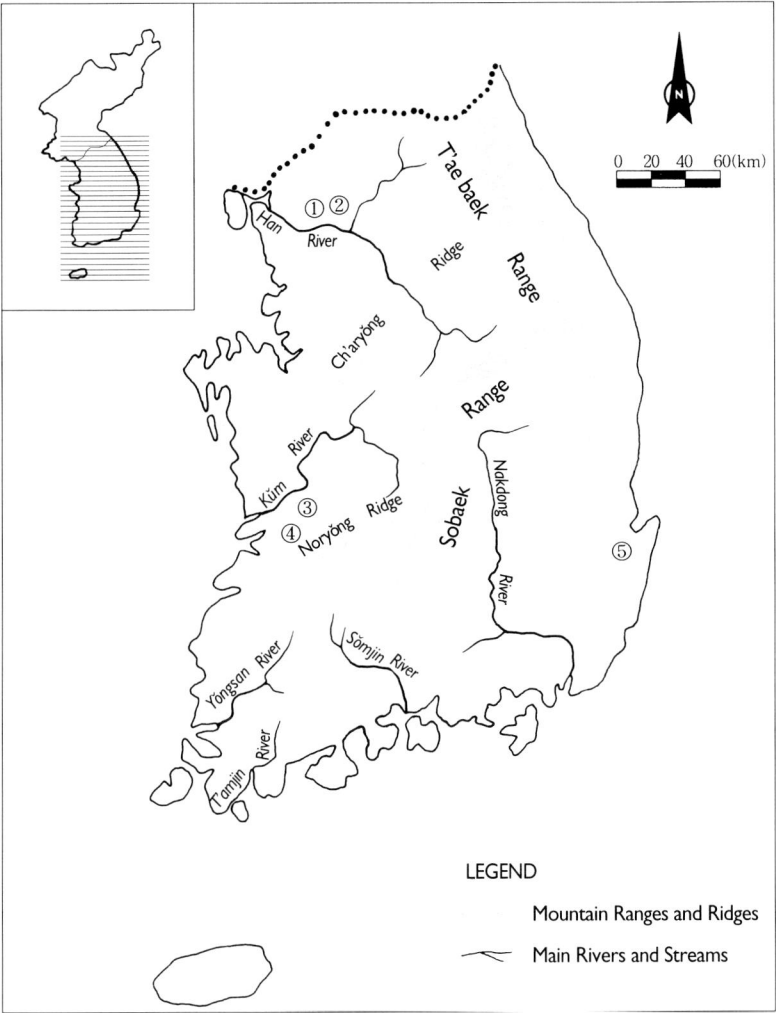

Figure 31. Locations of urban landscapes in Korea:
① The royal landscape in Seoul during the Chosŏn Period
② The colonial landscape in Seoul under Japanese occupation
③ The royal landscape in Chŏnju City during the Chosŏn Period
④ The colonial landscape in Chŏnju City under Japanese occupation
⑤ The royal landscape in Kyŏngju City during the Chosŏn Period.

1) THE ROYAL LANDSCAPE IN SEOUL DURING THE CHOSŎN PERIOD

During the Chosŏn Period, Seoul was known as Hanyang, which in Chinese meant a city located in the north of the Han River. Today, however, it is simply called Seoul in Korean, meaning "the capital." Not derived from Chinese characters, the name can only be written in the Korean alphabet called Hangŭl. When Sŏng-gye YI overthrew the last Koryŏ king in 1392, he decided to move the capital to Seoul and cut ties with the former ruling elite. Since then, Seoul has remained the administrative center of Korea for the past 600 years.

At that time, Seoul was situated at the center of the capital province called Kyŏnggi Province, not far from the largest river of the peninsula. It was also located at the focal point of the natural overland transportation routes, which converged from the north-northwest and the south parallel to the Yellow Sea coast, from the north-northeast across Ch'uga Pass furrow, from the east across Taegwan Pass and other low passes in the T'aebaek Range, and from the southeast across Ch'up'ung and Yihwa Passes in the Sobaek Range.

Seoul was not built on the river, but in a basin a few kilometers to the north, very efficient for military defense: in the south, Nam Mountain rises to the height of 265m; in the northwest, Yinwang Mountain to 338m; and in the north, Pukak Mountain to 342m (**Figure 32**). The more northern of these mountains have precipitous, grayish-black rounded slopes and peaks above moderately steep yellow slopes covered with pine scrubs. In addition to the opening to the east, the mountainous frames surrounding the basin had a few gaps through which

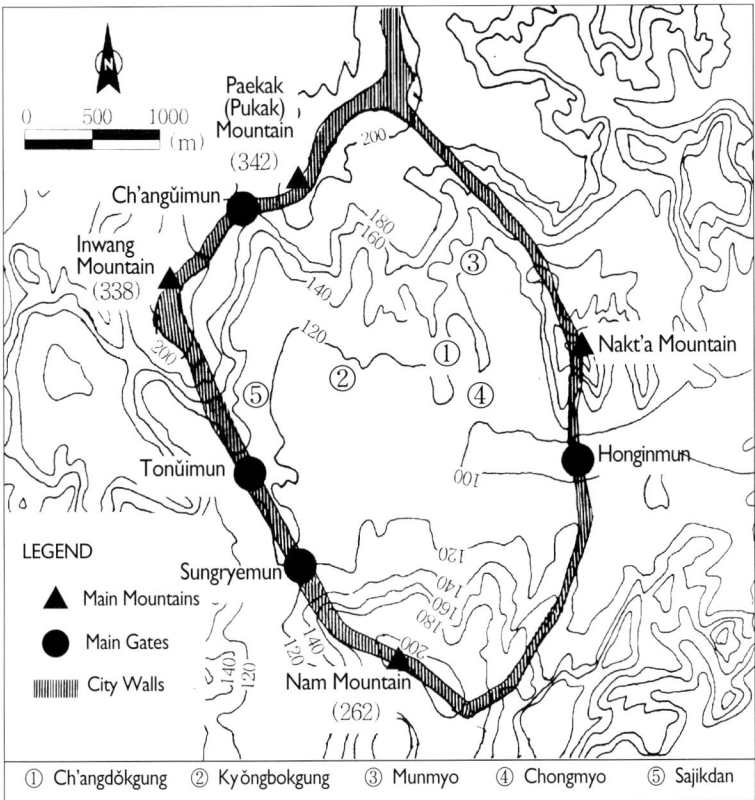

Figure 32. The site and layout of Seoul in the Chosŏn Period: The royal capital of the Chosŏn Dynasty, called Hanyang, was situated in a basin surrounded by a series of mountains. With the line connecting Paekak (Pukak) Mountain with Kyŏngbokgung (the Main Palace) as the main axis, Chongmyo was placed to the east in contrast to Sajikdan to the west.

transportation routes could develop (Lautensach, 1988:291). The encircling walls were built along these surrounding peaks, so that only at a few passes the built-up area could extend beyond the walls.

In Kaesŏng, the capital of the Koryŏ Dynasty, city planning relied exclusively on the doctrines in Feng-shui. The construction of Seoul, the capital of the Chosŏn Kingdom, however, was based on Confucianism as well as Feng-shui. In the city planning, King T'aejo consulted two intellectuals: a Confucian scholar named To-jŏn Chŏng, and a Buddhist monk named Muhak-daesa. The former supplied him with Churyegogonggi, or the knowledge on the classical principles of city planning in China, while the latter the knowledge on Feng-shui. From such a mixture of planning principles, emerged a unique urban landscape that was only to be seen in Seoul.

When King T'aejo moved his capital to Seoul, he immediately started construction of Kyŏngbokgung (the Main Palace or Palace of Shining Happiness) in 1394, Chongmyo (the Royal Ancestral Shrine), and Sajikdan (the Altars for the Earth-God and Harvest-God) (**Figure 32**). When determining the location of the main palace, the surrounding topography was examined carefully from the standpoint of Feng-shui. In palaces and public offices, the buildings and gates were often built and named in accordance with the ideals from Feng-shui. In the making of the city layout and district or gate names, Confucian ideology, in addition to Feng-shui, was intended to be expressed in order to demonstrate the royal authority. In fact, the urban landscape in Seoul under the Chosŏn Period was salient with iconography, symbolizing Confucian political ideology that would prescribe the relationship between the king, the superior and his subjects, the inferior.

The idea from Feng-shui was very much respected in the making of thoroughfares connecting main gates in four cardinal directions and streets running into official buildings. The east-west thoroughfare between the east gate and the west gate was originally a straight line, but later under the reign of King Sejong it was transformed into an arc-like curve based on

Feng-shui (Kim, 1933:151). It is said that the king accepted a geomancer's idea that curved lines of road were preferred in Feng-shui, and moved the location of the west gate to make the thoroughfare curved. The north-south thoroughfare between Kwanghwamun (the Main Gate of Kyŏngbokgung) and Namdaemun (the Great South Gate) was also curved in a line like an arc.

Nine gates punctuated the Seoul city wall: a main gate was located in each of the four cardinal directions, while four secondary gates were placed amongst them. To these gates were offered a variety of names full of Confucian symbols. The largest and principal of all was the Namdaemun, or the Great South Gate, which still today has a majestic structure. Although referred to by everyone as Namdaemun, its official name was Sungryemun, or the Gate of Exalted Decorum. Herein, the word, "decorum," indicates one of the five virtues that human beings must learn in Confucianism. Another main gate, Tongdaemun, or the Great East Gate, also has the official name, Hŭnginjimun, or the Gate of Flourishing Benevolence. The word, "benevolence," is also one of the five virtues that Confucianism suggests to be learned by people.

Moreover, on the mountains, in the south and north, called Nam Mountain and Paekak Mountain respectively, the halls were erected for mountain deities to be worshipped by the government and individuals as well. The deity on Paekak Mountain called Paekak-sanshin was female, whereas the deity on Nam Mountain called Mongmyŏk-daewang was male (Kim, 1989). The mountain in the north, Paekak Mountain, symbolizing royal authority, was closed to the common people, but the mountain in the south, Nam Mountain, was open to the common people.

As Paekak Mountain, the main mountain in Seoul, was the most highly valued in terms of Feng-shui, it was protected with much care from any private use. Moreover, soils were intermittently added to the mountain slope to strengthen its role as the protector of Kyŏngbokgung, and thus the king. In the eastern city, open to the outside without mountains, soils were piled up to create man-made hills and willow trees were planted there, in order to fulfill the ideal condition on Feng-shui topography (Kim, 1993:157).

According to Feng-shui, from the point that one stands facing southwards, there must be mountains both on the left and right hand sides, symbolized as an azure dragon and a white tiger respectively. In eastern Seoul, with lack of a natural mountain, the azure dragon, could not form an ideal type of Feng-shui topography. Here, a hill was made artificially with the intention to compensate for such a shortcoming in topography.

Following the idea of a Confucian scholar, To-jŏn Chŏng, the main palace was situated in the foothills of Paekak Mountain, or today's Pukak Mountain, facing toward the south. To-jŏn Chŏng insisted that in terms of Feng-shui doctrines, Paekak Mountain was the main mountain, symbolized by a black turtle, in the background of the entire city. By contrast, the Buddhist monk called Muhak-daesa insisted that Kyŏngbokgung had to face eastward because Paekak Mountain was not the main mountain. The result was that in the interpretation of Feng-shui topography, the Confucian viewpoint was accepted while the Buddhistic one was rejected by the king (Ch'oe, 1984:225). With such an idea on Feng-shui, all the other palaces except Ch'anggyŏnggung meaning the Palace of Bright Rejoicing were also built facing southward. Ch'anggyŏnggung was then facing eastward, as it had been first built by the Koryŏ Dynasty.

It seems that the first king, T'aejo, did not follow the traditional interpretation from Muhak-daesa, but the new one from To-jŏn Chŏng, because he liked the principle from Churyegogonggi that the emperor had to face toward the south. The king really wanted to reflect on the city planning and construction based on Confucianism more than Buddhism or Feng-shui, as he proclaimed Neo-Confucianism as the national religion and ideology. In particular, his intention on Confucian iconography was largely focused on the city layout and the street names.

One of the fundamentals from Churyegogonggi was that when the emperor in the palace was facing southwards with the south gate, the shrine be located on his left hand (eastern) side with the altar on his right hand (western) side. In Seoul with the north-south thoroughfare in the center, Chongmyo was placed on the east, while Sajikdan was placed on the west. The main thoroughfare, running from north to south, began from and ended at the front gate, Kwanghwamun (the Gate of Radiant Transformation), of Kyŏngbokgung in the central northern position (**Figure 33, 34**).

In its original form, it is said that Kyŏngbokgung, the main palace, had about 500 buildings. For the next 200 years it was the seat of government and the royal residence of the Chosŏn Dynasty kings. During the Hideyoshi Invasions, the palace was burned, and left abandoned until 1865, but about 200 structures had been reconstructed by 1872. However, through Japanese colonialism (1910-1945) only 10 of the structures remain today to attest to its former beauty and grandeur.

Figure 33. An old pictorial map of Seoul in the late Chosŏn Period: Herein, one can read the iconography that the Chosŏn Dynasty intended to realize with respect to urban design. The vision of the royal landscapes was stressed as they were exaggerated in the depiction of their physical sizes, Kyŏngbokgung, Ch'angdŏkgung, Kyŏnghŭigung, Chongmyo and Sajikdan. (Source: Chan Lee & Po-gyŏng Yang, 1995, *Old Maps of Seoul, Korea*, Seoul: Seoul Studies Institute, p. 35.)

6. Urban Landscapes

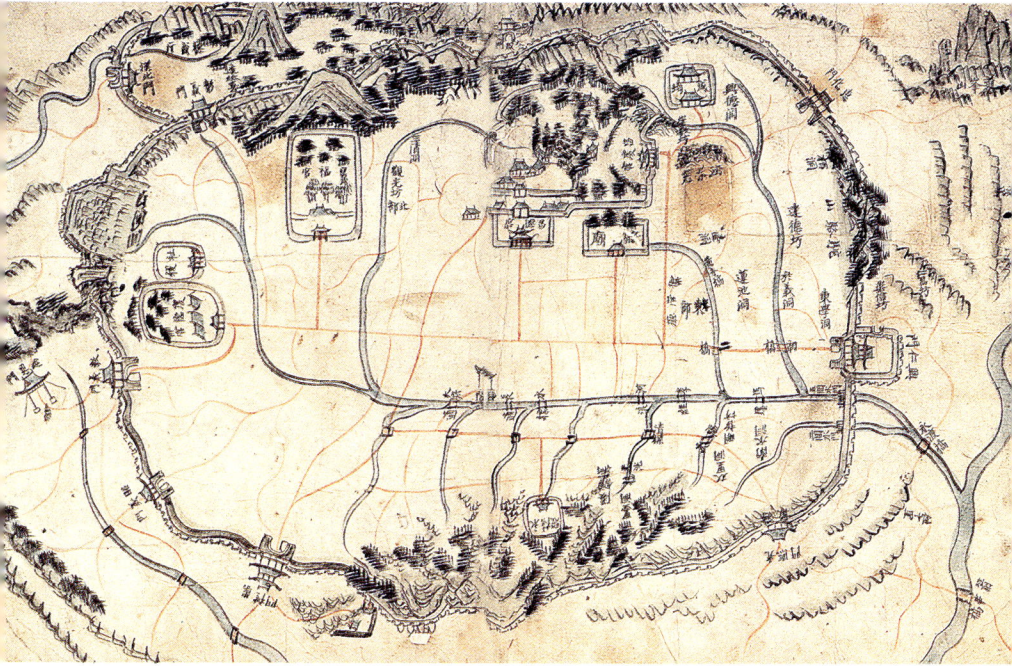

Figure 34. Another old pictorial map of Seoul in the late Chosŏn Period: Herein, only the royal landscapes were depicted in connection with roads, streams, walls, and mountains. (Source: Chan Lee & Po-gyŏng Yang, 1995, *Old Maps of Seoul, Korea*, Seoul: Seoul Studies Institute, p. 42.)

The throne hall called Kŭnjŏngjŏn, or the Hall of Government by Restraint was located inside Kyŏngbokgung and surrounded by the inner wall. Symbolizing the absoluteness of royal power, it was an enormous two-story building, the country's largest wooden structure (**Photo 39**). On the south wall of Kyŏngbokgung was the massive, three-arched Kwanghwamun that was the most impressive palace gate constructed in 1395. Its central door was used by the king, while side doors were used by the fortunate few who were allowed to enter the palace via this front portal.

At the same time Kyŏngbokgung was constructed, the most

Photo 39. Kŭnjŏngjŏn, or the Throne Hall, located inside Kyŏngbokgung, or the Main Palace: Many Koreans are proud of its architectural superiority, such as design, construction method and decoration.

important shrine in the country called Chongmyo was also built to house the tablets of four of King T'aejo's ancestors. Tablets for the Chosŏn Dynasty kings and queens (and a few crown princes who did not rule) have subsequently been added. Expansion of the original building followed periodically, and today two long buildings house these tablets. In 1995, UNESCO added Chongmyo and its ceremonies and music to the list of world heritage sites to be recognized and protected by the world community for its unique cultural value (Nilsen, 1997:162).

At Sajikdan, kings dedicated sacrifices twice a year to ensure successful planting and harvesting. The altars, eastern and western, were the only low flat mounds, and they were surrounded by stone walls. The eastern altar was used in spring to sacrifice to the god of earth; the western altar was used in autumn for the god of five major crops. Today this wooded sanctuary has been turned into a public park with walks and benches, a swimming pool and children's playground, city library, and the like.

2) THE COLONIAL LANDSCAPE IN SEOUL UNDER JAPANESE OCCUPATION

After the Japanese annexation in 1910, a completely new development plan was imposed on Seoul with the name changing into Kyŏngsŏng (Keijō in Japanese). In one generation the city had experienced the metamorphosis from royal capital to colonial base. The Japanese-led city administration ambitiously initiated the colonial transformation of the street network that had already begun in the last epoch of the dynastic period (Lautensach: 1988, 294-295). Two straight, wide east-west streets were intersected by four wide north-south streets, of which the two western ones converged on the South Gate. From there the main route out of the city to the south ran through the suburb of Yongsan to the Han River, and crossed it on a 450m long iron bridge.

Moreover, the Japanese usurped and transformed the dynastic symbols of royal authority in a number of ways. Upon their arrival in 1905, they immediately set about replacing the dynastic power structure and symbols of royal authority with their own. They had consciously set out to modify the landscape of Seoul to reflect their own values. The symbols of power from the Korean king had been eliminated, or taken over in associa-

Reading the Korean Cultural Landscape

Photo 40. An overview of Seoul from Nam Mountain under the Japanese occupation: The buildings for Chosŏn-ch'ongdokbu, or the Japanese Government-General, and Kyŏngsŏngbu, or Seoul City Hall dominated the scene. The Japanese-style houses also occupied the southern part of Seoul near Nam Mountain.

6. Urban Landscapes

Photo 41. The building for Chosŏn-ch'ongdokbu, or the Japanese Government-General in Korea: It had once been used as the main national museum until 1996, the colonial legacy in Korea. In 1996, the Korean government deliberately decided to demolish it in order to erase the shameful memory in Korean minds, and rebuild the palace buildings that had once stood there.

tion with the Japanese imperialism. Other new symbols were put in place to represent the power of the Japanese. The Japanese policy of creating new symbols of authority in Seoul went hand in hand with a policy of undermining the old symbols of authority. The parts of the palace that were not occupied by the government agent were allowed to fall in disrepair.

The northwestern part of Seoul, south of Kyŏngbokgung, became the seat of the colonial government, and there the enormous granite building of Chosŏn-ch'ongdokbu, or the Government-General, dominated the scene (**Photo 40**). It was built in an Americanized Renaissance style crowned by a dome 55m high, and conflicted flagrantly with the architecture of the other buildings in the former royal residence (**Photo 41**). It was constructed by the Japanese in 1926 as the administration office for the government-general. Significantly, it was placed within the boundaries of Kyŏngbokgung directly in line between Kŭnjŏngjŏn and Kwanghwamun, the figurative point of contact between the king and his people. This building symbolically severed any remaining royal authority, and replaced it with the supremacy of the Japanese governor.

The destruction of Kyŏngbokgung was actually begun in secret even prior to the construction of the office building for the government-general. In 1915, the government-general ordered that buildings be demolished to create an open space for an industrial exhibition to take place (Chŏng, 1995:42). This modern type of exhibition was to be the first experience for Koreans. The explicit reason to rationalize their destruction was to transform the Korean consciousness from the feudal into an industrial one, but in fact it was not true. Their implicit motivation was to wipe out the values and erase the symbols attached to Kyŏngbokgung, and thus the national consciousness centering around royal authority.

Kwanghwamun, the most impressive palace gate, was first constructed in 1395, and after being burned in 1592 it was not rebuilt until the late 1860s. During Japanese occupation, it was moved to the east wall, north of the east gate, so as not to block the entrance to the newly constructed office building for the government-general (**Photo 42**). The Japanese planned to demolish the gate, but a Japanese scholar named Yanagi Muneyosi saved it from destruction (Chŏng, 1995:49-55). During the Korean War its wooden top was destroyed when the Office Building for the Government-General was burned. In 1968 it was moved back to its original site, while the

Photo 42. Kwanghwamun, or the Gate of Radiant Transformation, before its relocation in the early Japanese rule: The contemporary architecture is not the original but the rebuilt one, with the name board written in the Korean alphabet, or *Hangŭl*, in 1968.

double-tiered roof was rebuilt in meticulous detail. Its signboard was then written in *Hangŭl* under the late President Chung-hee Park to promote the governmental emphasis on the Korean writing system.

Ch'angkyŏnggung in the northeastern part of the city center was originally built in 1104 on a spot chosen by the Koryŏ Dynasty for a summer palace, and in the 1390s its name was changed by the Chosŏn Dynasty to Ch'angkyŏnggung, or the Palace of Bright Rejoicing. Unlike the north-south orientation of other palaces this palace was laid out into the east-west orientation. During Japanese occupation, however, while a number of old buildings fell in disrepair, a modern red-brick structure in Japanese style was erected on the grounds. There also a botanical garden was started in 1907, and a zoo added in 1909, and finally the designation of *kung* meaning the palace was changed to *won* meaning the park (Chŏng, 1995:296-297). In order to make the park more Japanese-like, cherry trees in large numbers were planted there.

Tŏksugung, or the Palace of Virtuous Longevity was constructed in the mid 1400s as the private residence for the grandson of King Sejo. A great number of buildings in the immediate area disappeared over the years, and a disastrous fire in 1904 greatly modified its original shape and scope. This area was largely encroached upon by the district with the consulates-general from foreign countries, the houses of the Europeans and some of the Protestant mission buildings (Chŏng, 1995:280-283). The City Hall and its front plaza in triangular shape also ate up the space that the palace had once occupied. The principal gate in the south wall, called Taehanmun, was later moved to the east wall, opening onto the City Hall Plaza. Then, it once stood farther in the plaza, but was again moved to its present location because of the traffic problems it created.

On the other hand, Kyŏnghŭigung, or the Palace of Shining Bliss, erected in 1616 near the west gate of the city, completely vanished and was partly replaced by a Japanese school during Japanese colonialism (Chŏng, 1995:300). The palace grounds were planted in mulberry trees, and their leaves were used in silk making. It became known to foreign residents of the city as the Mulberry Palace. Over the years, most of its buildings were moved to other sites in the city for safekeeping. Ch'angdŏkgung, or the Palace of the Illustrious Virtue, is the best preserved out of the five palaces. It was constructed in 1405 as an annex to Kyŏngbokgung with a beautiful garden called Piwon, or the Secret Garden.

In the south, where the Japanese legation was constructed in 1885, the Japanese section spread out on the slopes and at the foot of Nam Mountain. There, stood one and two-story pure Japanese wooden houses with gray tiled roofs in little ornamental gardens. In the Japanese residential area around there, many street names were from personal, historical and geographical names in Japan. By contrast, the old city center, that is the eastern, the central and the central northern part, was still filled with a maze of Korean houses. In this Korean section, The Japanese style of street names could not be imposed because of the resistance from Korean residents.

Near Namdaemun, or the Great South Gate, Seoul Railroad Station was built in a Neo-Renaissance style in 1925. This and other prestigious buildings of the first rank, newly erected, dwarfed the gate. Around here were standing abruptly beside one another one-story old Korean shops, two-story Japanese stores and multi-storied Americanized or Europeanized buildings: banks, department stores, the Central Post Office, City Hall, Citizen's Hall with its tower, and the Chosŏn Hotel.

The narrow "Honmachi" that is now called Myŏngdong was also from the Japanese generic name for a main street, winding its way through the middle of this section in an east-west direction. Along it, multi-storied Japanese shops and restaurants were lined up side by side. Here, life and activity proceeded exactly the same as on a similar street in Japan. The southwestern suburb, called Yongsan, was not only the seat of the head office for national railways, but also the military center with the headquarters of the Japanese army in Korea. Here, too, the Japanese type of buildings and street names predominated the urban scene.

Moreover, when designing a city plan, the Japanese intentionally ignored the Korean traditional belief on environment such as Feng-shui. In the Chosŏn Period, according to Feng-shui, the mountains in four cardinal directions were treated as sacred places, where ordinary people could neither enter nor erect buildings. However, during Japanese occupation, in 1924, Seoul Imperial University was allowed to be established at the foothills of Nak Mountain, the sacred mountain in the east. At the foothills of Yinwang Mountain, the sacred mountain in the west, a nobleman's mansion of Renaissance style was erected in 1915 with permission from the government.

Nam Mountain, the sacred mountain in the south, was the most modified by the Japanese because of its location in the Japanese section. On the western slope of Nam Mountain, in

Photo 43. A Shinto shrine called Chosen Jingu on Nam Mountain: The shrine compound, with its entrance called *dori* in Japanese, occupied an immense tract of land on Nam Mountain. After the liberation from Japanese Colonialism in 1945, it was annihilated to be replaced by Korean monuments, buildings and parks. Only the stairways to the summit are relics from the former shrine compound established by the Japanese.

1925, the Japanese built a shrine for the Meiji emperor in Japan. It was called Chosŏn-shingung (Chosen Jingu in Japanese), and was the most important Shinto temple in Korea (**Photo 43**). This temple and its subsidiary buildings now dominated the mountain scene that had been heavily forested with pine trees. In the Chosŏn Period, on its summit a Shamanistic hall was erected to be dedicated to the mountain deity. It is said that an icon of a Buddhist monk named Muhak-daesa was retained in this hall, and he had once served King T'aejo, the founder of the *Chosŏn* Dynasty, as a royal advisor. In 1925, the Japanese forced this Korean traditional shrine to be removed and relocated at another mountain, called Yinwang Mountain, in order to create their own sacred place (Chŏng, 1995:95).

3) THE ROYAL LANDSCAPE IN CHŎNJU CITY DURING THE CHOSŎN PERIOD

Lying at the edge of the Honam Plain, Korea's largest rice belt, is Chŏnju City, the provincial capital of North Chŏlla Province. The growth of this city was intimately tied with the development of the nation as a whole, especially during the Chosŏn Period. Chŏnju City is the home of the Chŏnju Yi family, from which the long line of the Chosŏn Dynasty kings sprang. For this reason, the dynasty regarded Chŏnju City as an important place, and developed it into the provincial capital of Chŏlla Province, equal to the contemporary provinces of South and North Chŏlla Provinces. The dynasty also paid much attention to the city planning, because it wanted to impose iconographies and symbols on the city planning that represented the royal authority.

6. Urban Landscapes

Prior to the Chosŏn Period, Chŏnju City did not attract any special attention from the central government for political and economical reasons. At the end of the United Shilla Period, in 892, an upstart military leader, Kyŏnhwon, with his power base in Chŏnju City, rebelled against the Shilla Dynasty, and established the Later Paekje Kingdom. Before he was able to take control of the entire peninsula and make Chŏnju City the center of the nation, his troops were defeated in a battle by the Koryŏ army.

After reunifying the country, the Koryŏ Dynasty intentionally curbed the growth of Chŏnju City, by removing its military base and degrading its administrative status (Chang, 1994:32-33). Despite such public discrimination, however, from the late Koryŏ Period Chŏnju City began to grow rapidly as an urban center that dominated the surrounding area.

As in Seoul, the national capital, both Confucianism and Feng-shui were the ideologies being projected on the city planning of Chŏnju City. The city was built as a walled city on level land on the north bank of a stream called Chŏnju-ch'ŏn. The shape of the city was essentially rectangular, and its orientation was towards the four cardinal points of the compass (Ryu, 1987:73). Four gates were installed in the walls at these cardinal points, and these gates controlled the flow of people and goods in and out of the city. The south gate, called P'ungnammun, was particularly the main gate used by outsiders (**Figure 35**).

The south gate was originally constructed in 1389, while the present structure was built in 1768 with the reconstruction of the city walls. When the city walls were torn down at the dawn of Japanese occupation, only this gate, the largest in the province, was left standing. The sturdy stone wall is punctuated

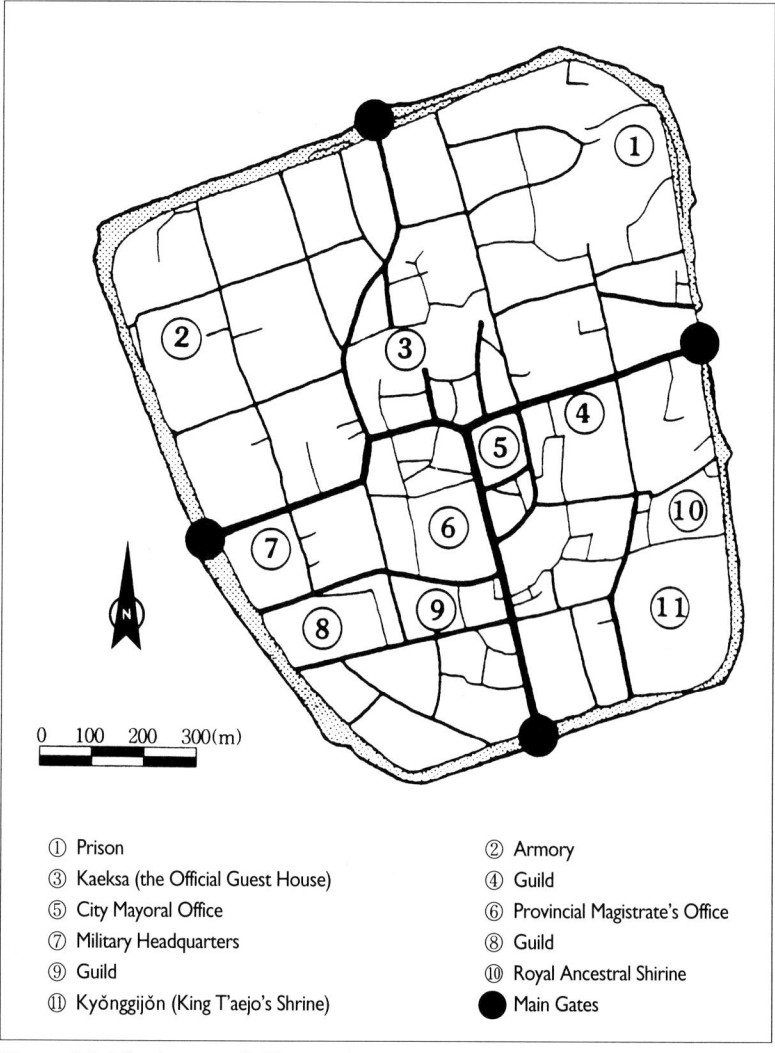

Figure 35. The layout of Chŏnju City in the late Chosŏn Period: Here, the orientation in spatial design did not conform exactly to the four cardinal points of the compass. Kyŏnggijŏn, or King T'aejo's Shrine, above all, occupied the largest tract of land within the walled city. (Source: Je-Hun Ryu, 1987, "Institutionalization and Cultural Adaptaton on the Honam Plain of South Korea: 1789-1982," Unpublished Ph.D. Dissertation, Department of Geography, The University of Texas at Austin, p. 74.)

6. Urban Landscapes

Photo 44. The south gate called P'ungnammun in Chŏnju City: The name in Chinese was borrowed from the home town of the first emperor for the great Han Dynasty in China. The obvious intention was to equal the Chosŏn Dynasty in Korea to the Han Dynasty in China.

by the wide graceful arch of the entry way, topped by a crenelated fence. Set over the entryway and surrounded by a low brick wall is a double-roofed pavilion. To each side is a small open structure; the one with staved sides contains the city bell, while in the other sits a cannon. Such a splendid and grandios architecture, undoubtedly, could manage to represent not only the height of administrative status, but also the greatness of royal authority (**Photo 44**).

Wide avenues from the four gates converged at the center of the city, where public buildings were clustered. Narrow avenues and lanes were densely interwoven in the city's interior. Following the doctrines in Feng-shui, the major avenues from the gates to the center of the city were intersected by irregularly curved, narrow lanes and cul-de-sacs. The main avenue from the south gate, P'ungnammun, served as the principal axis for the layout of residential quarters (Ryu, 1987:73).

Kaeksa, or the Official Guest House, occupied the north central city, interrupting the symmetrical grid pattern of streets. Built in two sections, the roof and veranda were offset on different levels. This building was used as a lodging house for representatives of the king who were in Chŏnju City on official business. The provincial magistrate entertained royal envoys and received royal orders in this building. Herein, a tablet symbolizing royal authority was retained, and in front of it he also held Confucian-style rituals twice a month to pay homage to the royal court.

Symbolically speaking, this building was the most important in the city, representing the royal authority. Probably, for this reason, it was located in the north central section of the city, an imitation of Kyŏngbokgung, or the main palace, in the national capital of Seoul. The main building and its secondary ones formed a building complex, occupying the huge area in the north central section of the city, much larger than any other public building complex. According to Feng-shui, moreover, a man-made mound was placed behind this building complex to create a mountain called Chinsan, symbolically protecting the walled-city of Chŏnju (Chang, 1994:163-164).

Except for Kaeksa and its auxiliary buildings, in the northern section of the city, few public buildings and private houses were constructed to be used. In the northwestern section was the armory; in the northeast section were the archery practice fields. By contrast, the southern section of the city was filled with public buildings and private houses. In addition to the military headquarters, Kamyŏng, or the Offices of the Provincial Magistrate and his assistants of Chŏlla Province, and guilds were located in the southwestern section. In the southeastern section were Puyŏng, or the Offices of the City Mayor and his assistants of Chŏnju Bu.

A Confucian-style shrine called Kyŏnggijŏn was placed in the southeastern section. Its iconography was unique to Chŏnju City, belonging to the Chŏnju Yi family (**Figure 36**). When King T'aejo died in 1408, his second son, King T'aejong, established this shrine in 1410 to commemorate his father (Chang, 1994:74). King T'aejo belonged to the twenty-second generation of the Chŏnju Yi family, and his ancestors from the first to the nineteenth generations continued to reside in Chŏnju City. Based on this historical fact, King T'aejong established a Confucian-style shrine there in dedication to his father, the founder of the dynasty. The shrine was set in a walled compound, within which there was a small hall to preserve a portrait of Sŏng-gye Yi.

Adjoining this shrine in the north, a Confucian-style altar called Chogyŏngdan was later constructed in 1771 (Chang, 1994:81). Here, on the side of a low hill, was the mound-tomb of Han Yi, the founder of the Chŏnju Yi family, and his wife from the Kyŏngju Kim family. Within a brick-wall enclosure to the side of this grave was a diminutive hall that housed their memorial tablet. This shrine, smaller than Kyŏnggijŏn, was sur-

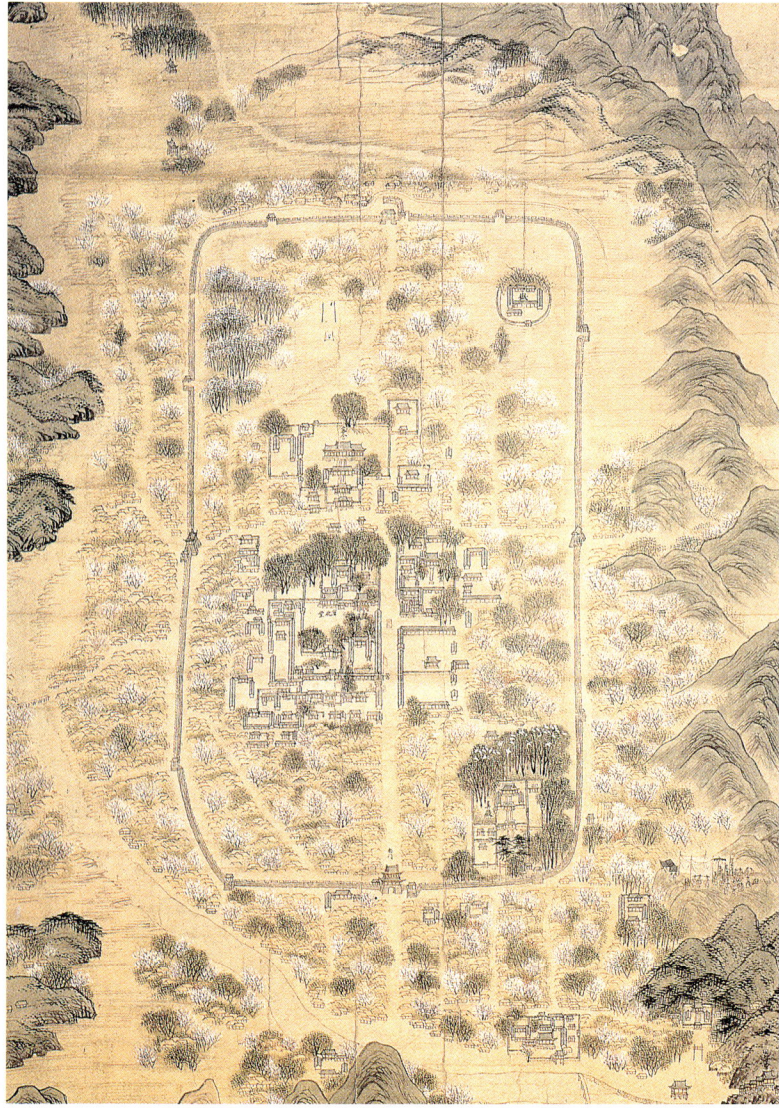

Figure 36. An old pictorial map of Chŏnju City in the late Chosŏn Period: Herein, one can also read the iconography that the royal court wanted to project on the formation of urban landscape. Kyŏnggi-jŏn (King T'aejo's Shrine) and Kaeksa (the Official Guest House) were depicted in exaggeration with dense forests surrounding them. (Source: Chan Lee, 1991, *Old Maps of Korea*, Seoul: Pŏmunsa, p. 291.)

rounded by thick forests resembling other sacred places (**Figure 36**).

The location of Kyŏnggijŏn in the southeastern corner also conforms to the principle in Churyegogonggi, or the knowledge on the classical principles of city planning in China, that the shrine be on the left-hand (eastern) side with the emperor in the center facing southwards. By contrast, here, Sajikdan, or the Altars for the Gods of Earth and Five Crops, were located on the right-hand (western) side, not inside, but outside the walled-city. This means that the fundamentals from Churyegogonggi were also faithfully followed in the city layout of Chŏnju City.

Before Kyŏnggijŏn was built there in 1410, a local Confucian school called *hyanggyo* stood in the vicinity. In complying to the complaints that the ancestral spirits of the Chŏnju Yi family were disturbed by the noise from students reciting books, the buildings of *hyanggyo* were moved further south to the outside of the walled-city in 1479 (Chang, 1994:77). The main hall called Taesŏngjŏn was still located there and rebuilt in 1603. It enshrined memorial tablets for Confucius and 49 other sages. In terms of political power being exercised over physical space, the founder of the Chosŏn Dynasty had surpassed Confucius himself, the founder of Confucianism.

Inside the walls, business and commercial activity agglomerated in a district sharply skewed in the direction of the city's main commercial trade routes, with its center in Kaeksa. Guilds were located in the southern section, where paper and fans were the specialized items. Artisans working there did not reside with the guild leaders inside, but outside the walls of the city. They commuted to their work daily from the southern suburb. Shops selling tins and brass containers were clustered along the avenue from Kaeksa to the north gate, while those of silversmiths lined the avenue that ran to the west gate.

In the late Chosŏn Period, periodic markets were held in front of the two gates: the west and south gates. The north and east gates were, however, closed to ordinary entrance. The south-gate market was the larger and busier one of them, because it was at the most convenient location for merchants from outside the city and consumers within to meet. Outside the walls, the southern suburb was the residential area for public servants, artisans and merchants (Ryu, 1987:76).

4) THE COLONIAL LANDSCAPE IN CHŎNJU CITY UNDER JAPANESE OCCUPATION.

Even prior to the Japanese annexation in 1910, many public buildings in the walled-city of Chŏnju began to be razed and replaced by modern buildings to be used as schools, post offices, banks, hospitals and police stations. The walls were torn down to broaden the roads that encircled the city. The Japanese built modern buildings for the provincial governor and his officials on the site where Kamyŏng, or the Provincial Magistrate Office, was once located.

The destruction of walls symbolically meant the disappearance of iconography from the urban scene that had represented the royal authority. During the dynastic period the walls served as not only physical, but also mental barriers, separating the rulers from the ruled. In the southwestern corner of the city, in particular, the walls were very important in protecting the sacred place, the shrine for the Chŏnju Yi family, from the secular world. At the turn of the century, moreover, the walls were viewed as preventing the Japanese from penetrating into the city. In Chŏnju City, therefore, the popular resistance to the destruction of walls was more fierce than in any other city in Korea.

Once the destruction of walls was publicly approved in 1907, the walls had all disappeared within four years, by 1911 (Chang, 1994:207-231). In other cities, by contrast, the walls were all gone at earlier times and at higher speeds: Seoul from 1907 to 1908; T'aegu City from 1906 to 1907. The materials from the walls were used either to reclaim the ponds and swamps or construct the modern buildings in the city. For instance, a Catholic church called Kijŏn Church was built in Romanesque style, and its building materials were earth and stone from the western-side walls.

After 1907, the new highway connecting Kunsan City, previously the Japanese concession settlement, to Chŏnju City entered the city at the west gate, and the road from the west gate to the south gate was widened (Ryu, 1987:141). Large numbers of Japanese merchants, craftsmen and artisans opened shops and established residences along this avenue between the west and south gates. This avenue, dominated by western and Japanese-style architecture, eventually emerged as the main Japanese business and commercial street in Chŏnju City (**Photo 45**). Meanwhile, the street from the south gate to the center of the city remained important in the commercial activity of local Koreans.

When straightening and broadening these streets, the Japanese forcefully got rid of any physical obstacles lying ahead in the direction of road construction. The street from the south

Photo 45. Japanese-style shops on the street in Chŏnju City under the Japanese occupation: Along the street named Taga-dong, one can easily recognize the colonial legacy in architecture. There are now several restaurants, still in business, with Japanese-style architecture in a good state of preservation.

gate to the center of the city was extended northward in 1914, and public buildings, including the building complex around Kaeksa, or the Official Guest House, were removed. The main east-west street was also straightened to form a more typical Milesian cross. Here, like other colonial cities in the 1920s, the street pattern became a more rectangular grid with major north-south and east-west thoroughfares, forming the main streets of the city (**Figure 37**).

In the meantime, the areas that Confucian-style buildings had once occupied, were largely replaced by modern buildings and streets (Chang, 1994: 254-259). In addition to Kaeksa, the major victims were the buildings of Puyŏng (the Mayoral Office), Kamyŏng (the Provincial Magistrate Office), and Kyŏnggijŏn

(King T'aejo's Shrine). In the Chosŏn Period, in fact, these buildings and the open spaces associated with them had once dominated the overall scene of the city.

When the Governor's Office of North Chŏlla Province was built in Renaissance style by the Japanese to replace the Magistrate Office called Sŏnhwadang, most of the old buildings were torn down by 1921, with the total built-up area being reduced by more than half. The Municipal Hall of Renaissance style, too, replaced the dynastic mayoral office, called P'ungrakhŏn, in 1934, while the total area was reduced more than ten times by 1945.

In 1911, in order to open a broad street between the south gate and Kyŏnggijŏn, once occupied by the walls, the eastern portion of Kyŏnggijŏn yielded to the street under construction. On its western portion, a girl's elementary school was established to provide education for the Japanese subjects. As a result, here, the total built-up area was reduced by less than half. In such a sacred place as Kyŏnggijŏn, the construction of secular buildings was totally unthinkable in the Chosŏn Period, and if so, it definitely caused a death penalty. By doing so, however, the Japanese deliberately wanted to weaken the symbolic power of the iconography associated with royal authority.

In 1912, local Koreans in Chŏnju City protested strongly against the construction of a main railroad called Honam-sŏn, and it had to run from Seoul through Yiksan City. In 1929, however, the railroad called Chŏlla-sŏn, the branch line from Honam Railroad, was finally extended from Yiksan City to Chŏnju City. Then, a railroad station was erected in the northern suburb beyond the former site of the north gate (Ryu, 1987:141). Consequently, the main north-south street was

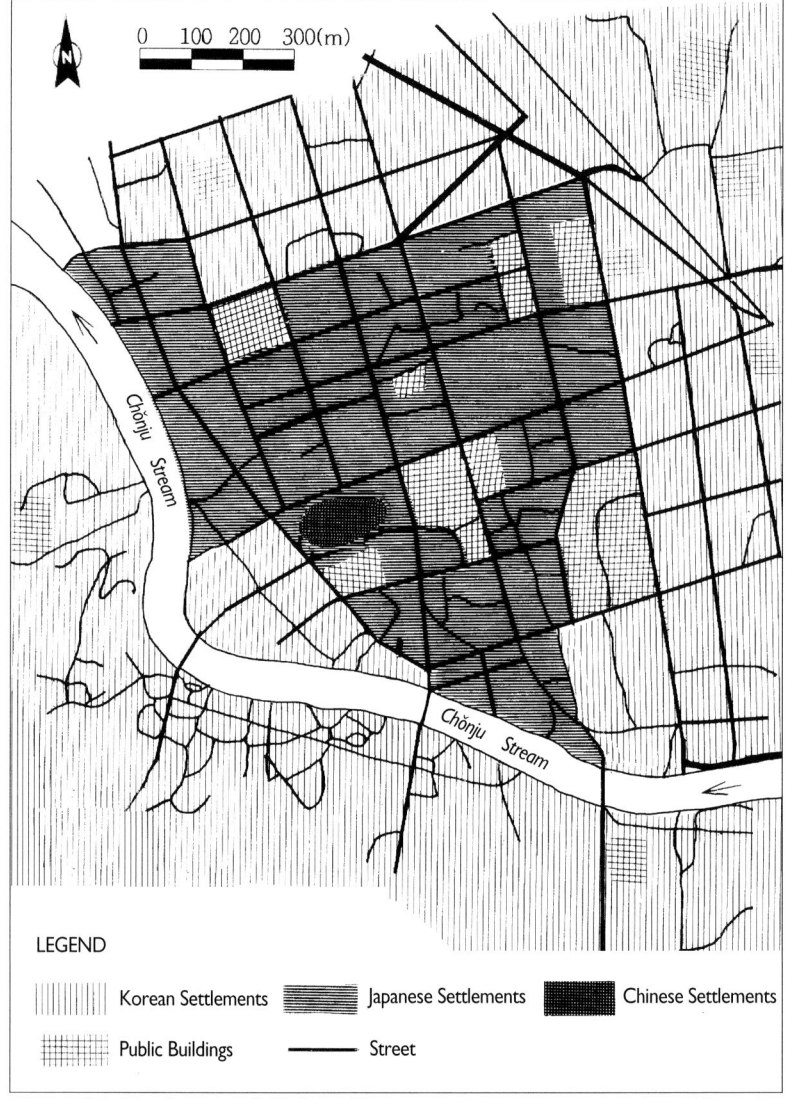

Figure 37. The layout of Chŏnju City under Japanese occupation: After the construction of the railroad called Chŏllasŏn in 1919, the Japanese expanded their residence into every direction including the core of the city, once occcupied by Koreans. The Chinese, by contrast, were more or less confined to a small portion of land in the southwestern corner of the city. (Source: Myŏng-su Chang, 1994, *A Study on the Development of City Walls and Urban Planning in Chŏnju City*, Seoul: Hakyŏnmunhwasa, p. 270.)

extended to this depot, attracting many Japanese business and commercial activities into this area.

The Japanese, once warily confined in the avenue between the south and west gates, were gradually encouraged to venture into the other streets of the city. With the support from the railroad along with the colonial government, the Japanese finally seized the power to dominate the local Korean in the competition over space (Chang, 1994:250-252). With this north-south thoroughfare serving as the main axis of commercial activity for the entire city, the core of the city, formerly dominated by dynastic officials and their families, came to be occupied by Japanese merchants, craftsmen, artisans and their families (**Figure 37**).

Here, many Japanese shops were unassuming wooden buildings, usually not more than two stories high, with two gabled roofs and walls paneled with horizontal boards that overlapped like tiles. However, in the construction of public buildings, such as the Governor's Office, pure natural stone, particularly granite, was chosen in addition to cement and reinforced concrete. Many banks, schools, barracks and department stores were built of brick, often having the ungainly box shape that was so easily connected with this material. In terms of architectural style, they were varied Europeanized and Americanized ones slightly altered by Japanese influence (Chang, 1994:263-264).

In the city development, moreover, the Japanese played down the traditional value of Feng-shui in an intentional effort not to respect it as an important principle to follow. The landscapes, artificially made in association with Feng-shui, had once created a sense of place whereby people could feel at home while sharing symbolic meanings in common. People, both the rulers and the ruled, indeed, attached special symbolic meanings to such landscapes as man-made forests and ponds, even though they had been originally made for a practical purpose. The physical destruction of these Feng-shui landscapes, therefore, meant the eradication of a special sense of place in the people's mind.

In the late Chosŏn Period, to fulfill the ideal type of Feng-shui topography, ponds were dug and trees were planted to form forests around them in the northern direction, both inside and outside the city. It was popularly believed that from the standpoint of Feng-shui, there, topography had a geographical shortcoming because of its plainness and openness. The mountains and hills surrounding the city did not stretch into the northeastern direction, where plain lands were open northwards. This symbolic interpretation also contained a practical meaning that once broken out in the north, fire would quickly proceed to the city in the south during the winter time when a strong northwesterly wind blew.

In 1767, it is said that a big fire in the north moved within a second on a strong wind, burning down about a thousand houses to the south. After this incident, in 1796, a pond, called Hyŏnmuji, with its circumference around 100m, was dug in the northeastern corner of the city (Chang, 1994:161-162). In the northwestern suburb, a Shamanistic hall was erected for the mountain deity in an old temple, called Chinbuk Temple, and trees were planted there in a row to form an artificial forest, called Supjŏngi. This forest, then, was supposed to protect the city from the wind, real or symbolic, blowing from the north.

Upon this folk belief, people decided to make artificial landscapes, such as ponds and forests, to solve this geographical problem. Based on Feng-shui, they interpreted that the natural disasters, the fire and the wind, usually from the north, would pass through the northwestern section into the city. They imagined that the water in the ponds would extinguish the fire while the trees in the forests blocked the wind from the north.

The Japanese, nonetheless, almost ignored this value of Feng-shui, because they wanted to create their own sense of place in the way they had been used to. First, they reclaimed all the ponds and swamps in the walled city into cultivatable lands. The small mound, called *chosan*, which was built behind the Official Guest House, Kaeksa, to create an enclosed Feng-shui topography, was completely demolished. The forests in the northwestern suburb were all gone due to the lack of public control.

The only Feng-shui landscape remaining then was a large pond called Tŏkjinji, which has continued to exist until today in the northwestern section of the modern city. It is said that this pond had been originally constructed as a moat to defend the city fortress about 1,100 years ago (Nilsen, 1997:670). However, in the late Chosŏn Period, it may have been reinterpreted as a Feng-shui landscape to make up the geographical weakness of the city.

5) THE ROYAL LANDSCAPE IN KYŎNGJU CITY DURING THE CHOSŎN PERIOD

Kyŏngju City, once the capital of the Shilla Kingdom, is known today as the most important of ancient cultural cities in Korea. UNESCO selected Kyŏngju City as one of the world's 10 most important ancient cultural cities (Nilsen, 1997:429). Of the ancient kingdom, however, only the stone structures, a portion of artwork, and its legends remain. Kyŏngju City and its environs contain hundreds of royal tombs, temples, palace sites, fortress ruins, pagodas and rock sculptures.

Before the first century, a walled town called Saro or Sorabŏl grew in size and influence, and took on a dominant role when the walled towns formed a confederation. This federation gradually developed into a state, called Shilla, and from its leading family clans (Pak, Sŏk, Kim) sprang the entire line of Shilla royalty. By the third century, Saro became known as Kŭmsŏng in Chinese or "the City of Gold," only later to be called Kyŏngju City. Eventually, Shilla became the first unifier of the peninsula, initiating 250 years of relative peace and prosperity of the United Shilla Period. During this time, the kingdom ushered in a cultural renaissance, with Kyŏngju City, the capital, receiving the most benefits.

By the early 900s, the United Shilla Kingdom had hit rock bottom, and by the 920s, it was a country only in name. Much of its land had been taken by the increasingly powerful Later Paekje and Koryŏ States, themselves vying for dominance on the peninsula. In the end, shortly after the surrender of the United Shilla Kingdom, the king named Kŏn Wang conquered the Later Paekje forces and once again united the peninsula under one monarch. A new capital was established in Kaesŏng City on the central-western coast, and with its diminished status the city's name, Kŭmsŏng, was changed to Kyŏngju City. From the Koryŏ Period, Kyŏngju City began to serve as the provincial capital of Kyŏngsang Province, which had lasted until the late Chosŏn Period when the provincial capital was moved to T'aegu City.

6. Urban Landscapes

Photo 46. The old city walls remaining in the center of Kyŏngju City: Most of the city walls were torn down even before the Japanese annexation in 1910. Even the remaining section, small in size, has not been preserved in its original shape.

Presumably, the Koryŏ Dynasty wanted to erase the iconography associated with the Shilla Dynasty's royal authority, and replace it with its own. However, few relics in the cultural landscape have remained up to today to contain the iconography from the Koryŏ Period. Only a few sections of the city walls can be seen in the center of the city (**Photo 46**). It was first built in 1012, and repaired again during the Chosŏn Dynasty (Han, 1993:85). However, it seems that the Chosŏn Dynasty simply took over the city-layout largely from the Koryŏ Dynasty, only with a minor modification. The street pattern, then, was basically the same as in the Koryŏ Period, similar to a grid pattern. The locations of important public buildings might have been the same as in the Koryŏ Period (**Figure 38**).

263

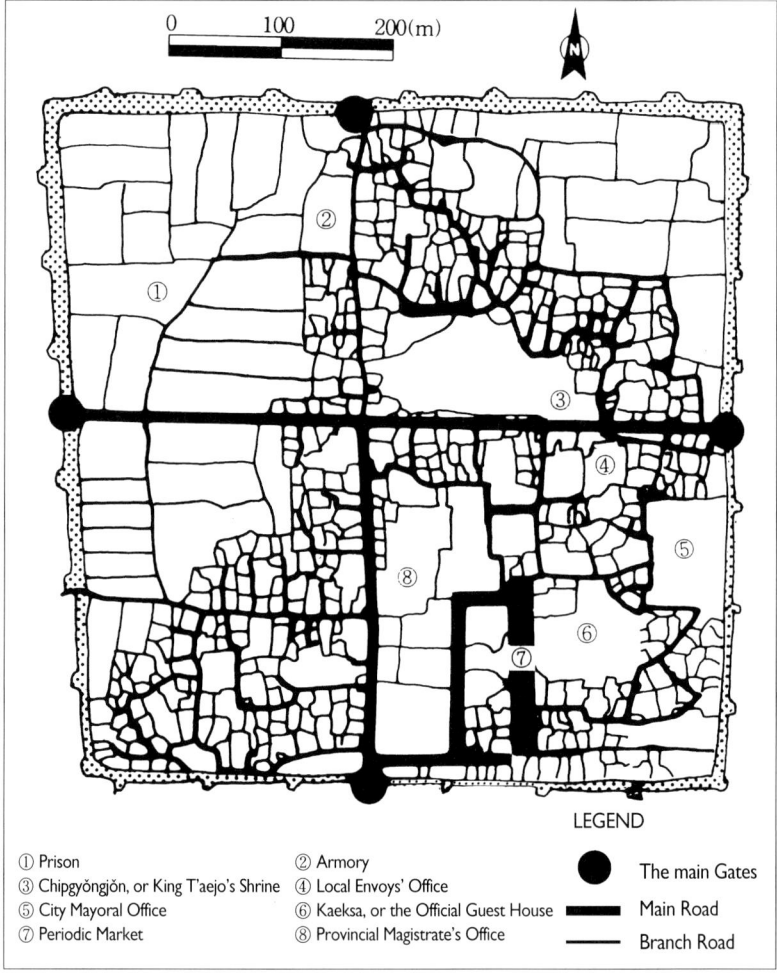

Figure 38. The layout of Kyŏngju City in the late Chosŏn Period: Unlike Chŏnju City, Kaeksa (the Official Guest House), Puyŏng (the Provincial Magistrate's Office) and their annex buildings were all located in the southeastern quarter of the walled city. The periodic market was unusually allowed to be open in front of Kaeksa inside the city walls. Chipgyŏngjŏn (King T'aejo's Shrine), above all, occupied the largest tract of land within the walled city. (Source: Sam-gŏn Han, 1993, "A Study on the Transformation of Urban Space in Kyŏngju City from Chosŏn Dynasty to Japanese Colonialism," Unpublished Ph.D. Dissertation, Department of Architecture, Kyoto University, p. 107.)

In the Chosŏn Period, on the other hand, the rulers imposed their own iconographies on Kyŏngju City to deliver the Confucian ideology and demonstrate the royal authority to the ruled. In the making of iconographies, they did not create entirely new landscapes, but decorated the ancient landscapes from the Shilla Period with their own reinterpretation. They reinterpreted the ancient landscapes from the standpoint of Confucianism as if they were texts. By ascribing their own ideological and symbolic meanings to them, the rulers forced the ruled to accept the new sense of place. Through imbueing their own sense of place, the rulers pursued to discipline the ruled to be docile while indoctrinating them with Confucian ideology

On a pictorial map drawn in the late Chosŏn Period, a Confucian-style shrine called Chipgyŏngjŏn was nearly occupying the whole northeastern quarter of the walled city. This map shows that the shrine compound consisted of a *pigak* (a pavilion for the stone monument), a *sŏksil* (a stone or sepulchral chamber), and a *hongsalmun* (a red gate with bars on top). A pavilion called *pigak* was placed in front of a stone chamber called *sŏksil*, while the red gate, *hongsalmun*, was located in front of the pavilion. The compound was also surrounded by a thick forest, demonstrating that it was an important sacred place.

Here, the Chosŏn Dynasty decided to construct a Confucian-style shrine because the stone chamber was there (**Photo 47**). It is said that during the Unified Shilla Period, a detached palace or a royal villa called Chipgyŏngjŏn was built around there. Upon his father's death, the son, King T'aejong, ordered that the portrait of King T'aejo be preserved in the stone chamber, and that the area around it be turned into a shrine compound. During the Hideyoshi Invasions, however, the por-

Photo 47. The Stone Chamber from the United Shilla Kingdom in Kyŏngju City: Under Japanese occupation, the royal shrine compound called Chipgyŏngjŏn was mostly encroached upon by secular buildings, and only the stone chamber remains today in imperfect form.

trait was moved to another place, and the shrine compound was completely destroyed. After that time, the buildings in the compound were never returned to the original state.

When King Chŏngjo (1752-1800) heard about this situation, he ordered that a pavilion be erected there to retain the stone monument on which five words were inscribed (Han, 1993:101-104). It is said that the five words inscribed on the stone monument were his own calligraphy. This inscription reads that this is the old location of Chipgyŏngjŏn. While writing the words with his own hands, he wanted to revive the place image that the shrine compound should belong to King T'aejo, the founder of the Chosŏn Dynasty. King Chŏngjo deliberately overlaid the old sense of place with the new one by juxtaposing them at one place.

In order to create a sense of place in association with the royal authority, the Koryŏ Dynasty made full use of Feng-shui and Buddhism. The Chosŏn Dynasty, by contrast, basically referred to Confucianism in the making of royal iconography and symbolic landscape. In the landscaping of a city, Feng-shui, once influencing most during the Koryŏ Period, now yielded its prime position to Confucianism. In Kyŏngju City, for instance, the royal tombs were often used as the means to express Confucian ideology as well as Feng-shui doctrines in material forms.

Between the 18th and the 19th centuries, the dynasty established the Confucian-style shrines at the royal tombs that had been constructed in Kyŏngju City during the Shilla Period. In 1723, the dynasty built a Confucian-style hall called Sungdŏkjŏn, to house the memorial tablet of Pakhyŏkgŏse, the first king of the Shilla Kingdom, at the group of five tombs called Onŭng (Han, 1993:148-149). It is believed that King Hyŏkgŏse and his wife Queen Aryŏng, and the kings of Namhae, Yuri and P'asa are buried here, all from the Pak family. Semi-annual memorial ceremonies were held in Confucian style here at the hall called Sungdŏkjŏn. The buildings at the front of the walled compound were used for the preparation of these ceremonies.

In 1888, to the west of the contemporary Taenŭngwon, or Tumulus Park, the dynasty established a Confucian-style shrine called Sunghyejŏn, where ancestral ceremonies were dedicated to the three kings with the family name Kim (**Photo 48**). Here, originally only the portrait of King Kyŏngsun had been retained in a hall called Kyŏngsunwangjŏn or Kyŏngsunwang-yŏngsa. With the memorial tablets of King Mich'u and King Munmu

Photo 48. Taenŭngwon, or Tumulus Park in Kyŏngju City: A cluster of royal tombs in the south of the walled city is now called Taenŭngwon, or Tumulus Park. These huge tombs are open to the public who are interested in climbing them, but the owners of these tombs are all unknown to the public.

being added, the name was changed to Sunghyejŏn, more Confucian in style. Inside the shrine were two buildings: one containing the memorial tablets for three Kim family members who became Shilla kings: King Mich'u, the first king from the Kim family; King Munmu who completed the unification of the country; and King Kyŏngsun, the last of the Shilla rulers (Nilsen, 1997:436). In the second building, there was the tablet of Alji, the legendary founder of the Kim family line.

As the shrines for the natural deities were publicly neglected, many of them usually located on the mountains disappeared from the scene. Moreover, people did not like to locate Confucian-style shrines in the remote mountains that were difficult to visit. In 1898, there was a petition from the members of the Sŏk family that the shrine of King T'al-hae Sŏk called Sŏkt'alhaesa,

6. Urban Landscapes

Figure 39. An old pictorial map of Kyŏngju City in the late Chosŏn Period: Herein, one can also interpret the iconography that rulers from the Chosŏn Dynasty wanted to impose on the formation of urban landscape. Ponghwangdae (Chinese Phoenix Height) was depicted much larger than in actuality, reflecting the importance of Feng-shui as an ideology at that time. (Source: Chan Lee, 1991, *Old Map of Korea*, Seoul: Pŏmunsa, p. 314)

Photo 49. Ponghwangdae, or the Chinese Phoenix Height in Kyŏngju City: In the Chinese myth, the imaginary bird, *ponghwang*, is believed to be an animal auspicious for human beings. Folks believing in Feng-shui, therefore, liked to visualize a hill or mountain of triangular shape as the flying Chinese phoenix.

be moved from the summit of T'oham Mountain down to the site of Panwolsŏng, or the Crescent Moon Fortress. At that time this fortress, built sometime around A.D. 100, lay in the south of the city. Upon this petition, the mayor of Kyŏngju City rebuilt the shrine at the site of Panwolsŏng, and changed the name to Sungshinjŏn, parallel with such shrine name as Sungdŏkjŏn or Sunghyejŏn (Han, 1993:155).

During the Chosŏn Period, though not so often as Confucianism, Feng-shui was also consulted in the use of tombs to create a sense of place in Kyŏngju City. In terms of Feng-shui topography, for example, a tomb called Ŭnryŏngch'ong was interpreted symbolically as a special mountain called *ansan*, on the opposite (southern) side of the city. It is the largest among the tombs that have been handed down from the Shilla Period, 22m in height and 250m in circumference (**Figure 39**).

On its slope they planted a few trees to make it look like a natural hill, and they placed an altar to perform the ritual in front of a tree. People also offered it a Feng-shui type name, Ponghwangdae, which literally means a "Chinese Phoenix Height (**Photo 49**)." They composed this symbolic name because the tomb had appeared to them on the opposite (northern) side like a Chinese phoenix, the imaginary bird. According to Feng-shui, this bird, though not real but imagined, is believed to bring much fortune and happiness to human beings. The name, therefore, was pregnating the popular wishes about their ordinary lives at that time.

7. Conclusion

7. Conclusion

A simple objective procedure for localizing cultural boundaries is to superimpose as many maps as possible of different traits, and establish boundaries where "bundles" cluster. Within these "bundles" of lines, taken as cultural boundaries, it should be possible to find "culture areas." The investigation of the past and present distribution of cultural traits constitutes the basis for recognition and delimitation of culture areas. The culture area, in geographic terms, may constitute a "region," forming a definable unit in space.

In this book, the method of mapping linguistic traits was applied to drawing linguistic boundaries in Korea. The result is that linguistic boundaries between northern and southern dialects appear as bundles of lines, on the east as well as west coasts. The isoglosses between them run from east to west across the territories of Kangwon Province and Ch'ungch'ŏng Province, and crisscross one another to form bundles on the east and west coasts.

On the east coast, isoglosses concentrate in the zone between Kangnŭng City and Samch'ŏk City, where a hybrid sub-dialect is widely spoken. The most important factors in the formation of this sub-dialect are the topography and geopolitical location. The T'aebaek Range serves as a natural barrier, and so it is difficult to cross over it from Seoul. By contrast, the movement between north and south along the coast was much easier.

The isoglosses from east to west are merged into a narrow zone, and the zone becomes wider as they get closer to the west coast. In the interior, the Sobaek Range acts as a natural boundary against which northern dialects confront southern ones. A series of isolgosses on the west coast form a wide zone, stretching from Asan Bay to the Kŭm River, topographically a hill country with elevation no less than 200m. Moreover, the relics of ancient language from the Paekje Kingdom are better preserved on the rim of the west coast, the T'aean Peninsula, where the delicate crenulation of the ingression coast with lots of small bays and peninsulas produces many small isolated places.

The typical association of geographical features within a region may be described as a "landscape." The cultural landscape, then, connotes the geographical content of a determined area, and serves as criteria for regional classification. In this book, using this method, a variety of religious, folk, linguistic, rural and urban landscapes could be identified, and their regions were recognized and delimited.

Within religious landscapes, it was discovered that each of Catholicism, Protestantism, Buddhism, and Neo-Confucianism showed a definable unit of distribution in the cultural landscape: Catholicism around Ansŏng Town, Protestantism around Yŏngdŭngp'o Railroad Station, Buddhism in southwestern Korea, and Neo-Confucianism around Andong City.

These religious landscapes, with their own distinctive architectures, are easily observable in the field trip. Catholic and Protestant churches with cross symbols can be distinguished from Buddhist temples with 卍 symbols. Neo-Confucian academies called *sŏwon* are different from Buddhist temples in building styles and colors. Protestant churches concentrated in the cities more than any other religious landscape including Catholic churches. Buddhist temples were basically seen in the countryside, but now appear once in a while in the cities. *Sŏwon*, or the private Confucian academies, are exclusively located in the countryside, where *yangban* families had once concentrated in the Chosŏn Period.

In the upper reaches of the Nakdong River, in particular around Andong City, *sŏwon* are most heavily concentrated to form a unique cultural region, called the Andong Culture Area. During the Chosŏn Period, this region served as a seed-bed for the private academies to proliferate after the first introduction. In the Yŏngdŭngp'o District, Protestantism, in particular Presbyterianism, has led the religious life of residents, and Protestant churches can be seen almost everywhere at favorable locations. In southern Korea, two out of three principal temples in Korea are situated at foothills of mountains considered sacred by Buddhists: T'ongdo Temple at Yŏngch'wi Mountain in southeastern Korea; Songkwang Temple at Chogye Mountain in southwestern Korea. Each of these temples has served as headquarters to extend its religious area around it. Southern Korea, by and large, has been relatively strong in Buddhistic culture as compared with other areas in Korea.

In Korea, folk beliefs are retreating in the countryside, while Shamanism is rampant all over the country. However, Kyeryong Mountain has been the most sacred mountain for shamans

7. Conclusion

to visit for their praying or rituals called *kut*. There are many places that tempted shamans to erect halls in Kyeryong Mountain. Deep valleys under high peaks are the locations where Shamanistic halls called *tang* have been concentrated. Many Buddhist halls are also scattered in the mountain, housing Shamanists who would come for night prayers. On Cheju Island, particularly in Tongch'on (the Eastern Region), *ponhyangdang*s (main spirit halls), have survived a series of oppressions in the Chosŏn Period. Shamans are usually invited to perform village rituals at these halls, normally hidden in the woods.

There are numerous deities in village rituals, and plurality of deities is an important characteristic of village rituals in Korea. In the upper valleys of the Kŭm River, village rituals have been preserved relatively well. Here, most of the deities at the entrance of a village are made from local materials, easily obtainable near the river stream: *sŏndol* (standing stone) and *tolt'ap* (pebble-pile or stone pagoda). The isolated locations and physical conditions made by the topography of the canyons contributed to the preservation of these folk landscapes.

On the islands in the southwestern sea called Tadohae, village deities are multiple, not only in numbers, but also in kinds, with some remnants of ancient origins. On an island, plural deities often co-exist in harmony with one another: animistic, Shamanistic and Confucian deities. The changes between islands in the kinds of village deities and styles of village rituals are gradual, overlapping on the islands between the near sea and the distant sea. The farther one travels from the mainland into the sea, the more likely one can observe Shamanistic rituals. On the islands in the distant sea, almost every village performs the ritual for the deity of the dragon king, and the deity type and ritual style are also exclusively Shamanistic.

On the other hand, rural landscapes that may best represent the national identity of Korea are *yangban* lineage villages, *chŏngja*s (pavilions), irrigation networks, folk housing, and village forests. Like religious and folk landscapes, these rural landscapes are basically universal all over Korea, but with some extent of regionalizaton or localization. Around Andong City, one can see *yangban* lineage villages with other Confucian landscapes more often than in any other area in Korea. The method of mapping the distribution pattern and tracing the diffusion process demonstrates a regional structure consisting of core and periphery. In the tributary of the Namhan River, *yangban* families competed with one another to build as many pavilions as possible. Pavilions, picturesquely set into nature at particularly attractive scenic spots in the vicinity of villages, have no side walls so that the eye can roam freely to enjoy the beautiful scenery to all sides.

Folk housing on the west bank of the Nakdong River represents the Korean invention to combine the wooden veranda called *maru* and the heating system called *ondol* under a roof of a house. Here, one can find a variety of house types, northern or southern, and even mixed ones. The northern and intermediate types frequently interrupt continuous distribution of southern types, and the mixed type between them does appear once in a while. On the Honam Plain, a system of web-like irrigation networks have developed as if it were a nerve system in the human body. From Japanese colonialism it emerged as the major rice belt in Korea at the same time with the integration of irrigation networks. In each valley of the Mangyŏng River and the Tongjin River, a single system of irrigation networks, large in size, evolved during Japanese colonialism.

On the south coast, one can often find village forests, once sacred by villagers, and here a variety of tree species form a vegetation community of multiple layers. From north to south on the coast, pine trees tend to lose their niches as dominant species, while zelkova and other trees replace them. Once in a while, evergreen trees, such as Camellia japonica or Torreya nucifera, appear in the middle of these trees. In Korea, this is the only place on the mainland where one can feel somewhat close to a sub-tropical landscape. These village forests, even with short evergreen trees intermingled with tall summergreen trees, sometimes form an exotic- and nice-looking vegetation community. Villagers used to perform village rituals regularly in these sacred forests, which in turn would protect the village from the wind.

The evolution of a landscape is a gradual and cumulative process and it has its own local history. The present landscape may reflect a local history of migration or diffusion. Cultural geography, therefore, is to discover four kinds of facts: the origin in time and place of given landscapes; the routes, times and manner of their dissemination; the distribution of former culture areas; and the character of former cultural landscapes.

However, first of all, to discover these four facts fully requires accurate information about cultural origin and diffusion or movement of people. A professional field work based on written documents can only supply materials to infer the facts about migration and diffusion. Moreover, if a cultural landscape has a relatively short history, field work may be much easier to carry out. In Korea, the cultural landscapes that make such inference feasible are some of the religious and linguistic landscapes, with written documents or short histories.

Catholicism was introduced into Korea in the late 18th century, and persecution was very intense from 1801 to 1869. During this time of persecution, Catholicism was spread into remote mountain valleys where Korean Catholics hid themselves. A mountainous area in the east of Ansŏng Town had geographical conditions, ideal for them to be secluded. Until religious freedom was given to Christianity in 1898, Korean Catholics were largely restricted to the countryside with their headquarters, and a mountain pass called Paet'i in this mountainous area was one of them. After a French priest was dispatched to Ansŏng Town in 1901, Catholicism was diffused rapidly into the plain areas to the west of Ansŏng Town, and around it an important Catholic region was formed.

In the upper reaches of the Nakdong River a private Confucian academy called Sosu Academy was established, and it was the first academy in Korea in 1542. Between the late 17th and early 19th century, private Confucian academies grew in large number, with the heaviest concentration in Andong City. After Tosan Academy was established by disciples of Hwang Yi in 1574, those who followed Hwang Yi's teachings were in competition to erect their own private Confucian academies.

The first Protestant missionaries did not arrive in Korea until 1884, and in the Yŏngdŭngp'o District the first Presbyterian church called Yŏngdŭngp'o Changro Church was established in 1903. Here, since then, believers in Protestantism have grown remarkably to outnumber those in any other religions. In the 1970s and 1980s, in particular, Presbyterian churches grew explosively in number along with urban population. Within

Protestantism, today, Presbyterianism maintains its prime position, and Methodist comes next to it in terms of church membership. The Presbyterians have been strategic experts at not only securing favorable locations, but also applying missionary tactics.

On the southwest coast, peninsulas, large islands and bays follow each other closely, so that there is no room for a straight stretch of coast between them. In the diffusion of language, the sea between peninsulas and islands served either as natural barriers or routes, depending on the situation at that time. Some linguistic elements were diffused easily by way of sea routes, while others were not. Then, if a place is almost inaccessible to linguistic diffusion, it may develop into a "linguistic island." On the southwest coast, two large peninsulas are separated by large bays, which in turn served as natural barriers to linguistic diffusion from the west. Among them, a peninsula called the Kohŭng Peninsula, in particular, represents not only a main divide of dialects, but a linguistic island preserving ancient vocabulary.

In reality, by both internal evolution and diffusion, a culture grows and spreads. Individual cultural landscapes can become widely distributed through contact of peoples, without any population movements taking place. In Korea, where folk cultures could spread without as well as with migration, it is difficult to relate the origin and diffusion of a certain folk landscape directly to migration. Instead, it is likely to be related to the internal evolution or local adaptation to environment, physical and social. It is a concrete product of the complicated interplay between a human community and its natural conditions. It is a heritage of many years of cultural evolution or many generations of human adaptation to physical environment: the overall pattern of mountains, hills and rivers; the climate; the ocean coasts.

It is the floor plan that shows strikingly regional and local contrasts in Korean folk housing. A certain regional type of folk housing can generally be recognized from the combination pattern of the wooden veranda called *maru* and the heating system called *ondol*. It is believed that *maru* and *ondol* were adopted together in the middle of Korea to overcome cold winter and hot summer. On the west bank of the Nakdong River where winter is much colder, a variety of house types, more open to outside, could develop. In other words, a region of folk housing, distinctive in floor plan, was formed on the west bank of the Nakdong River, owing to internal evolution as well as diffusion.

In the upper reaches of the Kŭm River, village rituals were also partly the outcome of interplay between villagers and their natural surroundings. In the village around Okch'ŏn Town, abundant with *sŏndol* along with dolmens, the transition from natural to human deities was deterred. The village locations near streams in the canyon, vulnerable to the danger from floods, made the villagers believe more in the supernatural power of *sŏndol*. Around Kŭmsan Town, heavy rainfalls and thin soils on steep slopes in canyons exposed villagers to the danger of flooding. A piling-up of pebbles, therefore, may have been originated from building a dike along a stream to protect a village from flooding.

However, cultural landscapes in Korea are so much more complex in their forming processes that they cannot be studied only from the standpoint of traditional cultural geography. Both traditional and new cultural geographies have their own merits

7. Conclusion

to be exploited in the study of cultural landscapes in Korea. In Korea, there are many traditional cultural landscapes, fully embedded with meanings and symbolism, transcending the scope and capability of traditional cultural geography.

First of all, language is a structure of signification that is reproduced in social practice. Like other practices, it does not exist outside social relations of power. A linguistic community is found around shared meanings which reinforce a group's identity and mark it off from neighboring communities. There is, in other words, a politics of language, and the study of dialect provides one of the best examples of the politics of language. New cultural geographers believe that cultural geography must go beyond the mapping of languages towards the study of language itself as a medium through which intersubjective meaning is communicated.

In Korea, place names have been linguistic media through which communication takes place within linguistic communities, characterized by the possession of shared belief systems, myths and ideologies, or a common language. Place names demonstrate an areal differentiation in assimilating into the Chinese style, depending upon the geographical locations and social positions that their users occupied. A comparison between Kyŏnggi Bay and Chiri Mountain shows an areal difference between place names being expressed in Chinese.

In Kyŏnggi Bay close to the political center, Seoul, place names have been easily transformed into written Chinese, including those on promontory landforms. People's intention to beautify their own place is hidden in the continuous transformation of place names on promontories. People may have intentionally erased phonetic meaning in their memory, because literal meaning is better than phonetic meaning. In Chiri Mountain distant from Seoul, by contrast, place names may have been resistant to the Chinese type. The name "Chirisan" itself is not a Chinese, but a Korean name which means a round mountain in an ancient dialect. Each of the names in Chinese about Chiri Mountain is an onomatopoetic (sound imitating) word, directly representing a pronunciation that had once dominated the local residents.

In Chiri Mountain, there are other place names which have been resistant to being Chinese. Being imbued with fantastic imagination and false image, these names have built up a local identity in association with history. They were originally meant to characterize certain physical features, but people have misinterpreted them consciously or unconsciously. The ordinary people relate the name "P'iagol" to human blood, and the name "Paemsagol" to snakes. Herein, popular knowledge painted with historical myths extorted their original meanings. A place myth was created from a historical fact that it was occupied by communist guerrillas during the Korean War.

New cultural geographers view culture as a domain in which social relations of dominance and subordination are negotiated and resisted. In other words, they look at cultures of socially marginal groups as well as the dominant, national culture of the elite. After all, they define culture as the way that social relations of a group are structured and shaped. This definition of culture may be helpful to explain cultural landscapes in Korea as a whole.

Understanding the regionalization or localization of a folk landscape in Korea does require the knowledge of social relations of dominance and subordination. Shamanism, in particular, has served as a domain within which socially marginal groups, including women, resisted the elite culture. In Korea, believers in folk beliefs including Shamanism were capable of rejecting the dominant mores of the ruling class. The dominant values of any social elite may be aspired to by the middle class, but they are likely to be rejected by those lower down the social hierarchy as unobtainable. In turn, members of the elite regularly condemn popular culture for its vulgarity, seeking to establish their hegemony.

Presumably, Shamanism remained alive in Korea because of the interest of women, more than anything else. For women in the Chosŏn Period, the Shamnistic ritual called *kut* was a domain where they resisted the oppression from patriarchs under Neo-Confucianism. In Kyeryong Mountain, a mountain peak named Sambul-bong (Three Buddhas Peak) has been one of the most sacred places for women to come to with or without shamans for prayer. This peak was named after a meld of Buddhist appearances with a Shamanist concept of *samshin*, or three spirits. *Sambul* (three Buddhas) or *samshin* are the deities that shamans resort to in their *kut*s for the birth of sons. In the time of Buddhism and Confucianism with hegemony in power, Shamanism disguised itself in Buddhist clothes and appealed to women's desperate needs for male descendants.

The extreme importance of male descendants made the shaman's performance undeniable as a sort of last resort. Usually, a lofty yangban man scorned the ritual as useless, but he would seldom forbid it if his wife asked for it as the last resort. Moreover, when women could go to shamanistic halls called *tang* in Kyeryong Mountain for *kut*, they could enjoy the open atmosphere with freedom to dance and sing. *Kut*, whether indoors or outdoors, offered women the opportunity to share their own identity by resisting subordination from men. Only when attending Shamanistic rituals, women, common or noble, were allowed to remain outside of the Confucian ideal.

On Cheju Island in Korea, Shamanism and other folk beliefs are better preserved than on the mainland, partially retaining their own identities in adapting themselves to foreign religions in power. In contrast to the mainland, *sanshin*, or the mountain spirit, are often Shamanistic deities, and identified as old women called *halmang* meaning grandmother in the Cheju Province dialect. Indeed, here, the women's higher status and stronger power in society had to do with the dominance of female deities in the sexual divisions of mountain deities. On Cheju Island, women did a great more physical work than the norm in Korea, and had more independence and freedom of movement.

In the eastern region called Tongch'on, in particular, main spirit halls called *ponhyangdang* could survive from a series of ordeals, owing to women's communal support. Here, in a village ritual for this hall, Shamanism is still intact, and women have led it. Women have been free to gather regularly in these halls outdoors to perform village rituals. Women's social power was strong enough to organize a village ritual in an open space for their own. In the early 18th century, during the persecution of Shamanism, main spirit halls largely disappeared in the western region, but survived in the eastern region. Here, main spirit halls served as domains within which Shamanism could resist the suppression from Confucianism.

However, in resisting the subordination from Confucianism, women in the eastern region did not only reject, but also adopted elements from it. They were very flexible in belief to accept other deities when it was necessary for their subsistence. It is, in fact, their resiliency, flexibility and practicality that underlie the dynamic changes in the deities and thus the survival of Shamanism.

On the islands in the southwestern sea, female deities also tend to dominate the sexual division of village deities. Here, the most common types of village deities are trees and stones, called grandmother and grandfather. In terms of function and location, these deities, animistic by nature, are the same with those on the adjacent mainland. However, even the islanders in the near sea usually dedicate village rituals to male deities called grandfather only after female deities called grandmother. On the islands in the distant sea, almost every village performs a Shamanistic ritual for the deity of the dragon king, in which the participation of an individual woman from each household is essential. It is suggested that on these islands, isolated from the center of Confucianism, women have retained their own social power better than on the mainland.

Around Kŭmsan Town, women have been active in the revival as well as the maintenance of village rituals for stone-pebbles, called *tolt'ap*. Here, in the past, a village ritual consisted of two parts or two levels: an upper and lower one. The upper one was for a *sanshin*, restricted only to men, while the lower one was for a stone pagoda, open to everybody including women. Recently, however, village women have increasingly paid attention to the lower one, in contrast to men who have gradually lost interest in it. The pagoda spirit has served not only as *hadangshin*, or deity in spirit hall below a village, but also as an individual woman's deity, listening to her prayers for the delivery of sons and the longevity of their children.

Likewise, subordinated groups can use cultural or symbolic strategies to resist subordination from the ruling class. The style in ritual may be a secret language, and can be a form of cultural insubordination that expresses an attitude of defiance and disrespect to those in authority. In Korea, rituals in folk beliefs, including Shamanism, show areal differentiation in terms of performance style. A ritual's assimilation into Neo-Confucianism or Buddhism has to do with the geographical location and social position that its performers had once occupied in the past. Village rituals, indeed, are so varied in style from village to village that one cannot recognize a typical form among them.

Even within Buddhist landscapes, moreover, those formed in association with women's power in the past can be recognized. Today, almost every temple contains non-Buddhistic halls, Shamanistic or Taoistic in origin, such as Sanshingak (the Mountain Spirit Hall) or Samsŏnggak (the Three Saint Hall). Even in T'ongdo Temple, Sanshingak in 1761 and Samsŏnggak in 1870 were built at locations adjoining the Main Worshipping Hall and the Kŭmganggye-dan, or the Diamond Ordination Platform, the most sacred space. A Buddhistic hall with Avalokitsvara was also newly built at that time to satisfy women's needs. In the Chosŏn Period, Buddhism no longer received much of the official patronage that it had earlier enjoyed. Without hegemony in power, Buddhism had to earn popular support from the common, including women, for its survival.

In terms of social power, Buddhism was in the middle between Shamanism and Neo-Confucianism at that time. As Buddhism aspired to the dominant values of Neo-Confucianim, the ideology of ancestor worship was projected on the formation of Buddhist landscapes. In T'ongdo Temple, an ancestral hall, Confucian in architectural style, was built in 1727 to commemorate a monk named Chajang, the temple founder. In the Songkwang Temple, a stupa of the monk named Chinul, the temple founder has been treated as if it were a tomb to which his descendent monks must worship as a common ancestor's. In the face of subordination from Neo-Confucianism, Buddhism could not but adopt such a dominant value as ancestor worship, however contradictory it might be to its morality.

There is a growing recognition that there are many ways of seeing and reading the landscape. If traditional studies of landscape stressed the outsider's view and concentrated on the morphology of external forms, recent studies seek to reverse this by discovering the identity and experience of the insider. A landscape has such symbolic dimensions, as it were, the symbolic and cultural meaning coined in landscape by those who have produced and sustained them, and who have come into contact with them.

In the new cultural geography, the concepts of ideology and hegemony are central to their landscape study, focusing on the processes through which dominant meanings are imposed, negotiated, and registered. Ideology, in particular, serves a crucial role in the reproduction of society, disguising the inevitability of class conflict and representing the interests of the ruling class as the interests of the whole society. In common usage, hegemony refers to a situation of uncontested political supremacy. It refers to the power of a dominant class to persuade subordinate classes to accept its moral, political, and cultural values as the natural order.

In Korea, even prior to the development of capitalism, urban landscapes, particularly in administrative centers, were embedded with symbolic representation of power relations. Landscape is an ideological concept, and represents a way in which certain classes of people have signified themselves and their world through their imagined relationship with nature. The rulers of the Chosŏn Dynasty imposed ideas from Neo-Confucianism and Feng-shui on the city planning to signify their own social role with respect to external nature. These ideas were often directly projected in the composition of street and gate names as well as the spatial arrangement of avenues and public buildings. The Japanese colonialists, then, tried to erase these urban landscapes and establish those of their own ideal versions.

In the city planning of Seoul, the first king of the Chosŏn Dynasty consulted Confucianism more than Feng-shui or Buddhism. Based on a Chinese classic on city planning, he decided to locate the main palace called Kyŏngbokgung at the foothills of a mountain named Paekak, facing toward the south. With the north-south thoroughfare in the center, Chongmyo (Royal Ancestral Shrine) was placed in the east, in contrast to Sajikdan (the Altars for the Gods of Earth and the Five Major Crops) in the west. This pattern of city layout, along with names on palaces, gates and streets, was meant to represent the ideology of Confucianism, and to persuade subordinate people to accept the king's moral, political, and cultural values as the natural order.

Since 1905, however, the symbols of a Korean king's power had been eliminated, or taken over in association with the Japanese imperialism. Creating new Japanese symbols went

7. Conclusion

hand in hand with undermining old Korean symbols. In northwestern Seoul, the southern part of Kyŏngbokgung became the seat of the colonial government, and there the enormous granite building of Chosŏn-ch'ongdokbu (the Government-General) dominated the scene. In the south, many street names were borrowed from personal, historical and geographical names in Japan. In the palace called Ch'angkyŏnggung, a number of buildings fell in disrepair, and a botanical garden opened there in 1907 and a zoo in 1909. The spaces of other palaces were also largely encroached upon by foreign users including Japanese colonialists or ordinary Koreans. On the western slope of the sacred Nam Mountain, the Japanese built a Shinto shrine in 1925 to worship the Meiji emperor in Japan.

Chŏnju City is home of the Chŏnju Yi family, from which the long line of the Chosŏn Dynasty kings sprang, and the dynasty imposed royal authority on its urban landscape. In the southeastern section, the second king established a Confucian-style shrine called Kyŏnggijŏn in dedication to his father, the first king. Later, adjoining with this shrine to the north, a Confucian-style altar called Chogyŏngdan was built in 1771 for the founder of the Chŏnju Yi family and his wife. In addition to Confucianism, Feng-shui was the ideology to be projected on the formation of urban landscape in Chŏnju City. Based on Feng-shui, the major avenues connecting the main gates were intersected by irregularly curved, narrow lanes and cul-de-sacs.

Even prior to the annexation in 1910, the Japanese began to erase the symbolic landscapes in the walled city of Chŏnju. In the time of straightening and broadening streets, they forcefully got rid of any physical obstacles lying ahead in the direction of the road direction. The major victims were buildings of Kaeksa

(Official Guest Houses), Kamyŏng (the Provincial Magistrate's Office), Puyŏng (the Mayoral Office), and their open spaces. In 1911, the royal shrine of Kyŏnggijŏn surrounded by walls, yielded its eastern section to the construction of a street, and on its western section, a girl's primary school was built. Moreover, the Japanese totally ignored the value of Feng-shui, and ponds and mounds that had been made artificially to create an ideal topography in terms of Feng-shui vanished. Artificial forests also rapidly disappeared in the north of the city as Feng-shui lost its own power as a dominant ideology.

In the Chosŏn Period, rulers projected Confucian ideology on the cultural landscapes in Kyŏngju City, the capital of the once great Shilla Kingdom. In the making of urban landscapes, however, they did not create new ones, but decorated old ones with their own symbolism. They reinterpreted ancient landscapes from the standpoint of Confucianism as if they were texts. Upon his father's death, the second king ordered that a portrait of his father (the first king) be preserved in the stone chamber, and turned the area around it into a shrine compound called Chipgyŏngjŏn. This stone chamber, however, had once been built as a detached palace or a royal villa by the United Shilla Kingdom. In the 18th and 19th centuries, the dynasty established ancestral shrines at the royal tombs that had been constructed during the Shilla Period.

Moreover, Buddhist and rural landscapes may contain the symbolic and cultural meanings coined by those who have produced and sustained them. As Chajang served as royal advisor for the queen of the Shilla Kingdom, he could excercise the hegemony in power to select and mystify the temple site of T'ongdo Temple. He located the temple beside a stream flowing through the foothills of a mountain, whose outlook resembled a holy mountain in India. In addition to this mountain, a myth concerned with a pond turned the site into a sacred place. It is said that Chajang dispelled nine dragons in the large pond and reclaimed it into land on which the temple was to be built. He also established the Kŭmganggye-dan with Sakyamuni's belongings in it to make the temple an authoritative place.

In the Koryŏ Period, Chinul, the founder of the Chogye Order, could also select and mystify the temple site of Sonkwang Temple. This temple is now located at the foothills of the mountain, whose name "Chogye" was borrowed from a holy mountain in China, the origin of a southern tradition of Zen (meditation). In the formation of Buddhist landscape, Chinul basically referred to ideologies from Hwaŏmjong (the Flower Garland Sect) and Sŏnjong (the Meditation Sect or Zen Sect). Buildings in the temple were arranged in concentric circles to reflect Pŏbgyedo, or the Diagram of Law-Realm in Hwaŏmjong, similar to the symbol "卍." Based on the ideology from the Zen Sect, the Meditation Practice Hall and the Law Lecture Hall were located on the highest spot behind the Main Worshipping Hall. Even higher than these halls, stupas of sixteen national-master monks were placed. All in all, the intention to impose these ideologies on Buddhist landscapes was to demonstrate the temple as a place of authority and power.

On the other hand, a pavilion is a distinctive rural landscape in Korea which has been coined with symbolism from Confucian ideology. The right to enjoy the scenery from a pavilion and share the leisure life with friends was restricted only to *yangban* men. The pavilion was not only a material landscape, but also a symbolic landscape which *yangban* men could share at that time. Once *yangban* men erected a pavilion, they offered it a specific name with a certain meaning, and composed poems to create a sense of place around it. Natural phenomena mentioned in them were the metaphors of the human mind that had been cited from classical Chinese. To grasp their meanings required a thorough reading knowledge of classical Chinese, a privilege restricted only to *yangban* men. Here, knowledge, power and landscape were interwoven to create a symbolic place securing a group identity among *yangban* men.

To summarize, dominant cultures are not identical with subordinate ones, neither is popular culture the equivalent of elite culture: they vary in terms of the scale of cultural power. Differences also exist between the "spatial strategies" of the dominating and the dominated. There is a conscious and unconscious use of space by all concerned, even within the context of such a heavily asymmetrical power structure. As a result, the existence of a hierarchical ranking of cultures, standing in opposition to one another in relation to domination and subordination along a scale of cultural power emerged. Therefore, regionalization or localization of a certain landscape can also be explained in terms of cultural power as well as cultural diffusion. From this perspective, an integrated cultural geography can emerge to be used in the study of cultural landscapes in Korea.

BIBLIOGRAPHY

Bibliography 1

Brandt, Vincent, 1971, *A Korean Village: Between Farm and Sea*, Cambridge, Massachusetts: Harvard University Press.

Buswell, Robert, 1989, *The Formation of Ch'an Ideology in China and Korea: The Vajrasamadhi-Sutra, A Buddhist Apocryphon*, Princeton: Princeton University Press.

Ch'oe, Kil-song, 1982, "Community Ritual and Social Structure in Village Korea," *Asian Forklore Studies*, Vol. 41 (1).

Clark, Donald, 1986, Christianity in Modern Korea, Lanham, Maryland: University Press of America.

Cosgrove, Denis and Peter Jackson, 1987, "New directions in Cultural Geography," *Area*, Vol. 19, pp. 95-101.

Cosgrove, Denis and Stephen Daniels, 1988, *The Iconography of Landscape: Essays on the Symbolic Representation*, Design and Use of Past Environments, Cambridge Studies in Historical Geography, Vol. 9, Cambridge: Cambridge University Press.

Cosgrove, Denis, 1984, "The Idea of Landscape," in Denis Cosgrove (ed.), *Social Formation and Symbolic Lanscape*, New Jersy: Barmes & Noble Books, pp. 13-38.

Covell, Alan Carter, 1986, *Folk Art and Magic: Shamanism in Korea*, Seoul and Elisabeth, New Jersey: Hollym Corporation Publishers.

Crang, Mike, 1998, *Cultural Geography: Contemporary Human Geography*, London and New York: Routledge Publishers.

Daniels, Stephen and Denis Cosgrove, 1988, "Introduction," in

Stephen Daniels & Denis Cosgrove (eds.), *The Iconography of Lanscape*, Cambridge: Cambridge University Press, pp. 1-10.

de Bary, William and Ja-hyun Kim Haboush (eds.), 1985, *The Rise of Neo-Confucianism in Korea*, New York: Columbia University Press.

Deuchler, Martina, 1977, "The Tradition: Women during the Yi Dinasty," in Sandra Mattielli (ed.), *Virtues in Conflict: Tradition and the Korean Women Today*, Princeton: Princeton University Press.

Deuchler, Martina, 1980, "Neo-Confucianism: The Impulse for Social Action in Early Korea," *The Journal of Korean Studies,* Vol. 2.

Eckert, Carter J., et al., 1990, *Korean Old and New History*, New Heaven: Korea Institute, Harvard University.

English, Paul Ward and Robert C. Mayfield, 1972, *Man, Space and Environment*, New York: Oxford University Press.

Foote, Kenneth E., et al., 1994, *Re-Reading Cultural Geography*, Austin: University of Texas Press.

Gramsci, Antonio, 1971, *Selections from the Prison Notebooks*, London: Lawrence and Wishart.

Grayson, James H., 1989, *Korea: A Religious History*, Oxford, England: Clarendon Press.

Huntley, Martha, 1984, *Caring, Growing, and Changing: A History of the Protestant Mission in Korea*, New York: Friendship Press.

Jackson, Peter, 1989, *Maps of Meaning: An Introduction to Cultural Geography*, London : Unwin Hyman.

Janelli, Roger L. and Dawn-hee Yim, 1982, *Ancestor Worship and Korean Society*, Stanford: Stanford University Press.

Joe, Wanne-J., (revised & edited by Choe, Hong-kyu), 1997, *Traditional Korea: A Cultural History*, Seoul and Elisabeth, New Jersey: Hollym Corporation Publishers.

Jordan, Terry G. and Lester Lowntree, 1986, *The Human Mosaic: A Thematic Introduction to Cultural Geography*, Fourth Edition, New York: Happer & Row Publishers.

Kang, Wi-jo, 1987, *Religion and Politics in Korea under Japanese Rule*, New York: Edwin Mellen Press.

Kendall, Laurall M., 1985, *Shamans, Housewives, and Other Restless Spirits: Women in Korean Ritual Life*, Stanford: Stanford University Press.

Kendall, Laural M., 1988, *The Life and Hard Times of Korean Shaman*, Honolulu: University of Hawaii Press.

Kim Harbush, Ja-hyunn, 1991, "The Confucianization of Korean Society," in Gilbert Rozman (ed.), *The East Asian Region: Confucian Heritage and its Modern Adaptation*, Princeton: Princeton University Press.

Kim, Kwang-ok, 1988, "A Study on the Political Manipulation of Elite Culture: Confucian Culture in Local Level Politics," *Korea Journal*, Vol. 28, No. Ⅱ.

Kim, Nam-Kil, 1988, "Korean," in Bernard Comrie (ed.), *The World's Major Languages*, New York: Oxford University Press.

Koo, John H. and Andrew C. Nahm, 1997, *An Introduction To Korean Culture*, Seoul and Elisabeth, New Jersey: Hollym Corporation Publishers.

Korean Buddhist Research Institute (ed.), 1933, *The History and Culture of Buddhism in Korea*, Seoul, Korea: Dongguk University Press.

Korean National Commission for UNESCO, 1998, *Kyŏngju: City of Millennial History*, Seoul and Elisabeth, New Jersey: Hollym Corporation Publishers.

Korean Overseas Culture and Information Service (Ed.), 1996, *Korean Heritage* Ⅱ, Seoul and Elisabeth, New Jersey: Hollym Corporation Publishers.

Lautensach, Hermann (originally published in German in 1965), translated by Katherine and Dege Eckert in 1988, *Korea: A Geography Based on the Author's Travels and Literature*, Berlin & New York: Springer-Verlag

Lee, Chan, et al., 1988, *Korea: Geographical Perspectives*, Seoul, Korea: Korean Educational Development Institute

Lee, Kwang-kyu, 1984, "The Concept of Ancestors and Ancestor Worship in Korea," *Asian Folklore Studies,* Vol. 43 (2).

Lee, Peter H. and William de Bary, (eds.), 1988, *Sources of Korean Tradition, Vol. 1*, New York: Columbia University Press.

McCune, Shannon, 1956, *Korea's Heritage: A Regional & Social Geography*, Rutland, Vermont: Charles E. Tuttle Company.

McDowell, Linda, Gregory, D., 1944, "The Transformation of Cultural Geography," in R. Martin and G. Smith (eds.) *Human Geography*, Macmillan, pp. 146-173.

Mikesell, Marvin W., 1968, "Lanscape," *Internatinal Encyclopedia of the Social Sciences,* Vol. 8, Crowell Collier and Macmillan Inc., pp. 575-580.

Nahm, Andrew C., 1988, *Korea: A History of the Korean People*, Seoul and Elisabeth, New Jersey: Hollym Corporation Publishers.

Nahm, Andrew C., 1988, *Korea: Tradition and Transformation*, Seoul and Elisabeth, New Jersey: Hollym Corporation Publishers.

Nahm, Andrew C., 1993, *Introduction to Korean History and Cul-*

ture, Seoul and Elisabeth, New Jersey: Hollym Corporation Publishers.

Nilsen, Robert, 1997, *South Korea Handbook*, Chico, Califonia: Moon Publications, Inc..

O'Brien, Betsy, 1997, *Let's Eat Korean Food*, Seoul and Elisabeth, New Jersey: Hollym Corporation Publishers.

Palais, James B., 1991, *Politics and Policy in Traditional Korea*, Cambridge Council on East Asian Studies, Cambridge, Massachusetts: Harvard University Press.

Palmer, Spencer J., 1986, *Confucian Rituals in Korea*, Berkeley, California: Asian Humanities Press.

Price, Marie & Martin Lewis, 1993, "The Reinvention of Cultural Geography," *Annals of the Association of American Geographers,* Vol. 83 (1), pp. 1-17.

Ryu, Je-hun, 1987, "Institutionalization and Cultural Adaptation on *the Honam Plain of South Korea: 1789-1982,"* Unpublished Ph.D. Dissertation, Department of Geography, The University of Texas at Austin.

Sauer, Carl O., 1941, "Forward to Historical Geography," *Annals of the Association of American Geographers,* Vol. 31, pp. 1-24.

Wagner, Philip L. and Marvin W. Mikesell, 1967, "The Themes of Cultural Geography," in Philip L. Wagner & Marvin W. Mikesell (eds.), *Readings in Cultural Geography*, Chicago and London: The University of Chicago Press, pp. 1-24.

Wagner, Philip L. and Marvin W. Mikesell (eds.), 1967, *Readings in Cultural Geography*, Chicago: The University of Chicago Press.

Williams, Ramond, 1977, *Marxism and Literature*, Oxford: Oxford University Press.

Won, Yi-beam and Byeong-ho Lim, 1992, *A History of Buddhist*

Culture and Some Essays: The Buddhist Pure Land & The Christian Kingdom of Heaven, Seoul, Korea: Jipmundang.

Yi, Kim Eun-hee, 1993, "From Gentry to the Middle Class: The Transformation of Family, Community and Gender in Korea," Unpublished Ph.D. Dissertation, University of Chicago.

Yun, Seung-yong, et al., 1996, *Religious Culture in Korea*, A Publication by Ministry of Culture and Sports, Republic of Korea, Seoul and Elisabeth, New Jersey: Hollym Corporation Publishers.

Bibliography 2

Ch'oe, Ch'ang-jo 崔昌祚. 1984. Hanguk ŭi p'ungsusasang. 한국의 풍수사상. *Ideas of Feng-shui in Korea*. Seoul: Minŭmsa.

Ch'oe, Hak-gŭn 崔學根. 1986-a. Hanguk Pangŏnhak sang. 韓國方言學 上. *Studies on Korean Dialectics*, Vol. Ⅰ. Seoul: Osŏngsa.

Ch'oe, Hak-gŭn 崔學根. 1986-b. Hanguk Pangŏnhak ha. 韓國方言學 下. *Studies on Korean Dialectics*, Vol. Ⅱ. Seoul: Osŏngsa.

Ch'oe, Ki-su 崔杞秀. 1989. "Kok gwa kyŏng e nat'anan Hanguk chŏnt'ong kyŏnggwan kujo ŭi haesŏk e gwanhan yŏngu." 曲과 景에 나타난 韓國傳統景觀 構造의 解釋에 관한 研究. "An Interpretation of Korean Traditional Landscape called *kok* and *kyŏng*," Unpublished Ph. D. Dissertation, Department of Urban Engineering, Hanyang University.

Ch'oe, Pŏm-hun 崔範勳. 1987. "Kyŏnggido sŏhaean 'koji' gye chimyŏnggo." 京畿道 西海岸 '고지' 系地名攷. A Study of Place Names with Suffix *'koji'* on the West Coast of Kyŏnggi Province, 畿甸文化, 第2輯. *Kijŏnmunhwa*, vol. 2, Kijŏnmunhwa yŏnguso. 畿甸文化研究所. A Society for the Study of Kijŏn Local Culture, pp. 5-27.

Ch'oe, Tŏk-won 崔德源. 1990. Tadohae ŭi tangje. 多島海의 堂祭. *Village Rituals on Southwest Sea called Tadohae*. Seoul: Hakmunsa.

Ch'oe, Wan-gi 崔完基. 1993. Hanguk sŏngrihak ŭi maek. 韓國性理學의 脈. *Traditions and Innovations in Korean*

Neo-Confuianism, Sahoesayŏnguch'ongsŏ 3. 社會史 研究叢書 3. Study Series in Social History No. 3. Seoul: Nŭt'inamu.

Ch'oe, Wan-su 崔完秀. 1994. Myŏngch'alsunrye. 명찰순례 (名刹巡禮). *The Pilgrimage to Famous Temples*, Vol. 1. Seoul: Taewŏnsa.

Chang, Myŏng-su 張明洙. 1994. Sŏnggwakbaldal gwa toshigyehoek yŏngu. 城郭發達과 都市計劃 研究. *A Study on the Development of City Walls and Urban Planning in Chŏnju City*. Seoul: Hakyŏnmunhwasa.

Chang, Po-ung 張保雄. 1996. Hanguk minga ŭi jiyŏkjŏk jŏngae. 韓國民家의 地域的 展開. *The Regional Variation of Korean Folk Housing*. Seoul: Pojinje.

Chang, Tong-su 張東洙. 1994. "Hanguk jŏnt'ongdoshijokyŏng ŭi jangsojŏk t'ŭksŏng e gwanhan yŏngu." 韓國 傳統都市 造景의 場所的 特性에 關한 研究. "A Study on the Place Characteristics of Traditional Urban Landscape, Unpublished Ph. D. Dissertation, Department Landscape Architecture," Seoul City University.

Chŏng, Chin-yŏng 정진영. 1997. "Wae antong enŭn yangban i manŭnka." 왜 안동에는 양반이 많은가? Why are there many *yangbans* around Andong City? in Yim, Chae-hae (ed.), Andongmunhwa ŭi susukkekki. 안동문화의 수수께끼. *Puzzles about Andong Culture*. Seoul: Chisiksanŏpsa, pp. 51-71.

Chŏng, un-hyŏn 정운현. 1995. Seoul shinae munhwayusandapsagi. 서울시내 문화유산답사기. *Field Notes on the Japanese Colonial Relics in Seoul*. Seoul: Hanwul.

Han, Sam-gŏn 한삼건. 1993. "Chosŏnocho yori Nitteijidai madeno Keishushi doshi kukan no henka ni kansuru kenkyu."

朝鮮王朝より日帝時代までの慶州市都市空間の變化に關する研究. "A Study on the Transformation of Urban Space in Kyŏngju City from Chosŏn Dynasty to Japanese Colonialism," Unpublished Ph. D. Dissertation, Department of Architecture, Kyoto University.

Hannam taehakgyo Ch'ungchŏng munhwayŏnguso. 한남대학교 충청문화연구소. 1990. The Institute of Ch'ungchŏng Culture, Hannam University, Kŭmsan ŭi maŭl kongdongch'e shinang. 금산의 마을공동체 신앙. *Village Rituals around Kŭmsan Town*. Taejŏn: Seminsa.

Kang, Yŏng-hwan 姜榮煥. 1993. Hanguk jugŏmunhwa ŭi yŏksa. 한국 주거문화의 역사. *A History of Housing Culture in Korea*. Seoul: Kimundang.

Kim, Hak-bŏm 金學範. 1991. "Hanguk ŭi maŭlwonrim e gwanhan yŏngu." 韓國의 마을園林에 關한 研究. "A Study on the Village Forests in Korea," Unpublished Ph. D. Dissertation, Department of Forestry, Korea University.

Kim, Han-bai 김한배. 1993. "Hanguk toshikyŏnggwan ŭi pyŏnch'ŏn t'ŭksŏng e gwanhan yŏngu." 韓國都市景觀의 變遷特性에 關한 研究. "A Study on the Changing Urban Landscape in Korea," Unpublished Ph. D. Dissertation, Department of Landscape Architecture, Seoul City University.

Kim, Ju-sŏp 金周燮. 1996. "Ch'ŏnjugyo shinang chiyŏk hyŏngsŏnggwajŏng e gwanhan yŏngu." 天主敎 信仰地域 形成過程에 關한 研究. "The Growth of Catholicism around Ansŏng Town," Unpublished Master's Thesis, Department of Geography, Korea National University of Education.

Kim, Kil-nam 金吉男. 1997. "Chŏnnam nambujiyŏk sach'al ŭi ipji wa kyŏnggwanyŏngu." 全南 南部地域 寺刹의 立地와

景觀研究. "The Locations and Landscapes of Buddhist Temples in the Southern South Chŏlla Province," Unpublished Master's Thesis Department of Geography, Korea National University of Education.

Kim, Kwang-ŏn 김광언. 1988. Hanguk ŭi jugŏminsokji. 韓國의 住居民俗誌. *An Ethnography of Korean Housing*, Daewoo haksulch'ongsŏ · Inmunsahoegwahak 29. 대우학술총서 · 인문사회과학 29. Daewoo Academical Series in Human and Social Sciences, No. 29. Seoul: Minŭmsa.

Kim, Su-dong 金秀東. 1997. "Kyeryongsan ŭi changsosŏng e gwanhan yŏngu." 鷄龍山의 場所性에 關한 硏究. "The Making of Places on Kyeryong Mountain," Unpublished Master's Thesis, Department of Geography, Korea National University of Education.

Kim, T'ae-gon 金泰坤. 1994. Hanguk minganshinang yŏngu. 韓國民間信仰硏究. *A Study on the Folk Religion in Korea*, Han'guk musokch'ongsŏ VI. 韓國巫俗叢書 VI. Study Series in Korean Shamanism, No. 6. Seoul: Chipmundang.

Kim, Yun-hak 김윤학. 1980. "Kyŏnggido hwadomyŏn ŭi ttangirŭm yŏngu." 경기도 화도면의 땅 이름 연구. A Study of Place Names in Hwado-myŏn, Kyŏnggi Province, Kijŏnmunhwa yŏngu vol. 11. 畿甸文化硏究, 제11집. Kijŏn hyangt'omunhwa yŏnguhoe. 畿甸鄕土文化硏究會. Institute of Kijŏn Culture Studies. Inch'ŏn: Teacher's College, pp. 157-239.

Kim, Yŏng-sang 김영상. 1989. Seoul yukbaeknyŏn. 서울 600년. *Six Hundred Years of Seoul*. Seoul: Hanguk Ilbosa ch'ulp'anguk.

Ko, Tae-kyŏng 고대경. 1997. Shindŭl ŭi gohyang. 神 (신)들의 고향. *Home Places for Deities*. Seoul: Chŭngmyŏng.

Kwŏn, Pŏm-ki 權範基. 1996. "Kyŏngbuk pukbu chibang sŏwon

munhwa chiyŏk ŭi hyŏngsŏng gwajŏng." 慶北 北部地方 書院文化地域의 形成過程. "The Formation of *sŏwŏn* Cultural Region around Andong City," Unpublished Master's Thesis, Department of Geography, Korea National University of Education.

Kŭm, Chang-t'ae 琴章泰. 1994. Yugyosasang gwa chonggyomunhwa. 儒教思想과 宗教文化. *Confucion Thoughts and Religious Culture*. Seoul: Seoul National University Press.

Kŭm, Chang-t'ae 금장태. 1995. Yuhaksasang gwa yugyomunwha. 유학사상과 유교문화. *Confucian Thoughts and Confucian Culture*, Tongyang munwhach'ongsŏ 7. 동양문화총서 7. Oriental Culture Study Series, No. 7. Seoul: Chŏntongmunhwa Yŏnguhoe.

Lee, Chan & Po-gyŏng Yang. 1995. Seoul ŭi Yetjido. 서울의 옛 지도. *Old Maps of Seoul*. Seoul: Seoul Studies Institute, Seoul City University.

Lee, Chan. 1991. Hanguk ŭi Kojido. 韓國의 古地圖. *Old Maps of Korea*. Seoul: Pŏmmunsa.

Lee, Ton-ju 이돈주. 1998. "Ttang irŭm (chimyŏng) ŭi charyo wa urimal yŏngu." 땅이름 (지명)의 자료와 우리말 연구. "Data on Place Names and the Study of Korean Language," *Chimyonghak*, Vol. 1, 지명학. 1권. Journal of The Place Name Society of Korea, Vol. 1, pp. 163-185.

MunhwaYŏksachiri No. 1-11. 문화역사지리 1-11호. Journal of Cultural and Historical Geography No. 1-11, Hanguk munhwa yŏksa chirihakhoe. 韓國文化歷史地理學會. The Association of Korean Cultural and Historical Geographers.

Nam, Ch'i-gyu 南治圭. 1997. "Namhangang yuyŏk jŏngja ŭi jangsojŏk ŭimi e gwanhan yŏngu." 南漢江流域 亭子의 場所的 意味에 관한 硏究. "The Meaning of Pavilion as a Place,"

Unpublished Master's Thesis, Department of Geography, Korea National University of Education.

Pae, U-ri 배우리. 1994. Uri ttangirŭm ŭi ppurirŭl ch'ajasŏ, Vol. 1. 우리 땅이름의 뿌리를 찾아서 1. *In Search of Korean Place Names' Roots*, Vol. 1. Seoul: T'odam.

Park, Chae-ch'ŏl 朴宰徹. 1999. "Seoul ŭi pŏpjŏng dongmyŏng e gwanhan yŏngu." 서울의 法定洞名에 관한 硏究. "A Study on the Names of Administrative Areas called *dong* in Seoul," Unpublished Master's Thesis, Department of Geography, Korea National University of Education.

Park, Mun-gyu 朴文圭. 1999. "Chonggyo konggan ŭi changsohwa gwajŏng." 宗敎 空間의 場所化 過程. "The Humanization of Religious Spaces in the Yŏngdŭngp'o District," Unpublished Master's Thesis, Department of Geography, Korea National University of Education.

Shin, Yŏng-hun 申榮勳. 1995. Hanguk ŭi sallimjip sang. 한국의 살림집 上. *Folk Housing in Korea*, Vol. 1, Yŏlhwadang misulshinsŏ 37. 悅話堂 美術新書 37. Yŏlhwadang Painting Series, No. 37. Seoul: Yŏlhwadang.

Song, In-jŏng 宋仁旌. 1998. "Chejudo ponhyangdang ŭi seryŏkgwŏn pyŏnch'ŏn e gwanhan yŏngu." 濟州道 本鄕堂의 勢力圈 變遷에 關한 硏究. "The Changing Spheres of *Ponhyangdang* on Cheju Island," Unpublished Master's Thesis, Department of Geography, Korea National University Education.

Taehan Chirihakhoeji No. 1-75. 대한지리학회지 No 1-75호. Journal of the Korean Geographical Society, vol. 1-34 (No. 1-75), Taehan chirihakhoe. 대한지리학회. The Korean Geographical Society.

Yang, Yŏng-sik 梁榮植. 1993. "Okch'ŏngun ŭi minsokmunhwakyŏnggwan ŭi punp'o e gwanhan yŏngu." 沃川郡의 民俗 文化景觀의 分布에 關한 硏究. "The Distribution Pattern of Folk Landscapes around Okch'ŏn Town," Unpublished Master's Thesis, Department of Geography, Korea National University.

Yi, Chong-gil 이종길. 1992. Chirisan. 지리산, *Chiri Mountain*, Sumun chumal series 8. 수문 주말시리즈 8. Sumun Weekend Series 8. Seoul: Sumum Publishing Company.

Yi, Ki-gap 이기갑. 1994. Chŏllanamdo ŭi ŏnŏjiri. 전라남도의 언어지리. *A Linguistic Geography of South Chŏlla Province*, Kukŏhak Ch'ongsŏ, No. 11. 國語學叢書 11. Series in Korean Language Study, No. 11, Kukŏhakhoe. 國語學會. The Association for Korean Language Studies. Seoul: T'apch'ulpansa.

Yi, Ki-yŏng et. al. 이기영 외 2인. 1991. T'ongdosa. 통도사, *T'ongdo Temple*, Pitkkal itnŭn ch'aek dŭl 110. 빛깔있는 책들 110. Shiny Book Series, No. 110. Seoul: Taewŏnsa.

Yi, Kil-gu 이길구. 1997. Kyeryongsan. 계룡산. *Kyeryong Mountain*. Seoul: Taemunsa.

Yi, P'il-yŏng 이필영. 1990. "Maŭl mingan shinang ŭi t'ŭksŏng gwa kujo." 마을 민간 신앙의 특성과 구조. "The Characteristics and Structure of Village Common Beliefs, In Kŭmsanŭp jubpyŏn ŭi maŭlje rŭl chungshim ŭro." 금산읍 주변의 마을제를 중심으로. *Village Rituals around Kŭmsan Town*, Ch'ungch'ŏng munhwa yŏnguso. 충청문화연구소. Institute of Ch'ungch'ŏng Culture, Hannam university. Taejŏn: Seminsa.

Yi, Sang-yun 李相潤. 1993. "Chosŏnshidae sŏwon ŭi ipji wa konggan kusŏng t'ŭksŏng mit pyŏnhwakwajŏng e gwanhan yŏngu." 朝鮮時代 書院의 立地와 空間構成特性 및 變化

過程에 관한 硏究. "The Location and Spatial Arrangement of *Sŏwon* under the Chosŏn Dynasty," Unpublished Ph. D. Dissertation, Department of Landscape Architecture, Sŏnggyungwan University.

Yim, Chae-hae 임재해. 1992. Andong Hahoemaŭl. 안동 하회마을. Hahoe Village in Andong County, Pitkkal itnŭn ch'aek dŭl 129. 빛깔있는 책들 129. Shiny Book Series, No. 129. Seoul: Taewŏnsa.

Yim, Chae-hae 임재해. 1997. "Andongmunhwa ŭi susukkekki." 안동문화의 수수께끼. "What are the Puzzles about Andong Culture" in Chae-hae Yim (ed.), Andongmunhwa ŭi susukkekki. 안동문화의 수수께끼. *Puzzles about Andong Culture*. Seoul: Chisiksanŏpsa, pp. 13-48.

APPENDICES

Glossary

absorbing barrier

A barrier that completely halts diffusion of innovations and blocks the spread of cultural elements in contrast with a permeable barrier. Usually, natural barriers (mountains, deserts, oceans) or artificial barriers (national boundaries) act as the absorbing barriers.

Altaic language family

A language subgroup, which is agglutinative with the verb inflected. Also referring to the racial groups that speak this type of language, with many scattered tribes in Siberia sharing this trait. In Europe the largest Altaic language groups are Finnish and Hungarian. In the area of the Middle East it is Turkish. In Northeast Asia, both Koreans and Japanese share this language pattern.

Berkeley School

A group of scholars who were trained by Sauer (the founder of the Geography Department at UC Berkeley) and those trained by Sauer's students, his student's students, and so on. It sometimes refers even to those who were indirectly influenced by Sauer's thoughts without training from Sauer or Sauer's students.

biotic zonation

A distribution pattern of vegetation forming horizontal or vertical zones. Such a zonal distribution is closely associated with the climate changing along with altitude or latitude on the surface of the earth.

Buddhism

A religion or philosophy that is said to have begun by Siddharta Gautama, scion of the Shakya clan, about 560 B.C. He is said to have found enlightenment, and preached that denial of craving is the way to bliss, and the end of the continuing cycle of rebirth, which is the cornerstone of the Hindu religion. This faith was spread throughout Asia, and reached Korea in 372 A.D.

ch'ilsŏngshin 칠성신 (七星神)

The Big Dipper deity, or Seven Stars that were worshipped as deities in a group, particularly for easier childbirth, healthier babyhood and also wealth, prosperity, long life and virility. The heavens always deserve respect, so the Seven Stars in the sky as a constellation became a potent subject in Korea's Shamanism.

Ch'ŏnt'aejong 천태종 (天台宗)

A sect in Chinese Buddhism that was called Tientai Zong. It represents an intellectual effort to reconcile the philosophical study of scripture with the method of religious meditation in order to facilitate sudden enlightenment. First brought into Korea during the Shilla Kingdom Period, it was founded as a sect in Korean Buddhism by a monk named Uich'ŏn or Taegak Kuksa in 1097 under the Koryŏ Dynasty.

chaeshil 재실 (齋室)

A Confucian-style hall built in front of a family graveyard where the eminent ancestors' tombs are arranged. It is normally owned by a lineage group in common, but the duty of taking care of it belongs to the direct descendant in the family line, that is the primary lineage and ages seniors. It became widespread in Korea from the seventeenth century when Neo-Confucianism took its firm roots all over Korea.

Chajang 자장 (慈藏) (590-658)

An eminent Buddhist monk during the Shilla Kingdom Period. He was ordered back home from Tang China in 643, and appointed the Taeguktʻong, the highest priest of the state. He was also called Yulsa, or the Teacher of Disciplinary Orders because he instituted the Kyeyul (Disciplinary Orders) Sect in the Shilla Kingdom. He made it mandatory that all clergymen receive their ordination on the Diamond Ordination Platform at T'ongdo Temple.

Chinul 지눌 (智訥) (1158-1210)

An eminent Buddhist monk known as Pojo Kuksa, or National Teacher Pojo under the Koryŏ Dynasty. He belonged to the Sŏn (Meditation) Sect which placed emphasis on sudden enlightenment into the mind of Buddha, the realm of Ultimate Emptiness. He seems to have identified this Emptiness with what the Flower Garland (Hwaŏm) Sect calls the Void or the Realm of Principle. However, in addition to the Sŏn method of meditation, he adopted scriptural or metaphysical studies and deliberations, thereby providing the basis for integrating the Kyo Sect into the Sŏn Sect called Chogye Sect.

chipsŏngch'on 집성촌 (集姓村)

A type of lineage village where the vast majority of residents are agnates. Here, the village social relations accord with the patrilineal principle and hierarchy. In villages where a single *yangban* lineage dominated numerically, called *panch'on*, systems of keeping order and sharing wealth tended to follow a strictly patrilineal hierarchy. Its overall settlement pattern would appear in an agglomerated form on a hilly slope with the clan-head house on the highest spot.

Choe's 최 (崔) family

A family group that had once dominated the military regime called Musinjŏnggwon in the middle of the Koryŏ Dynasty. Ch'ung Hŏn Ch'oe and his brothers seized political power in 1196, and his regime came to function in parallel with the royal government. Under the rein of his son, U Ch'oe (1219-1249), the military regime was more fully developed in terms of organizational and administrative efficiency.

Chogyejong 조계종 (曹溪宗), or Chogye Sect

The name of the Sŏn (Meditation) Sect that is believed to have been instituted by Monk Chinul, or Pojo Kuksa under the Koryŏ Dynasty. It is characterized by its comprehensiveness in allowing various branches in the Kyo Sect including Hwaŏm Sect into the practice of meditation called Sŏn. Since then it has been the majority sect of Korea's Buddhism until today.

chongga 종가 (宗家)

A clan-head house in a lineage village called *chipsŏngch'on*. It usually boasts of its architectural style, large in size and grandeur in decoration, that is distinguished from the ordinary houses.

Chosŏn Dynasty 조선왕조 (朝鮮王朝) (1392-1910)

A dynasty established in 1392 by Sŏnggye Yi who rose from a military leader to overthrow the Koryŏ Dynasty. The royal family named Yi continued to govern the dynasty until the Korean Peninsula was forcibly annexed into the Japanese Empire in 1910.

Churyegogonggi 주례고공기 (周禮考工記)

One of the six volumes written under Zhou Dynasty in China concerning the Confucian-style government, called Churye in Korean (Zhou Li in Chinese). It is divided into two parts that prescribe the principles of designing the urban form, street pattern and spatial arrangement of public buildings. The capital city of Han China, Changan, is thought to have been built according to these principles. It suggests that a city appear in a rectangular shape surrounded by walls, and within it divided into sixteen blocks by six lines of streets crossing one another.

Chŏngt'ojong 정토종 (淨土宗), or Pure Land Sect

A Buddhist sect believing in a paradise, or a pure land on the west that one can reach after death. It suggests that reciting the name of the Amitabha Buddha, or the Lord of Paradise, would take one to this paradise where this Buddha resides. The Monk Wonhyo (617-686) of the Shilla Dynasty wandered through villages, encouraging illiterate peasants to adopt the ideas from Chŏngt'ojong.

coastal flat

A flat land on the coast smaller in size than a coastal plain. It is usually formed from the deposition of silts and sands transported by seas and streams.

Confucianism

Teachings of a man who lived in ancient China, named Kong Chiu (551-479 B.C.), but who was known as Master Kong, or Kong Fuzi. The equivalent of that name is expressed in the Roman alphabet as Confucius. His teachings are sometimes called religious, but at other times are regarded as political philosophy. Unlike Buddhism, Confucianism is concerned with this life and world.

core-periphery pattern

A concept based on the tendency of both formal and functional culture regions to consist of a core or node, in which defining traits are purest or functions are headquartered, and a periphery that is tributary and displays fewer of the defining traits.

crenulation

A small-scale folding (wave length up to a few millimeters) that is superimposed on large-scale folding. Crenulations may occur along the cleavage planes of a deformed rock.

defensive side

A side of a meandering stream where sands and silts are deposited in contrast with the offensive side where the stream hits and erodes the surface.

deity

A god or goddess; one exalted or revered as supremely good or powerful. In Korea, people traditionally believe in a spirit, natural or human, as a supernatural being, or a deity.

diffusion

The two-dimensional spread of a phenomenon over space and through time; the evolution of its spatial distribution. Investigations of the processes of diffusion have focused particularly on information flow, the dispersal of innovation and the spread of settlement.

doksŏng 독성 (獨聖), or the Lonely Spirit

"Lonely Arhat," a spirit of Shamanistic origin now enshrined at many Buddhist temples, often in the company of *sanshin and ch'ilsŏng*.

estuary

The mouth of a river, where the channel broadens out into the sea and in which the tide flows and ebbs (for example, the Thames estuary and the Severn estuary). Most estuaries represent the lower parts of former river valleys which have been drowned by the post-glacial rise of sea level.

farm village

A clustered rural settlement within which farming people grouped together. It vary in size from a few dozen inhabitants to hundreds, and fields lie out beyond the limit of the village.

Feng-shui 풍수 (風水)

A different name of geomancy in China that is called P'ungsu in Korea.

flood plain

The surface or strip of relatively smooth land adjacent to a river channel, constructed by the present river in its existing regimen and covered with water when the river overflows its banks; That part of a valley floor over which a river spreads during seasonal or short term floods. During such events velocity of flow is less than that within the river channel, and in the relatively slack water over the plain suspended sediment slowly settles out; as a result the flood plain is also modified by shifts of the river course (in the development and migration of meanders), and flood plain deposits also comprise material from extended point bars. By definition flood plains are areas of gentle relief, giving an impression in the field of almost perfect flatness.

free meander

A stream meander that displaces itself very easily by lateral corrosion, especially where vertical corrosion is of no importance.

geomancer

A person who determines some special locational point for a capital, city, town, village and even grave by geomancy.

geomancy

The Taoistic science of locating construction sites so that the building or altar or tomb will be in harmony with the earth spirits, and the Guardians of the Four Directions. This served as the blueprint for such cities as Changan in China, Nara and Kyoto in Japan, and Seoul in Korea. It also served as a guide to grave site locations for Koreans who could afford it throughout the Chosŏn dynasty, even after Buddhism began to wane and Neo-Confucianism, with its Taoistic cosmology, went into ascendance.

halmang 할망

The grandmother in the Cheju Province dialect. A generic term for a female deity that appears in many myths on Cheju Island. The folk belief in *halmang* may have been the primitive religion that was popular in ancient times when matrilineal society once prevailed.

hamlet

A small rural settlement (often no more than a cluster of a few houses), too small to be called a village and usually lacking a church in Europe.

Hangŭl 한글

The name for the Korean alphabet, which is made of 28 symbols (19 consonants and 9 vowels). It is known as one of the simplest, most concise, efficient means of writing in the world. Korean may be written entirely in Hangŭl or in mixed script (i.e., Hangŭl and Chinese characters). The language can be written vertically or horizontally. Traditionally, it is written in vertical fashion from the right to the left. Today, horizontal writing from the left to the right is more commonly practiced.

harŭbang 하르방

The generic term for a male deity, meaning grandfather in the Cheju Province dialect.

hegemony

The power of a dominant class to persuade the subordinate class to accept its moral, political, and cultural values as the natural order.

heuristic

When used in the context of methodology and argument, it implies reliance on assumptions which, in their turn, have been based on previous experience; to discover by trial and error. It is a word increasingly used with reference to computerized problem-solving exercises.

hongsalmun 홍살문

Literally a red arrow gate in Korean. It was a red wooden gate, constructed of two posts and a lattice lintel set at the entrance to royal graves and Confucian shrines.

Hwaŏmjong 화엄종 (華嚴宗), or Flower Garland Sect

A Korean Buddhistic Sect, called Huayen Zong in Chinese, which was founded by Ŭisang (625-702) under the Shilla Dynasty. Its main tenet was based on the Avatamsaka Sutra which regards the teachings of Gautama Buddha as the historical manifestation of the greater Buddha, Variochana. In its all inclusive syncretism, it taught that all phenomenal existences partake of the Realm of Law, the ultimate reality; even every moment of thinking is rooted in eternity.

Hwaŏmgyŏng 화엄경 (華嚴經), or Flower Garland Sutra

The basic sutra containing doctrines of Hwawŏmjong; one of the most important sutras in Buddhism. It describes the state of enlightenment, or the Realm of Law as the state of the Flower Garland from which the sutra's name came.

hyanggyo 향교 (鄉校)

A public school, sometimes called *hyanghak*, and a state-supported institution established throughout the country. Under the Chosŏn Dynasty, there was one for each county teaching Confucian classics, and students registered in these schools were from families of low-ranking government officials or local gentry.

hyangri 향리 (鄉吏)

A low-ranking offical engaged in the administrative affairs in the local government during the Koryŏ and Chosŏn Periods. His job was hereditary in assisting the local administration by the magistrate who was dispatched from the central government. His social status lay at the middle layer called *chungin* (ideographically middle men) lower than the *yangban* class.

Hydeyoshi Invasions

A different name for the Imjin War (1592-1598). Hydeyoshi was from the personal name of the Japanese premier who twice supervised Japanese invasions into Korea.

iconography

A study which seeks to probe meaning in a work of art by setting it in its historical context, and, in particular, to analyze the ideas implicated in its imagery. Sometimes it also means the ideas and symbols themselves embedded in a visual art.

ideology

A system of beliefs in which ideas come to represent certain interest or to conceal them in a more or less consistent way.

Imjin War 임진왜란 (壬辰倭亂) (1592-1598)

The war between Korea and Japan on the Korean Peninsula caused by Japanese invasion in 1592. Usually Imjin War includes two wars: Imjin War (begun in 1592) and Chŏngyu War (1597-1598). But these two wars are often combined and called Imjin War.

interrogative end-form

The word at the end of a interrogative sentence, or a questioning sentence, which shows a remarkable regional variation in Korea.

isoglosses, or isoglotic line

The border of usage of an individual language or dialect that is normally drawn based on linguistic elements such as grammar, vocabulary, tone and pronunciation.

Japanese colonialism (1910-1945)

The period of colonial rule by the Japanese in Korea. During this period, Koreans were forced to speak Japanese in public and believe in Japanese Shintoism. The Japanese occupied all the high strata of public affairs including administration and military service.

Koguryŏ 고구려 (高句麗) Kingdom

The ancient kingdom in what is now North Korea and Manchuria. Its warriors were famous and feared in China as being great bowmen. The kingdom of Koguryŏ held off four major attacks by Sui dynasty China that occurred in a very short space of time. Also one of the "Three Kingdoms," and it was traditionally the first to receive Buddhism. Its Shamanistic heritage is copiously illustrated by tomb paintings.

Koryŏ Dynasty 고려왕조 (高麗王朝) (918-1392)

The dynasty established in 918 by Kŏn Wang who united the three kingdoms of the Later Paekje (900-936), Later Koguryŏ and Shilla on the Korean Peninsula. The royal family named Wang continued to govern the kingdom until Sŏnggye Yi overthrew it and established the Chosŏn Dynasty in 1392.

kut 굿

The Shamanistic ritual service in Korea which usually occurs over a two-day period. It consists of four elements: shaman clothes, music, dance and song. There is usually a group of shamans (singing and dancing) and musicians who perform the ritual together. It is performed for the purpose of securing good luck, for effecting a cure for physical or mental illness, or for pacifying a deceased spirit.

kwagŏ 과거 (科擧)

The state examination that the Koryŏ Dynasty adopted from China, and which lasted until the Chosŏn Dynasty. It was the gateway to become government officials for young students after a long period of concentration. After a century of practical application from 958, it became the most stable, well-functioning institution. The royal court constantly developed this examination as a means to strengthen the royal authority.

Kyojong 교종 (敎宗), or the Teaching Sect

A group of Buddhistic sects with emphasis on the study of sutras. During the United Shilla Kingdom Period, this sect was restricted to the ruling class who could read and write Chinese characters, and became challenged by Sŏnjong, or the Meditation Sect during the Koryŏ Period.

mudang 무당 (巫堂)

A term for a shaman in Korea. It is usually a priest in Shamanism who officiates at rituals called *kut*. The most important qualification is the experience of the so-called "shaman illness." A *mudang* has a shrine called *tang* in which her guardian deity and other instruments for her ritual services are kept.

Neo-Confucianism

The synthesis of traditional Chinese thoughts by the Southern Song scholars during the 11th and 12th centuries. It was the intellectual achievement of the greatest magnitude in Chinese history with some cosmological concepts and terminology appropriated from Taoism and Buddhism. Neo-Confucian metaphysics later branched into two schools: the School of Principle or Reason and the School of Mind or Intuition.

Paekje 백제 (百濟) Kingdom

One of the three kingdoms in the ancient period on the Korean Peninsula with the territory occupying the contemporary Ch'ungch'ŏng and Chŏlla Provinces. It emerged as a state around the century and fell down in 660 when the Shilla Kingdom, with military assistance from Tang China, attacked it.

Pakhyŏkgŏse 박혁거세 (朴赫居世) (69 B.C. - 4 B.C.)

The first king of the Shilla Dynasty and the founder of Pak's family. It is said that he was elected as the first king by six village-heads in the contemporary Kyŏngju City. Families Sŏk and Kim later succeeded Family Pak to become kings of the Shilla Kingdom.

permeable barrier

A barrier that permits some aspects of an innovation to diffuse through, but weakens and retards continued spread; an innovation can be modified in passing through a permeable barrier.

po 보 (洑), or weir

A fence or enclosure set in a waterway. It can also be a small dam in a stream or river to raise the water level or divert its flow.

posal 보살 (菩薩), or bodhisattva

Being analogous to saints in the Christian tradition, they are beings who have earned release from the realm of suffering, but out of compassion for the less advanced, have postponed their own final emancipation in order to offer assistance to others who wish to reach that same goal. Among them, Avalokitsvara (Kwanŭm or Kwanseŭm in Korea), the bodhisattva of unlimited compassion in the here and now, and Maitreya (Mirŭk in Korea), the bodhisattva who promised a better world in the future, were objects of particularly strong popular devotion; title of the lay female attendant at a Buddhist temple.

primogeniture

The state of being the first-born of the children of the same parents, or an exclusive right of inheritance belonging to the eldest son.

promontory

A high, prominent projection or point of land, or cliff of rock, jutting out boldly into a body of water beyond the coast line; a cape, either low-lying or of considerable height, with a bold termination; a bluff or prominent hill overlooking or projecting into a lowland.

pudo 부도 (浮屠), or stupa

A stone reliquary for the cremated remains of a distinguished Buddhist monk (also called *saripudo*).

Pukak Mountain 북악산 (北岳山)

The modern name for Paekak Mountain at whose foothill the main palace called Kyŏngbokgung was located during the Chosŏn Period.

sadang 사당 (祠堂)

A private shrine for ancestors within which spiritual tablets are preserved and worshipped regularly. In the Chosŏn Period, well-to-do families usually privately owned this type of ancestral hall at the rear of their houses.

sangmin 상민 (常民)

The name for commoners under the Chosŏn Dynasty, including a large number of farmers. Just below the farmers in social status, artisans and merchants also belong to this class. This class probably constituted over four-fifths of the population that economically supported the *yangban* and *chungin* classes. Still below these commoners were the *ch'ŏnmin*, or the despised people, such as butchers, grave-diggers and leather workers.

sau 사우 (祠宇)

A public shrine for an eminent *yangban* man where his descendants or followers dedicate Confucian ceremonies regularly toward his tablet or portrait. Its architecture tends to be more ornate in decoration and larger in size than the *sadang*.

Shilla 신라 (新羅) **Kingdom (57 B.C.- 935)**

One of the three kingdoms in the ancient period on the Korean Peninsula that finally defeated the other two kingdoms, Koguryŏ and Paekje, in the seventh century. During the United Shilla Kingdom Period (668-935), Buddhistic culture flourished with its center in the capital city of Kyŏngju.

Siberian Shamanism

The form of Shamanism common to the hunting and herding societies of Siberia. This type of ecstatic Shamanistic ritual was shared by Scythians on the Black Sea, and is also the basis for North American Indian Shamanist practices. The shaman is called by the spirits to serve as an intermediary between themselves and mankind.

Sik Cho 조식 (曺植) **(1501-1572)**

An eminent scholar in Neo-Confucianism who placed emphasis on the coincidence between behaviors and ethics. He spent most of his life in teaching his learning in a village on the southeastern slope of Chiri Mountain.

Sobaek Range 소백산맥 (小白山脈)

The mountain range branching out of the T'aebaek Range that separates the Yŏngnam Region from the rest of Korea. It runs from the T'aebaek Mountain and terminates at the 1,915 m Chiri Mountain in the southwest corner of the peninsula.

sound

A long broad inlet of the ocean generally parallel to the coast, or a long passage of water connecting two larger bodies (as a sea with the ocean) or separating a mainland and an island.

strewn farmstead

A farmstead wherein buildings lie spaced apart from one another in no consistent pattern, instead of being linked together around a central courtyard. This type of farmstead is especially common in zones of wooden construction where the danger of fire is greatest.

Sŏkjŏn Ritual 석전제 (釋奠際)

Originally the name for a ritual that was performed in commemoration of the sages. It later came to refer only to that at school such as Sŏnggyunkwan.

Sŏnggyunkwan 성균관 (成均館)

A national university established by the Chosŏn Dynasty to produce candidates for government officials. Its main buildings are Taesŏngjŏn (the Confucian shrine) and Myŏngryundang (the lecture hall).

Sŏnjong 선종 (禪宗), or Meditation Sect

A Buddhistic Sect that relies solely on intuitive meditation called Sŏn (Chan in Chinese and Zen in Japanese) as the one and only way to reach the Buddha's mind. From the middle of the ninth to the early tenth century, the nine most influential Sŏnjong groups in Korea came into being. With support from local elites, these groups founded their temples invariably in scenic mountain retreats. With the rise of Sŏnjong in the Koryŏ Period, all the traditional sects based on the scriptural authority came to be grouped under the banner of Kyojong, or the Teaching Sect.

T'aebaek Range 태백산맥 (太白山脈)

The backbone mountain range in Korea running southwards from the famous and scenic 1,500 m peaks of the Diamond (Kŭmgang) Mountains south of Wonsan to the Taegu-P'ohang Valley.

T'oegye 퇴계 (退溪), or Hwang Yi (李滉) (1501-1570)

Better known as T'oegye, he was the finest product of Korean Confucianism, and has been often referred to as Zhu Xi of the East. Although his official rank reached far above the ministerial level, he was never a politician or even a statesman. He longed for a life of learning, meditation, and writing based on his motto: Sincerity and Reverence. His metaphysical position was very much the same as Zhu Xi's, but he was thorough in viewing the interaction of *i* and *ki* as dualistic: yet he accorded an unmistakable priority to the *i*.

tang 당 (堂)

A generic name for a hall, indoors or outdoors, where a Shamanistic or village deity resides. It may sometimes include an open space without buildings if a deity is believed to reside there.

Taoism

A traditional belief that was originated in China and later diffused into Korea. Its doctrine is centered around the ideas of immortal beings on the earth. Unlike Confucianism and Buddhism, its founder was not clearly known but became popular enough to compete with these religions in China. In Korea, however, it has not been as popular as in China.

The Main Korean Tilt Block 경동지괴 (傾動地塊)

A landform feature peculiar to the Korean Peninsula, showing the contrast between the steep eastern slope and the much more gradual western slope.

To 도 (道)

The name for a province, the administrative area at the highest level. After being adopted from China under the late Koryŏ Dynasty, it continued to be used with some modification under the Chosŏn Dynasty and even during the Japanese colonialism. The Eight To of Chosŏn Dynasty were later divided into thirteen Tos during the Japanese colonialism.

To-jŏn Chŏng 정도전 (鄭道傳) (1337-1398)

A prominent politician and scholar who assisted Sŏnggye Yi to overthrow the Koryŏ Dynasty and open a new dynasty called Chosŏn in 1392. His scholarship and talents had been instrumental in the formulation of policies in such fields as military, government, history, law, literature, religion and music in the new dynasty.

Ŭisang 의상 (義湘) (625-702)

A Buddhist monk usually called Ŭisang Taesa (Greater Teacher) who went to Tang China to study Buddhism around 650 and returned to Shilla in 671. Under the patronage of King Munmu, he built ten great temples as major centers of Hwaŏmjong, or the Flower Garland Sect.

Wonhyo 원효 (元曉) (617-686)

A Buddhist monk who set the subsequent tone of Korean Buddhism as a whole. His religious philosophy in its sectarian form was close to that of Hwaŏmjong, but his cardinal concern was to synthesize all sectarian truths into T'ongbulgyo, or "One Unified Buddhism."

yangban 양반 (兩班)

A term most often used to denote upper-class landed gentry of the Chosŏn Dynasty; from the Koryŏ Kingdom denoting the two groups of civil servants: civilian and military. When used in modern speech, it means something akin to a respected male elder.

Yin 음 (陰) **and Yang** 양 (陽)

A belief in the duality of the nature of all things, represented by two enclosed symbols endlessly swirling around, separate, complementary and in balance.

Yushin 유신 (維新)

The name for a political event that occurred on Oct. 17, 1972. After this event, President Park set out an authoritative regime to suppress all kinds of political freedom of the people. It lasted for seven years until he was assassinated on Oct. 26, 1979.

Yŏngnamdaero 영남대로 (嶺南大路)

The main artery road connecting the capital city, Hanyang (Seoul), with Kyŏngsang Province called the Yŏngnam Region under the Chosŏn Dynasty. This road, beginning from Hanyang (Seoul), ran through Ch'ungju, Sangju and Taegu to terminate at Tongrae (Pusan).

Zen

The Japanese term for Sŏn in Korean or Chan in Chinese.

Zhu Xi 주희 (朱熹) **(1130-1200)**

A perfect Confucian scholar both in private life and in public conduct. His greatness lies in the clarification, as from those of Taoism and Buddhism, of Neo-Confucian philosophical concepts. His commentaries became the basic text of Neo-Confucianism.

Place Name Index

Andong City 안동시 (安東市) 47, 54, 58-60, 62, 178-180, 182, 184, 186
Anmyŏn Town 안면읍 (安眠邑) 143, 149-153
Ansŏng Stream 안성천 (安城川) 53, 152, 160
Ansŏng Town 안성읍 (安城邑) 46, 48, 50-51, 53, 56, 275, 279
Asan Bay 아산만 (牙山灣) 148, 160, 275
Ch'aryŏng Ridge 차령산지 (車嶺山地) 97, 153, 154, 190,
Ch'ilhyŏn Mountain 칠현산 (七賢山) 49
Ch'uga Pass 추가령 (楸哥嶺) 228
Ch'ungch'ŏng Province 충청도 (忠淸道) 138-139, 143, 150-154, 274
Ch'ungju City 충주시 (忠州市) 190-192, 194
Ch'up'ung Pass 추풍령 (秋風嶺) 168
Ch'ŏngju City 청주시 (淸州市) 150
Ch'ŏngyang Town 청양읍 (靑陽邑) 153
Ch'ŏnhwang Peak 천황봉 (天皇峰) 100, 168
Changhŭng Town 장흥읍 (長興邑) 158
Chech'ŏn City 제천시 (堤川市) 192
Cheju Island 제주도 (濟州島) 94, 104-112, 195, 218, 277, 286
Cheju Province 제주도 (濟州道) 138, 284
Chemulp'o 제물포 (濟物浦) 71
Chin Island 진도 (珍島) 131, 157, 159
Chiri Mountain 지리산 (智異山) 141, 165-172, 283-284
Cho Pass 조령 (鳥嶺) 150, 302
Choch'iwon Town 조치원읍 (鳥致院邑)
Chogye Mountain 조계산 (曹溪山) 47, 82, 84, 276
Chuk Pass 죽령 (竹嶺) 149-150, 167
Chŏlla Province 전라도 (全羅道) 137-139, 150-151, 153, 167, 251, 257
Chŏnan City 천안시 (天安市) 153
Chŏnju City 전주시 (全州市) 227, 246-249, 251-254, 256-259, 264, 291
Haenam Peninsula 해남반도 (海南半島) 155
Haenam Town 해남읍 (海南邑) 156, 159
Halla Mountain 한라산 (漢拏山) 104, 109-111
Hamgyŏng Province 함경도 (咸鏡道) 138-139, 143

Place Name Index

Hamp'yŏng Bay 함평만 (咸平灣) 154
Han River 한강 (漢江) 70-71, 148, 154, 160, 179, 187-192, 228, 237, 278
Hong Island 홍도 (紅島) 131-133
Hongch'ŏn River 홍천강 (洪川江) 190
Hongsŏng Town 홍성읍 (洪城邑) 150, 153
Hwanghae Province 황해도 (黃海道) 156
Hŭksan Island 흑산도 (黑山島) 130-133
Imjin River 임진강 (臨津江) 160
Inch'ŏn City 인천시 (仁川市) 71
Kaesŏng City 개성시 (開城市) 139-140, 262
Kanghwa Island 강화도 (江華島) 160, 162, 164
Kangjin Peninsula 강진반도 (康津半島) 158
Kangrŭng City 강릉시 (江陵市) 143-147, 274
Kangwon Province 강원도 (江原道) 138-139, 142, 146, 274
Kaya Mountain 가야산 (伽倻山) 152
Kimp'o Peninsula 김포반도 (金浦半島) 160
Kohŭng Peninsula 고흥반도 (高興半島) 155, 157-159, 281
Kongju City 공주시 (公州市) 98, 139, 152-153
Kosŏng County 고성군 (高城郡) 217
Kujwa Town 구좌읍 (舊左邑) 110-111
Kunsan City 군산시 (群山市) 255
Kup'o-dong 구포동 (九苞洞) 51-52, 54
Kurye County 구례군 (求禮郡) 170
Kwangju Ridge 광주산지 (廣州山地) 49
Kwangyang Bay 광양만 (光陽灣) 154-155, 157
Kwoesan County 괴산군 (槐山郡) 191-192, 194
Kyeryong Mountain 계룡산 (鷄龍山) 94-95, 97-100, 102-103, 276-277, 285
Kyodong Island 교동도 (喬洞島) 160-161
Kyŏnggi Bay 경기만 (京畿灣) 141, 152, 160-163, 283
Kyŏnggi Province 경기도 (京畿道) 55, 138-140, 143-146, 150, 153, 156, 158, 200, 228
Kyŏngju City 경주시 (慶州市) 78, 85, 139-140, 143-146, 150, 153, 156, 158, 200, 228
Kyŏngsang Province 경상도 (慶尙道) 138-139, 143-146, 150-152, 167, 217, 262
Kŭm River 금강 (錦江) 115-116, 123-124, 128, 150, 275, 277-278
Kŭmsan Town 금산읍 (錦山邑) 94, 123-125, 127, 129, 150, 282, 287
Mangyŏng River 만경강 (萬頃江) 207-211, 213, 278
Muju Town 무주읍 (茂朱邑) 150

Mungyŏng City 문경시 (聞慶市) 104, 200-201
Myŏngdong 명동 (明洞) 244
Naju City 나주시 (羅州市) 154
Nakdong River 낙동강 (洛東江) 58-59, 62-64, 148, 179, 195, 200-202, 276, 278, 280, 282
Nam Mountain 남산 (南山) 228-229, 238, 244-245, 291, 564
Namhae County 남해군 (南海郡) 219
Namhan River 남한강 (南漢江) 154, 160, 179, 187-192, 278
Nogodan 노고단 (老姑壇) 168-171
Nonsan City 논산시 (論山市) 98, 150, 153
North Chŏlla Province 전라북도 (全羅北道) 151, 246, 257
Noryangjin 노량진 (鷺梁津) 67
Noryŏng Ridge 노령산지 (蘆嶺山地) 203
Odae Mountain 오대산 (五臺山) 148, 190
Okch'ŏn Town 옥천읍 (沃川邑) 94, 112, 115-121, 282
Onyang City 온양시 (溫陽市) 153
P'iagol 피아골 169-170, 284
P'ohang City 포항시 (浦項市) 146
P'yŏngan Province 평안도 (平安道) 138-139
P'yŏngyang City 평양시 (平壤市) 139
P'yŏngch'ang River 평창강 (平昌江) 190
Paekdu Mountain 백두산 (白頭山) 167
Paemsagol 뱀사골 169, 284
Paet'i Pass 배티고개 49-50
Posŏng Bay 보성만 (寶城灣) 155, 157-159
Poŭn Town 보은읍 (報恩邑) 148, 150
Pukak Mountain 북악산 (北岳山) 232
Pukhan River 북한강 (北漢江) 191
Pusan City 부산시 (釜山市) 150, 168
Puyŏ Town 부여읍 (扶餘邑) 138, 152-153
Samch'ŏk City 삼척시 (三陟市) 143-146, 274
Sangju County 상주군 (尙州郡) 202
Sapgyo Stream 삽교천 (揷橋川) 152
Seoul 서울 47, 49-50, 57, 66-68, 71, 75-76, 111-112, 139-140, 143, 146-147, 149-152, 154, 157, 160-161, 168, 186, 191, 198-199, 202, 225-235, 237-238, 240, 244-245, 247, 250, 252, 255, 257-258, 275, 283-284, 290-291
Shinan County 신안군 (新安郡) 130
Sobaek Range 소백산맥 (小白山脈) 148, 154, 167-168, 190, 202, 228, 275

Place Name Index

Sohŭksan Island 소흑산도 (小黑山島) 130-133
Songni Mountain 속리산 (俗離山) 148-150, 167-168
South Kyŏngsang Province 경상남도 (慶尙南道) 217
Soyang River 소양강 (昭陽江) 190
Sunch'ŏn Bay 순천만 (順天灣) 155, 157-158
Sŏch'ŏn Town 서천읍 (舒川邑) 150-151, 153
Sŏmjin River 섬진강 (蟾津江) 168, 210
Sŏnsan Town 선산읍 (善山邑) 200-201
Sŏrak Mountain 설악산 (雪岳山) 148
Sŏsan City 서산시 (瑞山市) 150, 153
T'aean Peninsula 태안반도 (泰安半島) 143, 149, 151-152, 160, 275
T'aegu City 대구시 (大邱市) 146, 255, 262
Tadohae 다도해 (多島海) 130-131, 135, 157, 277
Taech'ŏn City 대천시 (大川市) 153-154
Taedun Mountain 대둔산 (大屯山) 129
Taegwan Pass 대관령 (大關嶺) 147-148, 228
Taejŏn City 대전시 (大田市) 154
Tangjin Town 당진읍 (唐津邑) 150-151, 153
Tanyang County 단양군 (丹陽郡) 191-192, 194
Tŏkyu Mountain 덕유산 (德裕山) 168
Wando 완도 (莞島) 155-156
Yellow Sea 황해 (黃海) 50, 130, 133, 154, 160, 204, 228
Yesan Town 예산읍 (禮山邑) 150, 153
Yihwa Pass 이화령 (梨花嶺) 150, 167, 202, 228
Yiksan City 익산시 (益山市) 257
Yinwang Mountain 인왕산 (仁旺山) 228, 245-246
Yongsan 용산 (龍山) 237, 244
Yŏmha 염하 160
Yŏngch'wi Mountain 영취산 (靈翠山) 75, 78, 276
Yŏngdongjibang 영동지방 (嶺東地方) 147
Yŏngdŭngp'o District 영등포구 (永登浦區) 47, 66-73, 276, 280
Yŏnghŭng Bay 영흥만 (寧興灣) 146
Yŏngsŏjibang 영서지방 (嶺西地方) 147
Yŏngwol 영월 (寧越) 188, 190
Yŏnp'ung 연풍 (延豊) 150
Yŏsu Peninsula 여수반도 (麗水半島) 155, 158
Yŏŭido 여의도 (汝矣島) 67-68, 72-73

Topic Index

absorbing barrier 149, 158
adaptation 23-24, 31-32, 197, 281-282
American cultural geography 22-23
ancestor worship 44, 81, 99, 113, 126, 132, 178, 215, 289
ancestral hall 81, 180, 289
ansan 161, 270
architecture 28, 37, 52, 56, 178, 182, 184, 187, 240, 242, 249, 255, 256, 264, 276
artificial forest 216-217, 219-220, 260, 292
Berkeley school 23, 39
British cultural geography. 23
Buddha's land 75
Buddhism 28, 30, 32-33, 35, 44-45, 56, 68, 75-76, 80-85, 92-93, 95, 99-100, 127, 166, 225, 233, 267, 275, 285, 288-290
Buddhist landscape 81, 288-289, 293
Buddhist temple 28, 56, 59, 65, 68, 75, 103, 106, 225, 276
built-up area 257, 259
bundle of lines 27
capital 34, 76, 78, 85, 139-140, 205-206, 209, 214, 228-230, 237, 246-247, 250, 261-262, 292

Catholic church 49-52, 68, 255
Catholicism 28, 44-46, 49-51, 54-55, 66, 275, 280
Ch'aryŏng Ridge 97, 153-154
ch'ilsŏngshin 81
Ch'ŏnt'aejong 84
chaeshil 180
chinsan 250
chinshinsari 78
chipsŏngch'on 107, 121
Chogyejong 82
Chongmyo 229-230, 233-234, 236, 290
Chosŏn 32-34, 37, 46, 48, 51, 53, 57-59, 63, 70, 76, 80-83, 85, 89, 93, 96, 98-100, 106-107, 121-122, 138-140, 162-163, 166, 172, 177-178, 181-182, 186, 191, 193-194, 202-203, 206-207, 212, 214-216, 218, 225, 228-230, 233-236, 238, 240, 242, 244-249, 252-254, 257, 260-267, 269-270, 276-277, 285, 288, 290-292
Chosŏn Diocese 51, 53
Chosŏn Dynasty 33, 37, 46, 48, 57-58, 63, 81, 83, 96, 139, 214, 225, 229, 233-234, 236, 242, 246, 249, 253, 263-267, 269, 290-291
Chosŏn Period 32-34, 37, 57, 59, 70,

76, 80-82, 85, 89, 93, 96, 98-100, 106-107, 121-122, 138, 140, 162-163, 166, 172, 177-178, 181-182, 186, 191, 193-194, 202-203, 206-207, 212, 215-216, 218, 225, 227-230, 234-248, 252, 254, 257, 260-262, 264-265, 269-270, 276-277, 285, 288, 292

Churyegogonggi 230, 233, 253
chŏngja 179-180, 188
chŏngji 198-199
Chŏngt'ojong 82
city planning 37, 229-230, 233, 246-247, 253, 290
colonial landscape 227, 237, 254
Confucian 28, 46-47, 56-61, 63-65, 76-77, 81, 89, 92-93, 96, 99, 107-108, 112-114, 121, 130, 132, 136, 166, 177, 180-181, 183-184, 192, 214-215, 225, 230-233, 250-251, 253, 256, 265, 267-268, 276-278, 280, 286, 289, 291-293
Confucian architecture 56
Confucian culture area 59
Confucian shrine 57, 180-181
Confucian temple 225
Confucianism 28, 30, 32-35, 37, 44-45, 56-57, 60, 63-64, 81, 93, 96, 99- 100, 104-108, 110, 112-115, 121, 126, 132, 176-177, 181, 187, 191-192, 215, 225, 230-231, 233, 247, 253, 265, 267, 270, 275, 285-292
Confucius 57, 63, 225, 253
core and periphery 278

critical social theory 40
cultural boundaries 27, 274
cultural diffusionism 23
cultural evolution 31, 281
cultural exchange 32
cultural geography 22-24, 26-27, 29, 31-32, 35, 37-41, 279, 282-283, 289, 294
cultural landscape 23, 28, 31, 92, 194, 263, 275, 279
cultural materialism 23
cultural power 40, 294
cultural region 61-62
cultural theory 23-24
cultural turn 22
culture 22, 26-33, 39-40, 59, 62, 93, 95, 124, 177, 201-202, 198-199, 274, 276, 279, 281, 284-285, 294
culture area 28, 59, 62, 274, 276
dialect 27, 138-140, 142-146, 148, 150, 153, 156, 174, 283
differentiation 35, 36, 283, 288
diffusion of language 148-149, 155, 281
distribution 24, 27-28, 31, 58, 102-103, 117, 124, 176, 201, 274-275, 278-279
doksŏng 81
dominant class 34, 289
dominant culture 93
dominant social group 33
elite culture 33, 40, 285, 294
end-form of speech 153
evolution 30-31, 46, 279, 281-282
female deities 105, 134, 286-287

Feng-shui 37-38, 88-89, 122, 127, 178, 215-217, 225, 229-233, 245, 247, 250, 259-261, 267, 269-271, 290-292
Feng-shui topography 232, 260-261, 270
filial piety 89, 177-178, 193
folk belief 94, 217, 260
folk housing 30, 32, 179, 195, 197, 201-202, 278, 282
folk landscape 24, 31, 33, 92-93, 124, 281, 284
generic name 64, 108, 162-163, 244
geographical knowledge 26-27
geomancer 127, 131
geomancy 127
geopolitical 146, 175
government-general 238, 240-241, 291
grave 251
hadangshin 113-115, 117, 121-122, 128, 287
haenyŏ 106
halmang 108, 286
Han River 70-71, 148, 160, 189, 190-191, 228, 237
Hangŭl 140, 228, 242
hegemony 33-34, 41, 45, 82, 100, 107, 285, 288-289, 292
Hwaŏmjong 84-86, 293
hyanggyo 57, 65, 225, 253
hybrid culture 202
hybrid dialect 144, 146
iconography 37-38, 56, 226, 230, 233-234, 251-252, 254, 257, 263, 267, 269
identity 35-36, 194, 278, 283-284, 286, 289, 294
ideology 26, 33-34, 44-46, 56-57, 63, 81, 85, 89, 93, 177-178, 194, 216, 225-226, 230, 233, 265, 267, 269, 289-293
independent dialect 145-146
integrated cultural geography 40, 294
interrogative end-form 146
intersubjective meaning 35, 283
irrigation 30, 32, 176, 179, 203, 205-213, 278-279
Irrigation Association 206-207, 209-210, 213
isoglosses 141-143, 148, 150-151, 274-275
Japanese colonialism 70-71, 73-74, 140, 203, 205, 213, 224, 226, 233, 243, 245, 264, 278-279
Kaeksa 248, 250, 252, 253-254, 256, 261, 264, 291
knowledge 26-27, 30, 33-34, 63, 83, 105, 169, 193-194, 230, 253, 284, 294
Koryŏ 33, 56, 59, 76, 80, 82-83, 85, 106, 135, 139, 162, 166, 171, 182, 184, 186, 228-229, 233, 242, 247, 262-263, 267, 293
kot 64, 162-165
kugok 64
kut 96-97, 99, 105, 127, 277, 285
kwagŏ 177
Kyojong 83-85

Kyŏngbokgung 229-236, 240-241, 243, 250, 290, 291
kyŏpjip 198-202
landform 161-165
landscape 23-24, 28-31, 33-34, 36-40, 46, 67, 81, 92-93, 124, 155, 176, 180, 193-194, 218, 224-228, 230, 237, 246, 252, 254, 261, 263, 267, 269, 275-276, 279, 281, 284, 289, 290-291, 293-294
language family 138
lineage group 65, 180, 194
linguistic boundaries 27, 274
linguistic community 35, 283
linguistic diffusion 155-156, 158, 281
linguistic element 158
linguistic island 140, 157, 159, 281
localization 33, 35, 38, 278, 284, 294
maru 142, 176, 195-201, 278, 280
migration 30-31, 278, 281
monk 76, 78-79, 84, 86, 88, 228, 232, 246, 289
natural barrier 146, 148, 279
natural boundary 148, 167, 275
Neo-Confucianism 28, 30, 32-35, 37, 56-57, 60, 63-64, 80, 100, 176-177, 180, 187, 191-192, 232, 275, 285, 288-290
new cultural geography 22, 24, 40, 289
nine-curves 64
nugak 65
ondol 178, 192, 195-197, 200, 202, 278, 282
origin 28, 31, 61, 76, 82, 111, 124, 127, 165, 170, 200, 279, 281, 288, 293
palace 215, 219, 229-230, 232-233, 235-236, 240-243, 250, 262, 265, 290-292
patrilineal 176-177
pebble-piles 94, 113-114, 123-124
periodic market 48, 264
permeable barrier 153
place name 140, 162-165, 169-170
plurality of cultures 22, 40
po 203
political power 58, 86, 84, 89, 107, 226, 253
politics 226, 283
ponhyangdang 94, 104-108, 110-111, 286
ponhyangje 107-108
popular culture 40, 285, 293
power 23, 34, 36, 38-39, 46, 65, 81, 84, 93, 96, 106-108, 122, 128, 177, 179, 194, 226, 237, 240, 247, 253, 257, 259, 282, 286-290, 292, 294
primogeniture 186
private Confucian academies 28, 47, 56-57, 276, 280
promontory landform 162-165
Protestantism 28, 44-45, 66, 68, 74, 275-276, 280-281
pudo 88
pyŏlshinje 112
railroad 67-68, 71-73, 153-154, 257-

259, 275
reclamation 53, 78, 209-210, 213
regional classification 28, 275
regional type 282
regionalizaton 278
relations of power 33, 283
religious landscape 46, 276
religious pluralism 45
reservoir 207, 210, 212-213
rice belt 203, 246, 278
royal authority 75, 225-226, 230-231, 237, 241, 246, 249-250, 254, 257, 263, 265, 267, 291
royal landscape 227-228, 246, 261
ruling class 33-35, 75, 285, 288-289
ruling elite 76, 228
rural landscape 24, 30, 34, 176, 293
sacred mountain 109, 245, 276
sacred place 78, 84, 95, 220, 246, 254, 257, 265, 293
sadang 180
Sajikdan 229-230, 233-234, 236, 290
sambul 99-100, 102-103, 285
samshin 99, 114, 285
sangdangshin 113, 115, 121, 134
sangmin 34
sanshin 81, 104-105, 112-115, 126, 130-131, 134-135, 171, 286-287
sanshinje 112, 126, 130
sau 180
secret language 35, 288
Shamanism 32-35, 56, 68, 76, 80, 92-93, 95-96, 99-104, 106-108, 110, 113, 115, 215, 276, 284-288

Shamanist 99
Shamanistic 81-82, 93-96, 99-100, 102-104, 107, 112-113, 127-128, 130, 134-136, 215, 246, 260, 277-278, 285-288
Shamanistic ritual 127, 134, 287
Shilla 75-80, 82-83, 85, 139-140, 152, 162, 166, 171, 214-215, 247, 261-263, 265-268, 271, 292
social power 34, 65, 76, 81, 106-108, 194, 286-288
spatial strategies 294
standard Korean 144-146, 151-154, 158-159, 170
standard language 139-140, 145
stone monument 165-166
stone pagoda 127-128, 277, 287
strategy 34, 107-108
strewn farmstead 200
sub-dialect 124, 143-145, 175
subordinate class 34
superstition 38, 76, 96
sutra 86
symbol 81, 85, 95, 99, 122, 186, 293
symbolic landscape 193, 267, 293
symbolic meaning 193, 215-216
symbolic place 194, 294
Sŏkjŏn Ritual 57
sŏnangdang 124, 126
sŏnangje 112
sŏndol 94, 112, 115-123, 134, 277, 282
Sŏnggyunkwan 57, 65
Sŏnjong 83-85, 88, 293
t'apje 126

t'apshin 126, 128
Tadohae 130-131, 135, 157, 277
taech'ŏng 117, 196, 198, 202
tang 77, 95, 105, 130, 139, 277, 285
tanggol 105
tangje 94, 113, 130
tangsanje 112
Taoism 92, 99, 123, 127
the local Confucian school 225
thoroughfare 230-231, 233, 259, 290
Three Kingdoms Period 56, 75-76, 140
three main temples 76
tolt'ap 94, 123-128, 277, 287
tomb 251, 270-271, 289
traditional cultural geography 22, 24, 39-40, 282-283
urban landscape 37-38, 67, 224-225, 230, 252, 269, 291
village deity 92-93, 134-135, 220
village forest 220-221
village ritual 107-108, 112, 115, 126-128, 286-287
way of seeing 38
Yangban 30, 33-34, 58, 81, 122, 177-183, 186-189, 191-194, 196, 202, 215, 276, 278, 285, 293-294
yangban lineage 30, 177-180, 182, 215, 278
Yangban lineage village 178
yin and *yang* 123
yongwang 130, 136
yongwangje 130
Zen Buddhism 28, 33

Photo Credit

cover, p. 87	Kang, Kŏn-gi et al., 강건기 외 2인, 1994, *Songkwangsa*. 송광사. Songkwang Temple, Pitkkal itnŭn ch'aekdŭl 150. 빛깔있는 책들 150. Shiny Book Series, No. 150. Seoul: Taewonsa. p. 38.
p. 98	月刊 山. Wolgan San. *Mountain*, A Monthly Magazine by Chosŏnilbosa (Chosŏn Daily Newspaper Company), May (1999), p. 104.
p. 184	Richard Saccone, 1996, *Having a Great Tour*. Elizabeth, NJ · Seoul: Hollym Corporation; Publishers. p. 208.
p. 236	Richard Saccone, 1996, *Having a Great Tour*. Elizabeth, NJ · Seoul: Hollym Corporation; Publishers. p. 4.
p. 238 - 239	Sŏmundang (ed.) 서문당, 1986, Sajinŭro bonŭn Kŭndae Hankuk Sang. 사진으로 보는 近代韓國 上. *Old Days of Korea through Pictures* (I). Seoul: Sŏmundang. pp. 10-11.
p. 240	Richard Saccone, 1996, *Having a Great Tour*. Elizabeth, NJ · Seoul: Hollym Corporation; Publishers. p. 67.
p. 242	Sŏmundang (ed.) 서문당, 1994, Minjŏkŭi Sajinch'ŏb: I. Minjŏkŭi Simjang. 민족의 사진첩 I. 민족의 심장, *Photo Album of Korea: I. The Heart of Korea*. Seoul: Sŏmundang. p. 28.
p. 245	Sŏmundang (ed.) 서문당, 1986, Sajinŭro bonŭn Kŭndae Hankuk Sang. 사진으로 보는 近代韓國 上. *Old Days of Korea through Pictures* (I). Seoul: Sŏmundang. p. 25.